FURNITURE
of the
PILGRIM CENTURY

1620-1720

*INCLUDING COLONIAL UTENSILS
AND HARDWARE*

BY

WALLACE NUTTING

*ILLUSTRATED WITH ONE THOUSAND PHOTOGRAPHS BY THE AUTHOR
HITHERTO UNPUBLISHED*

BONANZA BOOKS • NEW YORK

FOREWORD

THE interest in native wood early furniture is of recent growth. Many persons who formerly collected Sheraton types have gone farther back through the Hepplewhite period, through the Chippendale, to the Dutch period, and of late not a few persons collected only Americana, by which term, applied to furniture, is meant not merely furniture made in America, but made also of native woods.

The spirit of patriotism stirred by the great war, has stimulated interest in the work our fathers left. The study of American furniture has only recently reached the point of recognizing how desirable is the handiwork formed of local materials, as modified from foreign styles by the exigencies of the colonists. The late Empire furniture has acquired, without reason, in New York at least, the epithet Colonial. We should do what is possible to relieve our early fathers of the responsibility for such productions. Nothing is colonial that follows 1776, and so far as concerns those who desire to be correct the Colonial name should not be applied to any furniture later than Chippendale.

But what did the second generation of settlers, and to some extent the first generation, have as furniture? This fascinating question has begun to call to us until thousands ask it. This book is the effort to answer the question, and hence nothing is shown here that was not or could not have been made in America before the time of the cabriole leg, except the gateleg table, a style which continued half way through the eighteenth century; and pine cupboards, which for the sake of completeness, are shown to the close of their period.

No comparison can be made between the rich productions of England during the seventeenth century in furniture, and English books about it, with American furniture. A compendium such as is easy to produce, full of copies indiscriminately made of English and American pieces, is no longer satisfactory. This book shows few pieces of furniture that have been illustrated before, except in some instances of fuller restorations of pieces previously shown. This statement is made with trembling because no one can be absolute in knowledge of this kind. The main feature of the book, however, is that most of the examples here shown were until recently unknown.

The author is indebted to many persons for information and for the privilege of photographing their rare furniture. The names of these persons will be credited under the pictures of their pieces unless an owner has requested that his name be omitted.

The author has done most of the photographic work personally. In reproducing the photographs he has taken care where possible to avoid the serious error of working out backgrounds—a thing which cannot be done successfully. We thus have a richer variety of early American work than has hitherto been attempted.

The objects treated in this book are so confined in character and period that it has been thought best to depart from the usual custom of showing only museum specimens. Thus very many simple pieces are set forth, and even slight modifications in style are noted. For instance, the pine cupboard, now attracting so much attention, is treated by the exhibit of many quaint little examples, which twenty years since would have been scorned. The same attention to simple articles, possible to acquire by any furniture lover, has been given, under beds, cradles, chairs and utensils.

A few pictures including human figures have been used. This was necessary because the rooms containing the furniture are dismantled. The rooms themselves were so carefully furnished that it has been thought important to show them, despite the figures.

W. N.

CONTENTS

AN Architectural Chest. Owner: Mr. G. H. Buek, East Hampton, Long Island.

Mr. Buek's dwelling is that made famous as the inspiration of the poem, "Home, Sweet Home." The chest was discovered by Mr. Buek in his neighborhood. The tradition is that it was brought from Lynn in 1649, by a family of Osbournes. It has been very successfully restored by Mr. Morris Schwartz. There are two end-to-end drawers, a rare arrangement. The end carving is shown in the second picture. There the carving is from the solid, and the architectural front is merely imitated. Date 1640-1650.

[1]

AN elaborately carved chest belonging to Mr. William B. Goodwin of Columbus, Ohio. The chest, which has been restored by Mr. Morris Schwartz, has unusual carving on the stiles and top rail of a very handsome character. It departs from the conventional foliage pattern which appears on the bottom rail. This rail reminds one of the carving on the torus drawer of court cupboards, on page 126. Date, 1650-70.

Chests were the first furniture. The earliest need of man emerging from barbarism was a receptacle for valuable belongings. The Hebrew ark of the covenant was a chest. The word chest, under innumerable forms, appears in our earliest literature. The carving on ecclesiastical chests was inspired by reverence as well as by the innate necessity of man to express himself. Chests, as we first know them, originated in Italy, the cradle of arts. The English chests, our direct source of design, were brought to America more often than other forms of furniture. They were transported full of valuable goods and therefore occupied no extra cargo space. Further, they were the most cherished articles of property.

A CARVED Three-panel Oak Chest, owned by the author.

It is peculiar in having an oak paneled top, known in only two or three other American chests. This feature would indicate an early date since the earliest chests were closer imitations of the English than the later chests.

A good feature is the scrolled bottom rail. The carving on the inner stiles is also very uncommon on American chests. The bottom is pine but the back is oak. No English chests containing pine are known.

The origin of this chest is not definitely traced, but it is presumably Connecticut.

Size: 20x46 inches. Hight 27½ inches. Date 1650-60.

The fact that a chest has not a drawer does not necessarily indicate an early date, yet other things being equal, the absence of a drawer tends to throw the date back. The earliest chest had no drawer. The later chests occasionally had no drawer, but the second and the third drawer mark the approach toward a chest of drawers. Of course, all carved arches on chests represent a later substitution for an architectural arch such as appeared in the chest on page 1.

This remark applies to the lunettes on the upper rail of the chest before us which are, of course, incipient arches.

[3]

A CARVED Oak, Paneled Lid Chest. Owner: Mr. George Dudley Seymour of New Haven.   This piece is pronounced American, in spite of the fact that its lid is of paneled oak, a feature which, in over seventy chests shown in this book, appears in two cases only.   The date is therefore very early, 1650–1660.   The panels are carved in a Runic design.   The lower rail and the stiles are lightly carved.   The owner thinks the carving incomplete, which we might question.   The upper stile is faintly scratched, and prepared for intersecting lunettes.

The chest was found in Portsmouth, New Hampshire. It is now in Wadsworth Atheneum, Hartford.

These chests were convenient for the storage of biggins, boot-haunches, crosscloths, coifes, demicastors, leather doublets, forehead cloths, jerkins, kirtles, masks, portmantles, ruffs, safeguards, swashes, and such wearing apparel, used in those days.

AN Oak Chest.   Owner: Mr. H. W. Erving.   Date: 1660–70.

The ends, which do not show, are in single panels.   Though the short stiles are plain, the end stiles carry double rows of "pencil and pearl" carving. The top rail, between rows of pencil and pearl ornament, carries a scroll. The bottom rail carries one row of the pencil and pearl ornament.

The top is oak.

Size: Length, 47½ inches; hight, 26½ inches; front to back, 20¼ inches.

To a student of structure this chest is as good as any to illustrate certain peculiarities.   The molding on the inside edge of the leg-stiles is worked from the solid, apparently after the parts of the chest are assembled.   Thus this molding runs out to nothing at the top and bottom.   Again, the bottom rail is beveled on its upper edge, under each panel, which is not true at the top of the panels.   The practice in this respect varied.   The till at the top of the chest, at one end, was usually of pine, and generally framed in.   The back posts, projecting as they did beyond the back top rail, were cut away for an inch or so, at the top, to permit the lid to open and to stop the lid, when it struck the shoulder thus cut on the post.   Otherwise the lid would have been wrenched off its hinges.

AN Oak Four-Panel Chest. Date: 1660–70.

The decoration of the top rail is a type of lunettes and reversed lunettes which we see also on the next page, and on some other oak chests, and one pine chest in this work. The letters P. W. are, if our date is correctly estimated, a rather early instance of initials, though one other instance appears on the ship chest, page 34, as early as this.

It is a striking and beautiful chest. The laureling, which it bears on the short stiles, resembles that on the author's court cupboard, page 125. Also that on the chest, page 3, both early pieces, close to English influence. The absence of a drawer, the great length, and the careful work, all support the date given.

The author has expended a great deal of time in seeking to trace the source of this photograph.

In the matter of initials on furniture, they appeared in England in some instances very early. One piece bears the date 1533, and two names, doubtless those of a husband and wife. In instances also the faces of husband and wife appeared, carved on the panels.

Such chests were generally made to order. In fact most other furniture was so made. That is what gives early furniture so much individuality. It was designed for the house into which it was to go, and for a very specific purpose. A philosopher or a poet might start a train of reflection or sentiment on the fact that the furniture, and even the initials survive the memory of their owners, who are otherwise lost to us.

AN Oak Four-Panel Chest. Owner: William G. Erving, M.D., of Washington. Date: 1660–70. It is 54¼ inches long; 29¾ inches high; 22½ inches from front to back,—perhaps the largest no-drawer chest shown in this book.

The carving is as unusual as the size. The top and bottom rail are carved like the top rail of the chest on the opposite page, with lunettes and reversed lunettes, forming shuttle patterns. But the long stiles carry an extremely rare pattern, difficult to define; carvers characterize it as a "spade" motive. The short stiles show carving like an inset split-ball turning. The other features, on end and front, are obvious.

We notice that the bottom rail is not chamfered, as is usual, where it meets the panels.

This chest never had a drawer, but not a few chests, on careful examination, show that a drawer is missing. Sometimes the supports are entirely removed, but some trace of a framed rail for the drawer to rest upon can always be found, generally in the form of a rabbet on the back stile.

AN Oak Three-Tulip-Paneled Chest. Owner: Mr. George Dudley Seymour. Date: 1660–80. In having no drawer this Connecticut chest shares in honor with the more usual design, with sunflower center panel, on page 12. The design carrying three tulip panels is unique, so far as now known.

It is 47 inches long; 26 inches high; 19 inches from front to back. The new top should have been pine, not oak. It is otherwise original. It was found in the Capt. Charles Churchill House, Newington, Connecticut, nearly forty years ago. At that time it stood on end, and was in use as a harness cupboard.

A Connecticut Sunflower Court Cupboard was ejected from the same house to "make room."

AN Oak Tulip Chest. Owner: Mr. H. W. Erving. Date: 1660-70.
Size: Length, 49 inches; hight, 32 inches; front to back, 18½ inches.
The ends have three panels. The tulip design carved thus all over the piece, on rails and stiles as well as on panels, is very rare. It reminds us somewhat in this respect of the Hadley Chest, which is also completely covered with carving.

There is a two-drawer chest in the Connecticut Historical Society, in this fashion of rail and stile carving, though the panels are more like the tulip panels of the "Sunflower" chests. These are important and early examples of chests. It is hoped that more of them may be discovered.

It is to be noted that no moldings appear on this chest. They would be an over-enrichment, and insipid.

A PALM-PANEL Chest. Owned by the author. Date: 1650–70.

Quite generally the stiles and rails of oak chests are ornamented with the shadow molding, as here, when they are not carved. The palm carving was early. The three similar chests, which have come to the author's attention are of the same character as this chest, having the lunettes on the top rail, and the large and small rosettes on the drawer fronts. Mr. H. W. Erving's has two drawers. The length of the chest above is 52 inches; hight, 30½ inches, as three or four inches are missing from the feet; front to back, 21 inches.

The lid of this chest in pine, is a little too narrow, and bevels sharply, it being apparently cut from a slab, and left full width on the lower side, to cover as well as possible.

The regular number of lunettes on such chests is five, while there are seven large and six small rosettes. This chest has a three-pancl end. Mr. Erving's has a four-panel end.

AN Oak Tulip-Panel Chest, with the Connecticut Cross Panel, from the Henry Stearns Collection, Hartford.

This chest is quite like that on page 13, except for the center panel, where the cross, so characteristic of Connecticut architecture, is substituted for the sunflower panel. Of course, the large oval knobs are incorrect restorations for the proper original small knobs. The blocks at the feet are not a part of the chest.

The ramifications of the word chest, its analogies and synonyms, offer a suggestive by-path. Aged persons often pronounce the word *chist*, which follows the derivation, and was probably correct at one time. The word is almost unchanged from its Greek form, which indeed is precisely the Scotch *kist*.

The coffer and cassone are equivalents.

A CONNECTICUT "Sunflower" chest, without drawer, owned by Mr. James N. H. Campbell of Hartford. We arrive in this chest at a type which has without sufficient reason come to be more sought for than any other chest. As all these chests have been traced to Hartford County and most of them to Hartford, there is a strong presumption that they were all made by one man and his successor or local imitator. Efforts have been made to trace the maker but, such is human fame, none of the makers of our earliest pieces are known. The characteristics of this type of chest are a sunflower stock with three blossoms and foliage as the center panel, which is always chamfered at the corners to form an irregular octagon. The side panels are conventional tulips.

The no drawer type is very rare indeed. There may be in all some fifty to seventy sunflower chests in existence. There is a tradition that some of them came from England, and in one case the author saw an inscription on a lid giving the date on which his earliest American ancestor brought it over. Against this tradition there is the insuperable objection that the bottoms and backs and lids of these chests are invariably in pine. Lyon, in his very accurate work, states that English collectors have never seen an English chest, oak and pine in parts.

Size: 44¼ inches long; 24½ inches high; 18 inches from front to back. Date 1670-80.

A ONE-DRAWER Sunflower Chest. Owner: Mr. H. W. Erving.
Date: 1660–80.

Size: 44½ inches long; 31 inches high; 19¼ inches from front to back.
The measurements given are generally, as here, on the frame. Lids usually
overhang about three-quarters of an inch in front, and twice as much at
the ends.

The lid is pine. There are two end panels. The upper end panel has
beveled corners, and four small bosses around the central boss. The
fashion of slanting the "turtle backs" or bosses, on the drawer is interesting.
The one drawer Connecticut sunflower chest is very rare, the two drawer
pattern being more numerous.

While the name "sunflower" chest has been bestowed on this style, it is
understood that there are always side panels with conventionalized tulips.

A PANELED-LID Oak Child's Chest. Date 1670–1700. Owner: Mr. George Dudley Seymour. It is the only miniature chest in oak of this date, so far found, in America. The front rail is charred, perhaps by rush lights, a common thing in English chests. Hight, 14⅞ inches; lid, 12½ by 20⅞ inches. The miniature chest below with four ball feet, and double arch mold, belongs to J. Milton Coburn, M.D. Date: 1700–1710.

A TWO-DRAWER Sunflower Chest. Date: 1660–1680. This specimen has not lost any considerable portion of its feet; the top is original except the cleats; so are most of the ornaments. It was restored many years ago, perhaps forty, by Hartford craftsmen, inspired by the interest just then awakened by Dr. Lyon and his friends.

It completes the series of sunflower chests, begun on pages 12 and 13. It is 45 inches long; 20¼ inches from front to back; 40 inches high; legs, 6 inches, probably never more than 6½ inches. There is an interesting variation in the carving of these chests, showing the individuality so dear to the collector. Owner: the author, who bought the chest near Hartford.

A CARVED and Painted Chest. Owner: Mr. M. A. Norton, of Hartford. Date, shown on the central panel, 1704.

This chest is really a variant of the sunflower pattern, with the sunflower left out! Instead of applied spindles and chamfered corners on the drawers, we find painted tulip decoration, thus carrying out the carved tulip design in the side panels.

This chest is undoubtedly later than the pattern shown on the previous page, of which by the way, Mr. Norton has two examples.

The date is very valuable. It is very seldom found on chests, except in the last decade of the 17th or the first decade of the 18th Century.

A ONE-DRAWER Hadley Chest. Owner: Mr. Brooks Reed, of Boston.
In this chest we reach a style in much request. The specimens found
are in one, two and three drawers; the one drawer style being extremely
rare; the two drawer style predominating; and there are but two known
pieces in the three drawer style.

The dates run from 1680, or more certainly from 1690 to 1710. The
material, as that of nearly all carved chests, is oak, with pine in lid, back,
bottom and drawer bottoms. The size is about 44 inches long and 19
inches "deep," that is, from the front to the back. The hight varies according to the number of drawers, from 37 inches upward. The chests are
almost always initialed. The crude carving varies somewhat in pattern.

A HADLEY Chest, with Full Name. Owner: Mr. Philip L. Spalding, of Boston. Date: 1690–1700.

The material as usual is oak, with pine lid. It is extremely rare that a full name is carved on an American chest of this date.

The piece was found near Deerfield, about 1916, by Dr. Miner of Greenfield, who also found in the same vicinity the three-drawer Hadley Chest, on page 22. The condition of both pieces was very good.

AN Oak Hadley Chest. Owner: Mr. B. A. Behrend, Brookline. Date: 1690–1700. A very beautiful specimen. Its general surface is the soft age-worn front, so pleasing in its mellow effect.

Instances are known of the absence of initials on Hadley chests. But usually either initials, or in two or three instances a full name, appears.

Sometimes a Hadley is locked by passing a flat bar vertically down through a slot, just inside where the 'scutcheons would otherwise appear. The top is then locked, and all drawers are secure.

The making of a good early lock was no small part of the labor of construction on a chest. Most locks are lost. The hinges on nearly all early American chests are "pin," that is, cotter pin. The so-called chest hinge, a strap with an offset, is seldom seen.

A ONE-DRAWER Hadley Chest. Date 1690–1700. The variations between this chest and that on page 17, are to be marked, as indicating that the designer, while following in general the style of carving peculiar to the Hadley chest, did not confine himself to slavish copying. For instance, a grotesque head appears on the center of the drawer, page 17, whereas here a different motive prevails. This chest was found in Southeastern New Hampshire, in the hands of an owner who had brought it from the Connecticut river, in Southern New Hampshire. It is of very recent discovery and bears out the uniform source of this class of chests—on the Connecticut river section of Massachusetts. Size: 41½ inches long; 18⅞ inches from front to back; 35¼ inches high. It is owned by the author.

A TWO-DRAWER Hadley Chest, owned by the author. Date: 1690–1700. The carving here differs slightly from that on the preceding chest, especially in the bottom rail. This chest is in a remarkably good state of preservation, and, in this particular, it stands rather high on its legs. The initials here are H. A., and are carved in the conventional style on the center panel. Size: 44 inches long; 42¾ inches high, and 18¾ inches front to back.

A remark of Mr. H. W. Erving inquiring in 1883, if a certain friend had seen his "Hadley" chest apparently originated the name. Give a piece of furniture a specific name and at once you enhance its desirability to many collectors. We, of course, absolve Mr. Erving from any malice aforethought, as no one had then discovered this tendency of the collector.

[21]

A THREE-DRAWER Hadley Chest, owned by Mr. Chauncey C. Nash. The only other Hadley chest known with three drawers is in the Deerfield Museum. It will be seen that all the Hadley chests here shown with two and three drawers have four end panels, which are plain. The Hadley chests were, as a rule, painted in black or red. Of course the carving is very simple. Date, 1680-1700.

AN Oak Diamond-and-Arch Chest. Owner: Mr. H. W. Erving. Date: 1760–80. Size: Length, 45¾ inches; hight, 33½ inches; front to back, 19¾ inches.

An elaborate chest, with legs of unusual length. The ends have three panels, all plain. The turned incised ornaments at the sides of the arch are simple but effective. The number of features on this chest leave little out from the possibilities. The interesting enumeration includes: drops, bosses, nail-heads, shadow mold, diamonds, rosettes, blocked corners, turned ornaments, an arch, keystone and other arch-structure blocks, and moldings around panels and drawer.

The question of correct taste in chest ornament is not the only question as regards desirability. Quaintness, rarity, odd features, even the over-doing of some features, are all elements entering into the matter. The historical record is often completed, or a mooted point of structure or decoration is cleared up by an unusual chest.

AN Oak Chest, with Double-arched Center Panel. Owner: Mr. M. A. Norton. Date: 1660–80.

An important feature of this chest is its two sets of end-to-end drawers, scarcely known elsewhere. The double arched panel, with its keystones and capitals, reminds us of similar details on court cupboards. The pointed dentils above, and the three lines of notched carving below are excellent, and rare features. The additional decoration afforded by the pencil and pearl molding renders the chest very rich

The feet have lost somewhat by wear. The chest was found in Connecticut, the home of most American oak chests. It had been for many generations in the family from which it was purchased. The chest opposite has so many similar features, that the two should be compared carefully.

AN Oak Chest, with Diamond Center Panel. Owner: Mr. B. A. Behrend, of Brookline. Date: 1670–80.

This chest has the rare arrangement of two drawers end-to-end. It is enriched by pointed dentils under the lid, and by three rows of tooth or notch carving. The similarity of this to the opposite chest make it morally certain that the two came from the same neighborhoods. The principal variation in style is in the center panel. Each also carries two lines of molding with sets of duplicate notches, roughly resembling the pencil and pearl motive, which, however, is absent from this chest. What we have called pointed dentils are nothing other than the immediate juxta-position of dentils with the Norman tooth carving.

It may be presumed that the infrequency of the two drawers end-to-end was the greater convenience of a long drawer for laying clothing with fewer folds. This convenience was found to be so great that it no doubt was re-sponsible for adding drawer on drawer, until the chest disappeared, and the chest of drawers alone was left.

AN Oak Three-Panel Chest. Owner: Mr. H. W. Erving. Date: 1670–1680. Size: 44 inches long; 25½ inches high; 18 inches from front to back. The foliated scroll on the center panel, with the initials W. B., differentiates the chest from the simple three panel chests. The absence of a drawer might suggest a date ten years earlier.

The chests of this general type have the corner blocks, of triangular shape, painted black. The shadow molding is also, as a rule, black; and the applied ornaments are, we believe, uniformly black. These last are generally of maple, but sometimes of beech or pine, or perhaps birch. Fine birch seldom grows as far south as Connecticut, except on the highlands. These were settled later, and even then were far from a cabinet shop and so precluded an extensive use of birch.

A SEVENTEENTH Century Carved New England Oak Chest, owned by Mr. George Dudley Seymour. Front and end panels of oak, original pine lid. The Renaissance carving of the stiles and top-rail is perhaps copied by the maker from the copper-plate frontispiece fly leaf of an old Bible.

Height, 26½ inches; width of top, 22⅜ inches; length of top, 45 inches. Date 1650-1680. The chest was sold many years ago at an auction of the effects of Josiah Herricks, of Antrim, New Hampshire, and, therefore, called the "Antrim Chest."

It is generally understood in this volume that the lids of all chests and boxes are pine unless otherwise stated. Also that the frames are oak.

Chests were made when the passion for solidity ruled. But the American could not resist making his lid, at least, of pine, not merely because it was readily available in fine wide boards, but because it was easy to work, and to lift.

A THREE-PANEL, Corner Block Chest. Owner: Mr. H. W. Erving. Date: 1770–80. Size: 50 inches long; 33½ inches high; 21¼ inches, front to back.

This chest has two end-to-end drawers and other features which cause it to resemble closely the chest on page 25.

There are three end panels. To the student this chest is very effective with its numerous black blocks and drawer fronts. The effect of the lighting does not show the quartering of the grain of the left panel.

An interesting, possibly desirable, feature is the half-leg, turned, superimposed on the stile leg, and not fully reaching the floor. This feature does not appear on any other chest in this work.

We consider the tooth carving lends a marked degree of strength and the feeling of great antiquity.

A CARVED Oak Chest, with Drops. Owner: Mr. James N. H. Campbell. Date: 1670-80. Size: Length, 48 inches; hight, 37½ inches; front to back, 20 inches.

This very rich front exhibits many features, which are too clearly shown to require full description. A peculiarity is the very wide bottom rail. The carving between the rosettes is very unusual. So also are the four little sections into which each side panel is divided. The rosettes are carried out even on the feet, and foliage is carved below them.

AN Architectural Chest with Four Panels. Owner: Mr. Stanley A. Sweet, New York City.

This chest is an amazing instance of individuality. That a carver should desire in 1776, the plainly original date of this chest, to copy the architectural arched chest of at least a hundred and fifty years before, certainly shows a decisive and independent mind in the maker. He was not satisfied with a simulated arch, but must needs "do it right" and put the arch into the framing. The fine scale-like, lattice-like tracery on the stiles and the lower rail are noticeable, as well as the handsome rosettes, some being "doubled." The brackets are very striking. The same repeated S scrolls, carried around the arches and just under the lid are seen on the chest, page 5.

Regarding the authenticity of dates on chests, it is obvious that if one had desired to create the impression of great age, by a false date, he would have chosen an earlier date for this chest. That chests are sometimes falsely dated, we are certain. Nor is it always easy to detect the fraud. Experts in carving are themselves deceived in this matter.

A TWO-DRAWER Carved Pine Chest. Owner: Mr. B. A. Behrend. Date: 1680–1700.

This is the earliest and best pine chest that has come to our attention, in this style. It will be seen that the arched grooving is like that of the oak box, page 102. The lunettes are like those on numerous oak chests. The maker apparently loved his material, but strangely did not copy the legs of oak chests, but followed the style in his frame of the six board pine chest. It is hard to understand the three hearts carved above the lunettes, so as to interfere with them. All the heavy moldings are carried around the ends, a feature which is perhaps unique in pine. This chest was bought in Boston, but found, probably, in Connecticut. The discoverer is not living to verify the origin.

A ONE-DRAWER Carved Pine Chest. Owner: Mr. G. Winthrop Brown. Date: 1680–1700. This chest like the preceding, is a rare specimen. Its drawer was pulled by reaching under the front, so that it required no knobs. This style, which omits a rail below the drawer, while a rare feature is nevertheless present on some of the oldest cabinet pieces in this work. The little gouge notches cut in the ends of the front boards are often seen on boxes, cradles, and other cabinet pieces. A very peculiar line of carving under the large lunettes suggests small horizontal arched flutings, overlying each other.

Altogether we have here a series of carved pine chests which the collector of oak may hold lightly, but which are, in spite of that, very quaint and very important in the history of furniture.

A SIX-BOARD Pine Chest. In the former collection of the author. Date: 1690–1710. An amusing instance of quick appreciation in values is connected with this chest. It passed, within seven years, through the hands of two of the best known dealers in antique furniture, at a very small price. As it was the first carved pine chest of any consequence which either had handled, they failed to appreciate it properly.

It is easy, by comparing the simple carving with the modified lunette carving on several oak chests in this work, to see the source of the maker's motive.

We have also, bordering the carving, the arch molding, done in the solid, which was usually applied to the chests of drawers of the period. The writer knows of one or two other chests with different carving but of the same plain six-board construction.

The central sunflower very much adds to the effect. We have seen how popular it was on Connecticut chests. This one also came from Connecticut.

A CAPTAIN'S Six-Board Sea-Chest. Owner: Mr. George F. Ives, of Danbury, Connecticut. Date, appearing in three places on the front, 1677. Initialed, M. S. The term ship or sea chest has been erroneously applied to chests with V or "boot-jack" ends. Sea chests are always low, to prevent the danger of overturning. They could not have legs, owing to the manner in which they are stowed in the forecastle. They always have backs slanting forward, to fit the ship's side, and the lid is consequently narrower than the base.

The specimen before us is the best we have seen. The hearts may suggest an early date for the chest on page 31. Certainly they, with the style of carving, make a very early date plausible, and even probable.

This chest has the usual rope handle.

The lid measures 21 by 53 inches. The chest is 19 inches high.

It is a little to be wondered at that sailors, who are fond of carving, did not oftener expend their talents on ship chests. But if we begin to wonder at what was not done in early furniture our field will be too wide. It is even more wonderful that the present day sees so little real taste exhibited in furniture.

Pine is not the best material for carving. Late architectural carving was often done in pear wood, the favorite medium of Grinling Gibbon. The best wood was one with a hard, fine grain. Oak itself, while the classic material for Gothic carving, is not susceptible of the daintiest cutting.

AN Oak Two-Drawer Chest with Drops. In the Metropolitan Museum.
Date: 1660–80. The desire for variety led, in the usual fashion, to the
difference in moldings seen on the two drawers. The diamond blocks are
effective. The curious triangular blocks just below the lid are an oddity.
The favorite motive of stopping the heavy molding by returns on the front
is seen here in perfection.

A CHEST with Drops. Owner: Mr. G. Winthrop Brown, Brookline. A two-drawer chest with single panel ends. The decoration is extremely rare. The motive of the fronts of chests always tended to straight lines. In this case we have a series of curved moldings.

There are four ball feet. The chest bears initials, A. D. Date: 1680–1700.

The drops are also rare in form. The long drops on the leg stiles are symmetrical from their centers, like turnings in the stretchers of chairs.

It is a feature of ball-foot chests that their base molding runs around the end as well as the front. This may or may not be true of stile-foot chests.

HEAVY Two-Drawer Ball-foot Chest. Owner: Mr. Brooks Reed. Date: 1660–70.

The heavy effect of this chest suggests its early date. The habit of simulating drawers in the front of the chest part proper shows, however, that at the time this chest was made, complete chests of drawers were well known. The back legs are stiles. Later chests with ball feet were more likely to have the four feet alike.

AN Oak Chest, with Drops.   Owner: Mr. Harry Long.   Date 1670-1680.
This chest is peculiar in having its stiles run down below the base molding
before the balls are attached.   It has the appearance of a chest on which ball
feet are out of place, but the feet appear to be original. There can be no
doubt that some restorations have been made, in the interest of ornament,
using ball feet where a plain stile was originally used.

On pages 61 and 66 there are also stiles running below the body of
the chests before the ball-feet are attached.   We do not consider this
feature a merit.

The reader will notice the entire absence, on the ends of chests, of long
drops on the stiles.   The makers were content, at most, with affixing
bosses in the end panels, though sometimes even these are omitted.   Chests
were often so placed that the ends were not prominent, and so not important.

The embossed central square on the panels is a pleasing feature, and the
chest altogether is very attractive.   As restored, the moldings are in red.
We err in supposing the color decoration of early furniture was quiet.   It
was brilliant in the extreme.   The old reds which we admire are merely the
result of age.

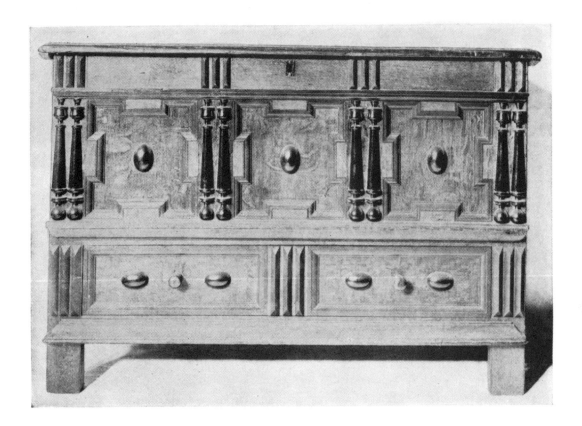

AN Oak Chest, with Applied Ornament. Owner: Mr. H. W. Erving.
Date: 1680-1690.

This chest shows no very marked variation from some that have preceded
it, except that we have now passed out of the carved styles, and shall find
only such decoration as variations in moldings and in applied turned pieces
can supply. The moldings on this chest are of Spanish cedar. There are
two panels in the ends. The triglyphs, which appear here in numbers, give
a strong series of vertical lines. Size: 45½ inches long, 33 inches high, 20½
inches from front to back.

It has not hitherto been mentioned, but the reader will have seen that
oak chests were made of riven lumber, and therefore they almost uniformly
show the quarter grain. This is sufficient ornament in itself. In fact, we
count it a defect that carving should ever appear on any except plain oak.

AN Oak Chest, with Applied Ornaments. Owner: In the former Wallace Nutting Collection; then owned by Mr. Chauncey C. Nash; then by an owner unknown to the writer. It is marked by very handsome quartering, apparently left free of ornament on the top rail to show its beauty. Date: 1670-90.

At the top of the next page is a chest of oak owned by Mr. Dwight Blaney of Boston and Weston. It is wisely left in the rough. Date: 1660-70.

At the bottom of the page opposite is an oak chest owned by Mr. H. W. Erving. It has the characteristic shadow moldings strongly emphasized. The end panels are varied with blocks, forming short armed crosses. It has two-panel ends. It is 43 inches long, 31 inches high, and is 20½ inches from front to back.

AN Oak Chest, with Applied Ornaments. Owner: Mrs. Hulings Cowperthwaite Brown, of Boston and Brookline. A chest with interesting ornaments, inherited from the Waters Estate. Date: 1670-90.

On page 43, at the top, is a chest belonging to Mr. H. W. Erving. It has three-panel ends. It was made as seen with no rail under the drawer. Its date is 1660-80. It is 45½ inches long, 24½ inches high, the feet having been shortened, and 18¼ inches from front to back.

A chest at the bottom of page 43, belonging to Mr. H. W. Erving, has pine panels, with the usual oak frame. There is a one panel end.

Date: 1670-80. It is 41¾ inches long, 28¼ inches high, and 18½ inches from front to back.

Chests should not be judged in this book by the space accorded to them. The exigencies of space, with so many specimens, must be apparent.

AN Oak Chest, with Chamfered Feet. Date: 1670-90. It is 47 inches long, 29 inches high, and 20½ inches from front to back.

The shadow mold is the only ornament on stiles and rails. The student will easily discern that the panel mold at the top and on the outside stiles is worked in after the panel is put together, whereas the similar mold, on the inner stile, is worked before assembling the panel. The reason is easily seen. A miter was avoided; yet the general effect was preserved.

The chamfering of the legs seems original, though why it should have been done, it is hard to say, as no one would now suppose any use or beauty was conserved. Owner: the author.

With this chest we pass from the ornamental panel to simpler fashions coincidentally with the short and delightful excursion in painted decoration which arose about 1700, and continued perhaps twenty years, in a very limited territory. Of course the plain, or nearly plain oak chest was used by all sorts of persons, as to worldly condition. It is sufficient to show a few.

AN Oak Chest with Painted Pine Panels and Painted Drawer-Front. (Branford, Connecticut.) The oak carcass of the chest is painted black, evidently in imitation of the contemporary English imitations of lacquer work brought into England from the far East. The end panels are painted in a thistle design while the central panel is dated 1705-6. The painting is much plainer as seen on the chest than in the photograph. There was a tradition of painting furniture in the shore towns of Connecticut, including Branford, Guilford, Madison, and extending up the Connecticut River

to Middletown. The chest is now in the Wadsworth Atheneum, Hartford. Mr. George Dudley Seymour, owner. Date: 1690-1700.

The little chest at the bottom of this page is painted in very effective decoration, but the photograph does not bring out its features. The chest is owned by the Metropolitan Museum. Date about 1700.

A ONE-DRAWER Oak Chest. Owner: Mr. Dwight Blaney. Date 1660-80.

The striking feature is the extraordinary repetition, above, below and on, the drawer-front, of the same molding. We cannot deny it is very effective. The motive is that found on the choicest sheathed paneling of our earliest houses. The same idea is carried out on the top rail. The stiles show, on each side, a triple bead which also appears at the top and the bottom, that is on the rails, above and below, the drawer. The top of the panels is chamfered, on the rail as well as the bottom—a rare feature. Mr. Blaney's other numerous pieces have previously figured in works on furniture. We seek to show, almost entirely, what has not hitherto been made public.

On page 48 are two miniature pine chests, made to go together. Owner: Mr. Geo. D. Seymour. They are in the Wadsworth Atheneum. Date: 1710-20.

A SIX-BOARD Single-Drawer, Whitewood Chest, with front paneled in the Jacobean manner. Formerly in the collection of George Dudley Seymour. Now owned by Miss Mary Miles Lewis Peck, of Bristol, Connecticut. An heirloom of the Lewis Family, of Farmington. Found in Bristol, Connecticut, an offset of the town of Farmington, by Mr. Seymour about 1895.

The panels are painted black, as well as the incised moldings in the rails and stiles. The applied moldings are painted red. A peculiarity in this chest is the running of the molding on the outside stiles down through the width of the drawer. The central block of the panels is very thick, protruding far beyond the face of the chest. Date 1700-20.

In 1920 Mr. Seymour found another six-board, single-drawer Whitewood chest in Bristol of the same style. The two chests are so much alike that they appear to have been made by the same hand. In 1920 the author of this book found another chest of the same character, which piece also is believed to have come from Connecticut. These three chests are all that have come to light thus far of this style.

ABOVE is a pine chest, owned by Mr. G. Winthrop Brown. Date, 1710-20. It has pleasing lines.

Below, on the left, a miniature chest in pine. It is 16¾ inches high; the top is 19 x 13 inches. On the right is another little chest in pine. It is 20 inches high; the top is 23 x 13¾ inches. Both are owned by Mr. Chauncey C. Nash. Their date is 1710-20.

A TURNIP-FOOT All Pine Chest.   Owner: the author.
The single arch mold suggests the date: 1690-1710.
The small chest below is a six board pine chest, dating about 1710.

ON the right is a little chest with painted decoration of a very fine type. It is owned by Mr. Chauncey C. Nash. The upper drawer is treated as a unit with the chest section, in the decorative motive. The lower drawer has birds, probably doves, in addition to the floral design. The single arch molding gives us a date, with other considerations, between 1700 and 1710. This chest belongs with the small class with this decoration, found in the south central portion of Con-

necticut, sometimes as framed, at other times as board chests or chests of drawers. Of course the framed chests are more important, as they are also more rare.

THE little ball-foot chest below is owned by Mr. Arthur W. Wellington of Boston and Weston. Date: 1700-10. The miniature chest is always appealing. Whether is was made for children, or to place above another piece, for specially valuable belongings, we do not always know. Doubtless it was at times put to both uses. This chest is pine.

It is often the case that the front feet are balls, while behind the board end is carried down.

A PAINTED Chest of Whitewood. The property of the State of Connecticut, in the Stone House, at Guilford. These decorated pieces are mostly in whitewood, otherwise called tulip wood, with pine in parts. The whitewood front presented a finer grain for painting than oak or pine. The frames are oak. A goose painted on the end panel gives this piece its name of Goose Chest. The outside scroll does not differ much from other examples in this book. The design on the upper panel shows a handsome vase of flowers. Compare pages 51, 45, 62, 63 and 74.

Within a triangle whose north apex is Middletown, east apex Madison, and west apex Branford, all these pieces, together with the whitewood chests shown or mentioned on page 47, have been found.

A PAINTED Chest, with Two Drawers. Owner: Mr. Geo. F. Ives.
Date: about 1700.   Size of lid: 20 by 42 inches.   Hight of chest, 40 inches.

This chest belongs to the class shown on page 74, and elsewhere. But the
design is different from the thistle and crown. To give room for a handsome
spray between the drawer panels, the latter were set very far apart.

There is a large tulip on the ends, as on page 62, and the whole design is
very attractive.

The feet are missing, which is not so noticeable, as owing to the unusual
hight of the chest, the proportion is well maintained.

A SMALL Painted Chest. Owner: Mr. H. W. Erving. Date: about 1700.
When purchased the chest was entirely covered with a thick coat of brown paint which had been on for many years. On carefully removing this, the figures all came out, and have simply been touched up line for line, with absolute fidelity. One interesting fact brought out is preserved to us by this protective coating of paint. That is the brilliancy of the coloring. It is often imagined that the colors on decorated pieces were soft. They were in reality quite strikingly bright, almost painfully so. Some of the parts of the color on this chest were unbelievably red.

As retraced the fascinating little chest teaches us much. The background appears black, but is a few shades off, rather green-black. The thistle blossoms and buds and the crown are the most intense and varied centers of color.

Size: 25¼ inches long, 16¼ inches from front to back, 19 inches high. The overhang of the lid is ⅞ of an inch in front, and 1½ inches at the ends. The material is whitewood. The origin is south central Connecticut.

AN Oak Six-Board Chest. Owner: Koopman's, Boston. This example shows the gouged notches at the ends of the front, and a mold at the joints of the boards of the front, similar to that on the earliest sheathing.

The chest was the one indispensable piece of furniture in an old civilization or in a new country. Men could, and did for ages, eat from a board. They sat on the chest. They could sleep on the ground, and did, even in a highly civilized country, taking up their beds, that is, rugs, and marching on. Or they slept on a chest. So the chest is the central symbol of house furnishing. It was the repository of treasures, the emblem of family dignity; the object of bequest by will, more than any other property. It was the first effort at joinery, and the last achievement of art. Among nomads, where it was set down, there was home; when it was taken up, the march followed. It was the family ark.

Romance, tragedy, the joy of the bride, the last memory of a long dead owner, all gathered about a chest. The poorest could have something that was called a chest. The wealthy or the devout summoned craftsmen to put forth the best powers of their cunning and their genius upon this symbol of family importance, or churchly devotion.

A CHEST in pine owned by Mr. W. of Boston. This piece should be compared with the wardrobe of pine and whitewood, owned by the same person, on page 145. Doubtless the reason why chests of this character are very rare is that at the period of wall panel work in pine the chest had, for the most part, passed out of style. For this very reason the piece before us is of the more interest with its numerous panels which are raised, and with its bracket feet, which do not go with any of the chests that precede this. Somewhat is lost from the feet, perhaps an inch.

The question of the date of pine paneling is mooted. The best antiquarians who study houses place it at 1720. It would therefore hardly be possible to name a much earlier date for this piece. There is in Mr. Geo. F. Ives' collection a room of paneling into a side of which a secretary is built with the same panel work as that used in the walls, and resembling this chest. The date is agreeable to that already named.

The increased demand for labor doubtless works against artistic developments in furniture. If the Indians had been hurried they would never have thought out the designs in fabrics which are now sought after. Beautiful and worthy work doubtless requires also a higher appreciation than it now receives from the American public. As a politician must die before he becomes a statesman, an artist or an artisan is seldom a genius so long as he is with us.

A SEVENTEENTH Century Ship Model. Owner: Mr. Geo. F. Ives. It stands on a decorated chest with slender legs. Owing to the difficulty of bringing out the red and black decoration we do not attempt to show the chest, merely using it to serve as a base for the model. Those who know, state that every rope on an ancient ship is shown here. It is all original requiring no restoration. The very sharply cocked bowsprit, and the high poop, are peculiar to ancient vessels. The subject of ship models is worthy of extended treatment, which it receives elsewhere, and we can hardly enter farther into the subject in a work of this scope.

The chest, by the way, on its high legs, is said to have been placed, as now, at the foot of a bed, to hold extra bed coverings.

A SIX-BOARD Pine Chest. The panel work is cut from the solid. The original coat of red paint is in place. Date: 1700-20. Owner of this and the chest below: Mr. George Dudley Seymour. Origin: Capt. Chas. Churchill House, Newington. Below is a chest on shoes. The scratch carving running around the front is discernible on the left end. Date: 1710-20.

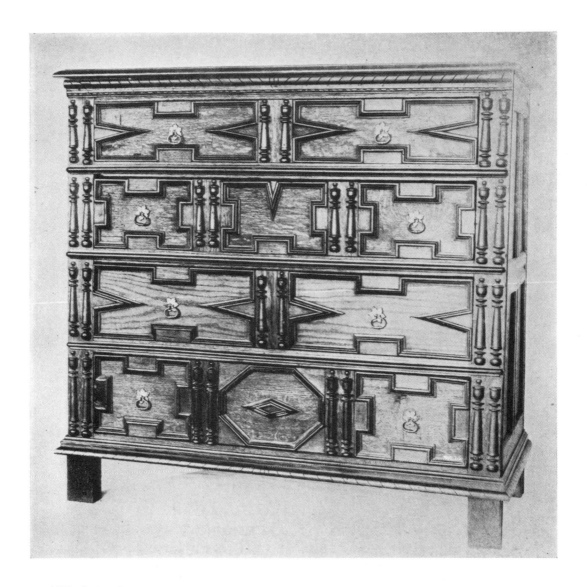

AN Oak Chest of Drawers owned by the author. The extraordinary amount of ornament applied to chests and chests of drawers as the 17th Century drew to its close, is no doubt quaint, but is a distinct decline from the more artistic types of the 16th Century. Yet we love the work of the fathers, in that they did what they could, and eagerly groped after beauty, which their children do not, always. The decorations are shown too clearly to need rehearsal in the text. Date 1680-1700. It is 46 by 21¾ inches and 43¾ inches high—a large article.

AN All-Pine Chest of Drawers. Owner: Koopman's, Boston. This piece is probably within the limits of the 17th Century. The little gothic arches into which the feet are cut, and the character of the drawers, incline us to date it about 1690, for the single arch molding may go back to that time. The discovery of the piece is said to have been made in Maine. It is odd in having all the drawers alike. It is a question of taste, on which there might be a difference of opinion whether a piece is more attractive in this form, or with a variety in the drawer fronts.

A CHEST of Four Drawers. Owner: the author. Date: 1690-1700. There is one heavily embossed panel at the end. Size: 39¾ inches long, 38 inches high; 19¾ inches from front to back.

The top and bottom drawers are blocked, that is, they protrude beyond the body of the piece, and match the end panel.

The feet are flattened balls, sometimes called onion feet. They are strikingly odd from being set on extended stiles. Origin: Connecticut, again!

A DECORATED Chest of drawers, shown from two positions on this and the following page. Owned by the author. The tulip design of the end view is very bold and is practically the same at as the end of the Davidson highboy, page 74, where the reflection prevents its being well shown.

A half dozen articles of furniture in this decoration have come to light very recently. They are in whitewood which is, otherwise, and properly, called tulip wood. It is rather commonly found in New England, but structurally, in old furniture, it seems mostly to have been confined to articles made about 1700. Thus the three chests like that on page 47 are in tulip wood. This material shows little grain and less color, and is a semi-hard wood. It had no beauty unless decorated. The front of this piece shows a different design for each drawer, and the lines are very delicate. On the two drawers at the top an excursion in portraiture appears, the faces having vines issuing from the lips. They are in flat, light color, and make us wish

that the decorator had not essayed his skill! The coloring of the tendrils is nearly white. That of the rest is in shades of yellow, old red, pink, etc.

Some original handles remain. The drawers are of the heavy early construction and are made with side runs, a fashion which went out about 1700. The body is 19 by 42 inches; it stands 43 inches high. The author has spliced the feet about three inches. It is otherwise original.

The decoration while a little worn, is better and in a better state of preservation than we remember having seen elsewhere.

Date about 1700.

AN Oak and Walnut Chest of Drawers. Date: 1690-1700. The carcass is 33 inches high, 36 inches long, 22 inches front to back. The molding projects to give an over-all length, both top and bottom, of 39 inches.

Top, half inch walnut. Frame and end rails, oak; the end panels plain pine, there being two, one above the other, sunken, with perfectly plain rails and stiles. Drawer fronts pine, covered with ⅛ inch walnut; and all moldings walnut. The posts are 2 by 1½ inches. The two wide drawers are blocked. The drawers have the grooved side runs. The piece was bought in the rough, by the author, in Boston, 1921, and is in his collection. The feet were missing. Added, they are five inches high, which length is conservative. We notice a tendency during the latter years of the 17th Century to construction in walnut, and to smaller posts. With the exception of the feet the chest is practically original.

A CHEST of Drawers in Walnut, owned by the author. It is somewhat smaller than the average chest of drawers, being 38¼ by 21 inches, and 33½ inches high. It has undergone some repairs and the handles are not original. It is low enough to satisfy the modern taste for a dressing case. A very interesting and unusual feature is the series of small panels on the stiles. They add not a little to the appearance. They are instead of the usual applied half spindles. It will be noticed that the first and the third drawers are alike; also the second and the fourth—a familiar arrangement adopted for variety's sake.

The date is difficult to determine. If we say 1680–1700 we shall not greatly err.

AN Oak Ball-Foot Chest of Drawers. Date: 1680-90. The center panel of the top drawer contains the initials "R. B." while the center panel of the drawer below contains the initials "A. P." The ends of the chest contain two panels separated by the returned ends of an applied molding extending between the two upper and two lower drawers. The other applied moldings between the drawers extend only to the outer edges of the stiles. The ball feet should be compared with those on page 61. Mr. George Dudley Seymour, owner.

Below, is a chest of drawers the picture of which is furnished by Mr. H. V. Weil, of New York City, who owned it at one time. Let us say here quite emphatically that none of the pictures in this book are made to scale. This piece is larger than it appears. The end panel is blocked like those on pages 61 and 56.

AN Elaborately Paneled Chest of Drawers. Owner: Mr. Brooks Reed.
Date: 1680-90.

Features to which one should attend are the blocking of the top and
bottom drawers, the difference in the depth of the drawers and the system
of moldings on the end panel to enhance the blocked effect. Compare
with central blocks on chest, page 38. Compare also the panels formed on
the stiles by moldings with the author's chest of drawers, on page 65.

OAK and Pine Chest of Drawers. This piece has effective ball feet. The drawers, including the moldings, are of pine. The drop handles are very unusual and pleasing. The termination in a ring is a device graceful in itself and convenient in use. The rosettes behind the drops match well the handsome 'scutcheons.

In the former collection of the author. Owner: Mr. I. Sack. Date 1690-1700.

The transition from the chest of drawers with decorative moldings, to a plain front, doubtless may be accounted for by the coming in of the highboy, which used decoration of another sort. The legs were elegantly turned, and veneer of an elaborate character supplanted the molded front. There was a gain in the filling of wall space. But the modern return to the chest of drawers shows it a more convenient piece of furniture.

AN Oak Two-Part Chest of Drawers. Owner: Mr. George Dudley Seymour. The two-parts are separable on the medial line, which should be covered by a molding, over the joint, but was not so covered when the chest was found in the rough state. The brasses are in part original. The piece was, so it is said, brought into Boston to sell, from Dedham. It was put in order by Patrick Stevens, then employed by Robbins Bros., of Hartford. Date: 1660-70. Hight, 56¾ inches; the top is 20½ by 38¾ inches.

A MINIATURE Chest of Drawers. Photograph furnished by Mr. H. V. Weil, who owned the piece. The handles, which of course are of the usual size for a large chest of drawers, display very quaintly the comparatively small size of the drawers. It is such pieces as these, so rare, so appealing, that make the quest of antique furniture what it is. Date: 1690–1700.

Below is a miniature pine chest of drawers: Owner: Mr. Harry Long. In the moldings we have the style of a somewhat earlier time. The pine feet, being part of the end board, give a date perhaps as late as 1700-10.

These little pieces are sometimes called child's furniture. They may have been so intended, or they may have stood on larger chests of drawers, to store small articles of the wardrobe.

A TWO-PART Oak Chest of Drawers. Owner: J. Milton Coburn, M. D., South Norwalk. Date: 1670-90.

The applied ball-turned molding is a most interesting feature. There is the not unusual arrangement of decorative moldings, whereby the second and fourth drawers are more elaborate than the first and third; and in this case, as frequently, deeper than the others.

Handles on furniture in America, as the end of the 17th Century approached, were sometimes wooden knobs, always small in diameter, and to be differentiated from the 19th Century knob—and sometimes brass drop handles. The brass gradually supplanted the wood on the finer pieces. But in the case of tavern tables, and other simple articles, the small wooden knob persisted to the middle of the 18th Century.

ON pages 73-85 appear a series of high-boys, called in England tall-boys, or high chests of drawers. While these are impressive from their size, and offer good opportunity for the display of veneer, and of style in turning, they are somewhat ungainly, their very name being a sly poke at their awkwardness. The period we treat here excludes the "bonnet top". Highboys began as flat tops, logically, as they were simply chests of drawers on legs. A very few, like that belonging to the author, on the opposite page, had scrolled legs, influenced by the Flemish style of chairs. Most had turned legs in the trumpet pattern, clearly shown on page 77, and modified on pages 74 and 75 to a cup and ball. There were usually four legs in front and two behind, all connected by a scrolled stretcher, which followed the contour of the arches on the frame above.

The material was usually a walnut veneer, varied by solid wood pieces like the oak specimen on page 73, the butternut on page 76, or by pine or maple, as in specimens shown. On page 74 we have an extraordinary example in decoration, reminding us of the similar crown and thistle work on pages 62 and 63. It is owned by Mr. James Davidson, of New London.

The early example on page 75, owned by Mr. Chauncey C. Nash, shows the heavy frame, considerably larger than the top, a feature of importance for very early styles. This piece is also a five-legger, and the frame is without arches. The brasses on these pieces begin with drops, and are followed by plates and bails, a style which is found in a considerable number of instances as early as 1700. The earliest highboy here shown scarcely goes back beyond 1690, and the latest may be 1720. An instance of an ornamental molded panel is known, possibly more than one. These examples before us are now shown for the first time.

The specimen on page 76 is owned by the author.

Incidentally the highboy on page 73, shows, or may show, the origin of the heavy Flemish scroll base on Victorian furniture. But this middle 19th Century furniture carried the scroll into huge clumsy proportions, and applied it, in many cases, to the frame instead of making it a part of the structure, as a supporting member.

The frame of the highboy on page 73 extends beyond the top. This is an early feature, where the extension is so considerable. It will be seen that the frames on highboys on pages 73, 74, and 75 have the single long drawer. This feature is also shown on the pieces on pages 78 and 85. The plain, table-like frame suggests an earlier period.

A FLEMISH-LEGGED Highboy, owned by the author. Mr. James Davidson also owns one, and another exists in New York. This piece is in American oak, even to the backs of the drawers. The curved legs, however, appear to be bass wood. Date, perhaps 1680-1700.

A PAINTED Highboy. Date· 1700. The end does not show, owing to reflections, the large single tulip, like that on page 62. The decorative scheme of the front also bears a close resemblance to the chest of drawers on page 63.

A FIVE-LEGGED Highboy, owned by Mr. Chauncey C. Nash. A rare specimen, in walnut, practically all original. Date 1690–1710.

ON page 77 is a rare arrangement of highboy legs, following the usual design of the corresponding cross-stretcher lowboy. The incipient pair of missing legs is represented by the acorn drops. One should note the thin flat strip which lines the under edge of the frame and, by a slight projection, forms a bead. This is characteristic. This piece is in walnut. The present owner is unknown. It was in the former collection of the author. Date: 1700-10.

On page 78 is a specimen in herring-bone walnut veneer. The brasses are good. The turning is not as delicate as the preceding. It was bought by the author in Boston, and taken to the Webb House, Wethersfield. Present owner unknown.

On page 79 is a remarkably good curly maple effect. It is the property of Mr. Geo. F. Ives. The interest centers in the country-made turnings, which were probably done from memory. The turner "did himself proud" in the drops, not stopping short of seven rings. Date: 1700-20.

On page 81 is the most perfectly preserved old highboy the author has seen. It is owned by Mr. W. of Boston. Every part, including every handle, is original. The veneer is in fine condition. It is in the herring-bone pattern. The date can be hardly later than 1690-1700. The frame, below, is 38½ by 21¼ inches. The upper part is 36½ by 20 inches. The total hight is 61 inches, and outside measurement on the table mold is 40½ inches, and 22¼ inches from front to back.

The piece has never been cleaned.

The highboy on page 83 is the only one we have seen with two small end-to-end drawers over the central arch. On page 76 there is no central drawer, also a rare feature. But on page 77 we find two small drawers on each side of the frame. In the odd piece on page 84, there are two abutting drawers. The conventional type is supposed to have three drawers in the frame, the central one being shallower than the others to allow for the arch under the frame. These variations in detail have no little interest for collectors, though they are otherwise more curious than important.

When we enter upon highboys we are as likely to find them in Massachusetts as in Connecticut, which is supreme in its oak treasures.

A HERRING-BONE Walnut Highboy. Date: 1700. Owner: the author.
On the next page is the fine example of a curly maple highboy owned by
Mr. W. of Boston. Its turnings are beautiful. It is painted black, and is
in all respects original. Date: about 1710.

A SIMPLE Highboy, without stretchers, owned by Mrs. E. B. Leete of Guilford. It is a great rarity. The leg turnings are quite like those of some tables. While the need of stretchers on highboys is apparent, this piece has existed without them since about 1720.

A SIMPLE Five-legged Highboy, owned by Mr. I. Sack. Its 17th century turnings suggest tavern table legs. It is a piece of much interest. The single arch mold suggests 1690–1700 as the date.

THE ORIGIN and purpose of little chests on frames is hazy. They are close cousins to the boxes which follow. Besides the descriptive name they are also called Pilgrim Chests and Desk Boxes on Frames. Their size would indicate their probable use for more precious contents than were placed in the great chests, but as the tops were always flat they could scarcely have been used for writing purposes, unless one stood while at work.

The same impulse which brought in the highboy was evidently at work to bring in the box-on-frame, that is, greater convenience.

The charm of the piece we are considering lies in the obvious artistic impulse that created it. Undoubtedly it was a labor of love, constructed with ingenious care and thought, stimulated by an ambition to produce a masterpiece. All the little refinements, together with the more important features, suggest this conclusion. The popular habit of naming all chests "dower chests" or "hope chests" is not unnatural, and we are not prepared to say that most chests did not come into being as wedding dowers. It was quite the thing that the bride-to-be should find it useful and appropriate to have a chest of some sort wherein to accumulate the various stock of household linen that she would require.

The one drawer which always appears in this type of chest was convenient for the more precious or the smaller articles.

Until a recent period such chests were exceedingly rare and even now there are perhaps only twenty to thirty known. The notable piece next following is unique. It was found in York, Maine, and is far more ornate as well as earlier and quainter than any of its humbler brethren on the following pages.

Its American origin should not be challenged as it has pine in the lid and bottoms of the frame and drawer. Its most striking feature is the doubled stretcher work of the ball-turned base, a markedly good design for strength, and possibly unique in this respect also.

Another astonishing feature is the beautiful urn turning of the front posts reminding one of court cupboards. The piece is in an unrestored state and therefore shows only one of the two arches of the side panels. The star of the center panel also originally had eight points. These minor marks of years, however, only endear the piece to us. It is painted black. One may hope to see it restored ultimately, as the somewhat glossy appearance it presents makes a good picture of it impossible.

Date: 1670–90.

The fortunate owner is Mr. Chauncey C. Nash, of Milton.

AN unique little chest-on-frame. Owner: Chauncey C. Nash. Hight 36 inches; length 27 inches; depth 18½ inches. Oak, with pine lid and drawer bottom. Date: 1660–90.

A CHEST on frame partly restored. Property of the Wayside Inn. Date: about 1680. The sizes of all these pieces are about the same as that on page 87.

A CHEST-ON-FRAME, from the collection of Miss C. M. Traver, New York City. This fine specimen is in its original condition. It is a question, mooted among antiquarians, whether these chests, with square stretchers, had a shelf upon them. If the chest opposite this is correct the shelf must have been original as the applied molding on the bottom stretcher laps over the lower edge of the shelf. Further, there was a shelf on the piece above, but it was destroyed. Date: 1670–90.

A CHEST-ON-FRAME owned by the Rhode Island School of Design. The foliage decoration, a branch of delicate sprays, is clearly discernible. This decoration is usually in black on a red ground. These simple little chests are of the class desired because of their size, their variety, and their merit.

THE description of this chest-on-frame appears on the following page.

[91]

ON the previous page is a good example of the decorated panel chest-on-frame. It is the property of Mr. Arthur W. Wellington of Boston and Weston. For the most part the decorations are in colors which are not picked out by the camera. The turnings are attractively done.

On the following page is a similar piece, but with a deeper drawer, and with decoration which shows somewhat. It is owned by Mrs. F. G. Patterson, of Boston, and is further described on its page.

Instituting a comparison between the little chests here shown, we may place the Nash chest in a class by itself. The others are divided between decorated chests, with turnings below, and chests with carving and applied turned decorations. These latter are the older. The most perfect is the chest on page 89, which is unrestored.

Most or all of the chests-on-frames originated in New England, within narrow limits from southern New Hampshire to Cape Cod. They are a type so marked as to attract much attention. Many collectors have never seen one. At least half of them have come to light within a year, as their distinctive features made them sought as soon as they were known to exist. They now hold values parallel with those placed on large spindle-decorated chests. There is a difference of opinion as between the two styles, with perhaps a slight present leaning to the decorated pattern.

A specimen of this style of chests in the possession of Mr. H. W. Erving has the spray decoration on an unpainted panel, and is fully more attractive in method of application. The leafage is green, the stem black. Another specimen of the style in the possession of the Rhode Island School of Design lacks the front stretcher, but is otherwise very admirable. Mr. B. A. Behrend owns three specimens. Most of the others have been mentioned in previous works on furniture.

We lament the going out of style of an article so attractive and convenient. It certainly adds to the realism of a family about to be instituted to have one receptacle into which its treasures can be gathered. Around such a piece one's heart strings twined. It was the symbol, in substantial form of the greatest social institution, and held that proud position until the cradle supplanted it.

A CHEST-ON-FRAME described on the previous page. This piece is in beautiful condition and the turnings are very handsome—the best perhaps to be found on a decorated piece of the kind. Date about 1700.

ON the next page is an oak chest-on-frame, which differs strikingly from the other examples we show. Its back legs follow the style of the court cupboard, instead of being turned like the front legs. The side and back stretchers are also plain. The turnings of the front legs and stretcher are extremely rare, being what we may call the reverse of the ball turning, or a series of turned flutes, into which a ball-turned piece would fit exactly. The lid is of yellow pine. The false drawer has knobs instead of the usual bosses. The chest is 36 inches high, and the frame is 27½ by 16 inches. The lid overhangs ¾ of an inch in front, and 1¼ inches at the ends. The date is 1680-90. It is owned by the author.

On page 96 is an example of an all-ball-turned chest-on-frame, made with painted panels. It is owned by Mr. B. A. Behrend. Its date is about 1680-90. The frame is oak; the lid pine. It is peculiar in having a perfectly plain drawer front. The mold on the rail below the drawer is not seen on some of the other chests-on-frames.

A few years since there were not above a half dozen chests-on-frames known. If they are found in the next few years as rapidly as in the five years just passed, they will rival the sunflower chest in numbers. In passing from the treatment of these pieces we cannot fail to see how closely they resemble the boxes which follow, where the boxes have flat tops. The chests are generally a little larger and may have suggested desks. There is a close resemblance.

Properly following analogies, we should look for antique chests, of a large size, on frames. One is shown on shoes. But we know of no large chests, set on legs, and with a drawer under. Their place was taken by the highboy. The discussion of this matter in Lyon is very interesting, but developments since his volume should have added more to our knowledge than we can claim to have gained. One thing, however, we feel more clearly: the little chests on frames were not designed as desks. We have, it is true, almost no desks of the period, but we do find slant top boxes. Why, if these little chests were for desks, were the tops never slanted? The decision must be that they were not designed as desks.

INTRODUCING the subject of boxes we present a miniature box, owned by Mr. George Dudley Seymour. We can call it a toy box. Its entire surface is covered with carving in the Friesian manner. The body of the box is worked out from a single piece of wood, which appears to be whitewood. The cover, also of a single piece, has thinned edges running in grooves formed in the edge of the body. Midway of the length of the cover are the initials A. C., while the initials N. J. are incised on the end of the cover. Length, 4½ inches; width, 2½ inches; thickness, 1½ inches. As we have found Friesian designs, carved in America, we are allowed to assume that this box may be native. Certainly whitewood is native. Date: about 1700. The box was found in Cheshire, Connecticut, about 1900.

On page 109 is another minute box, owned by Mr. Hollis French, of Boston. It rests on top of a larger box. There is in this box, again, a Friesian design, with beautifully notched carving on the base and the lid. While these boxes are very rare, they were useful, more than the name toy box would imply. Probably they were used as jewel boxes to be placed, if need were, in a large "strong box." Many simple boxes of about this size are found with slight ornament. They are in some cases attractive but, of course, never important.

THE Box, otherwise called Bible box or desk box, is a small article designed to rest on a table. Undoubtedly it was sometimes used for a great Bible. But in general it was a receptacle for valuable papers or other articles too small or too important to place in a chest. Where boxes have cabinets as well as slant fronts, of course they are designed for desks. It is unfortunate that they should be named, indiscriminately, Bible boxes. It is better to use the shorter term box.

The English box has a lid, back and bottom of oak, and is usually very dark. We have tried in the following pages to exclude boxes of a foreign character. The American box was rarely all oak, and the wood is lighter than the English box.

The hinge for slant top boxes is, in best forms, a butterfly. The flat tops generally have pin hinges like chests.

Probably several hundred American boxes are known. Certainly this estimate is not too high if we include plain pine boxes. The specimens of a finer character may be confined to 150 or 200 in number. The design of the carving follows closely the carving of chests. Almost invariably there is a molded base. The locks are likely to be missing. It is very probable that where no lock was ever fitted the box was used for a Bible. The writer has never seen this distinction made, but it is very reasonable. It will be noted that many of the most beautiful specimens never had locks.

The Bible no one would steal, not because it lacked value, but owing to the fear of sacrilege. Hence it needed no key to protect it. The Bible was in many cases, a huge, very expensive volume. It contained of course a family record more important then, when the state kept no vital statistics. In fact history would lack much if deprived of these records. At a time also when optical knowledge was small, a Bible with large print was necessary for the aged, who had recourse to it often. And it was so heavy that it required a rest. Hence, the Bible-box.

On the other hand, nearly every slant top specimen, which was made for a desk, had a lock, at least the examples before us would so indicate.

The ends are more likely to be plain than carved. The presence or absence of a cabinet has no bearing on desirability. The cabinets are always very simple. The box passed out of fashion with the general introduction of desks. But a modern desk box persisted, and is found today in mahogany in many homes. It opens on a slant, being flat on top.

A BOX of Oak. Owner: Mr. H. W. Erving. Date: 1660-80. Size: 21¼ by 14½ inches, and 8½ inches high. There is some difficulty in naming the carving running across the upper front. Perhaps the best name is arched fluting. The lunettes familiar on chests run across beneath the fluting. The same carving is repeated on the ends, which is unusual.

The box at the bottom of the page also belongs to Mr. Erving. The short half-moon carvings in three rows near the bottom were seen on one chest we have figured. Date: 1670-90. The top line of carving is unusual and attractive. The box is 27¾ by 17 inches, and 11 inches high.

The base mold on boxes is often of the very simplest character—surprisingly so, since so much elaboration was expended on the other parts of the box.

A BOX owned by Mr. Dwight Blaney. The carving is artistically designed and executed.

Boxes are usually put together with nails. The only paneled box we have to show appears on page 102. Occasionally we find dovetailing. It is obvious that panel work was a device for covering large surfaces, and not ordinarily indulged in for beauty's sake alone.

Below is an oak box belonging to Mr. George Dudley Seymour. It is asymmetrical, one panel having the initial W. The design is a tulip pattern, less conventionalized than usual. The corners are notched. Date: 1670-90. Now in the Wadsworth Atheneum, Hartford. Origin: Guilford, Connecticut.

AN Oak Box belonging to Mr. H. W. Erving. Date: 1670-90. The aster or sunflower is a design found on much 17th Century work. An example appears even on the pine chest, page 33. As a matter of fact, of course the flower may be something else. It looks more like a rose. There are turned ornaments on the ends.

Size: 25½ by 17 inches, and 9½ inches high. Initialed, E. D.

At the bottom of the page an oak box appears. Owner: Mr. Arthur W. Wellington.

The carving of arched flutes is like that on Mr. Erving's box on page 99. Below is a handsome rope pattern with rosettes. Date: 1660-80.

AN Oak Box, with two rows of arched flutes. It is unusually large, being 23½ by 19 inches, and 11⅛ inches high. Date: 1660-80. It carries carving on the ends also.

Another oak box, below, in paneling, is a rare design. It bears the initials, H. S. The applied drops and bosses are mostly original. Size: 27⅝ by 17⅜ and 9¾ inches high. Date: 1670-90.

Both of these boxes are owned by the author. Only one who loved ornament for its own sake would have taken pains to work out so many little panels as we see in this box. The maker really delighted in design.

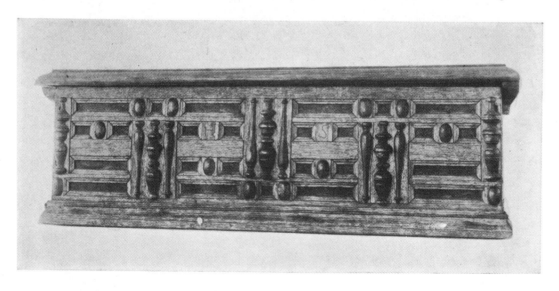

A POND Lily Box, with raised carving. Owner: Mr. H. W. Erving. The carving is asymmetrical, and rather more attractive on that account. The dimensions are: 25½ by 16¾ inches. It is 9 inches high. Date: 1670-90.

Below is a pine box with starfish design. There are one complete and two half lunettes, each with tooth carving to form the outlines. The carving is raised. The design is striking. The battle-ax shaped designs between the lunettes are difficult to understand. No base molding appears.

Origin: Connecticut. Owner: Mr. George Dudley Seymour. Date: 1670-1700.

A PINE Box on Ball Feet. Owner: Mr. B. A. Behrend. This delightful specimen has fine butterfly hinges. We have seen but one other box on feet and that was later in date. We give 1690-1700 as the probably date of the box before us.

Below is a carved pine box belonging to Mr. Chauncey C. Nash. The carving is combined with heavy moldings, which gives an appearance of solidity. Date: 1690-1700.

Boxes occasionally had tills at the ends, like chests. Sometimes boxes were carved on the slant top. In such cases of course they were designed to hold Bibles, not papers. We have not seen an American box so carved.

A HADLEY Box. Owner: Mr. B. A. Behrend. Date: 1690-1700. At least one other Hadley box is known, perhaps two, but they are sufficiently rare to excite much interest. This specimen is very shallow.

A box with painted rosettes appears below. The ends are of oak, the front and back of pine, as is the lid. It belongs to Mr. H. W. Erving. It is suggestive of the starfish design on page 103, but of course has no special reference to it. The design was a very obvious one, easily outlined by a compass. Red and black paint appears in the cutaway sections of the rosettes.

Size: 23½ x 18 inches, 8½ inches high.

Date: 1700-10.

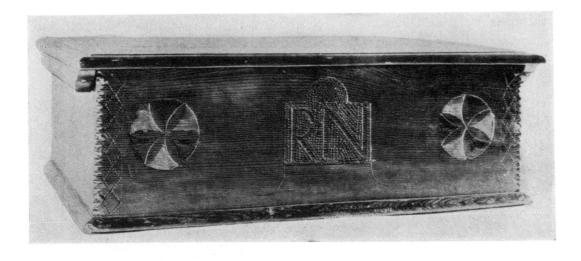

A SMALL Box, from Norwichtown, Connecticut. Fanning Family. Front, ends and lid profusely enriched with carving in the Friesian style. Made, according to family tradition, by David Fanning, of Norwichtown, when he was nine years old, which would give the box a date of 1736, as his birth was in 1727. Fanning, who died at Groton, Connecticut, January 8, 1817, was a soldier in the French and Indian War, a man of considerable local prominence. The box was recently bought from one of his descendants. Made of whitewood, pine and soft maple.

Length, 20⅜ inches; width, 10⅜ inches; hight, 6⅜ inches; lid, 21 by 10½ inches. George Dudley Seymour, owner.

Below is a Carved and Stippled Front Pine Box. This rude piece, related in its type of carving to Friesian carving, was evidently the work of a tyro in design. Date 1675-1700. Owner: Same as above.

AN Oak Box, belonging to Mr. B. A. Behrend. The foliated design here compared with Mr. Seymour's box under it is interesting. Mr. Behrend's box shows something resembling the acanthus. Mr. Seymour's is a conventionalized tulip. The initialed box may date from 1670-1700.

Mr. George Dudley Seymour's box below is of about the same date. Both boxes show the notches at the corners, simple touches which the carver loved, and used frequently.

Did any one ever connect the remarkable mechanical ability of the people of Connecticut, especially of the Connecticut Valley, with the fact that they so long kept the traditions of the Pilgrim generation? If a wooden nutmeg had ever been made by the Connecticut artisan it would have been because he was the only person in America with sufficient skill to make wood look like a nutmeg.

AN Oak Box. Date: about 1670. It has its original butterfly hinges. The size is 21 by 18 inches, and 10½ inches high.

Below it is a walnut box, dating perhaps 1720. It is dovetailed, not nailed like other boxes, and has ball feet. It is 19½ by 11½ inches, and 14½ inches high. It opens down, desk fashion, and has a cabinet. There is a chain covered with leather to hold it from swinging too far. Both these boxes are owned by the author. They are without decoration, but belong to the simple substantial sort, many of which have doubtless been destroyed.

A CARVED Oak Box. The property of Mr. Hollis French. Date: 1660-90. The scrolls and the foliations resemble those on the press cupboard, page 139. The little box on top was described on page 97.

Below is a tulip motive box, owned by Mr. H. W. Erving. The carving is attractive. The box is 27 by 15 inches, and 10 inches high. The date is 1660-80. There is every reason to suppose that these boxes were made about the same time as the tulip chests. One may see in the carving at the center that the artisan tried his hand at a very successful 'scutcheon in wood.

A PAINTED Pine Box. Owner: Mr. George Dudley Seymour. Date: 1700-10. The piece was bought in Hartford. The bottom molding is a restoration. The painting, not restored, shows a vine enfolding large flower-forms.

The box is now in the Wadsworth Atheneum, Hartford.

The vine just mentioned resembles closely the decorations on the panels of chests-on-frames, as for instance that on page 90.

At the bottom of the page appears a box in pine, the property of Mr. B. A. Behrend. It is initialed E. A. At the center, within a diamond marked out in scratch carving is the date 1694. We see again in this instance that pine carving was used very early.

A LITTLE Box, with scratch carving. It is owned by the Connecticut Historical Society at Hartford. The outlines of the carving are filled in with white, but a decorative border of carving is not so filled. The size is 10½ x 7 inches, and 5½ inches high. The lid overhangs ½ inch front and sides.

The use of nails in early furniture is not well understood. The impression prevails among many persons that nails indicate a late date. Also the use of hand wrought nails is reckoned by some a mark of antiquity. All nails were hand wrought up to the year 1795. Before that period nails were freely used where experience showed them to be appropriate. Thus the bottoms of many of the oldest chests and the drawer sides of court cupboards were attached with nails, in the earliest examples we know. In fact the sides of the drawers of court cupboards and chests were gouged, where they met the rabbeted ends of the drawer front, in order to make room for great nails to set in deeper than they otherwise could. Small dovetailing is a proof of late work. The early dovetail, when used, was very broad.

Nailers, that is persons who made, not drove, nails formed a guild. A good nailer could make several hundred nails a day. There were nails of very many shapes and sizes, as there are today.

ON the next page appears a secretary, dating about 1700. The marks of its age are found in the single arch molding, in the shape of the door panels, in the ball-feet and in the sliding panel of the table, under the cabinet. The greater number of the handles are original. The wood is walnut. Later feet would have been more delicate. The earliest ball-feet were very clumsy. The secretary is owned by the author. As books of record became necessary the top became indispensable. Also the tops were used, as they still are, as library shelves.

The rarity of early secretaries is to be accounted for by the fact that the ordinary family found it convenient to move a desk box from place to place, and also from the circumstance that in those days less writing was done than at present. In other words, the piece was more a luxury than a necessity. When, however, the convenience of a cupboard above a desk was felt, transforming a piece into a secretary—though why it should be called a secretary rather than a desk, the author does not know—the fashion of secretaries rapidly came in and reached in the block fronts the finest development of cabinet work ever attained in America, in the marvelous creations of John Goddard of Newport.

The French scrutoire was a creation beyond the limits of our work. Secretary tops on 17th Century desks are very rare.

The wood of secretaries and desks, in this country, was at first pine, for the simpler specimens, and walnut for the finer examples. An occasional whitewood secretary, like the above, is found. We do not recall any American oak desk with legs.

Then came maple, which followed along with the walnut, and continued in use during the mahogany period, for the simpler desks. Desks with maple frame and pine for the desk proper are not unusual.

A fine cabinet is not found in the 17th Century desks. As a rule desks are made with base attached. Occasionally we find an early desk which maintains the tradition of a separate upper section, like a desk box. The fact that almost every desk had a lip on the drawer indicates that few were made before 1700. Nor do we find any carving on American desks, in the early time. This again shows that they are later than the boxes and the little chests on frames. They are essentially a part of the furniture of a developed country, and a secondary age.

As a consequence the variety of desks before 1720 is small, and we have seen none that appeared to be older than 1690, possibly 1700.

In this connection we notice that the portion of Connecticut where early furniture was made comprised a rich agricultural district, and was settled in many cases by men of substance.

Put in another form, one reason why we find so much good furniture before 1700, in Connecticut, is that her people could afford it.

ON the previous page appears a picture of a secretary with ball feet, the property of the author. The features which mark the close of the Seventeenth Century and some which also appeared in the early part of the Eighteenth Century are here manifest, namely the ball feet and the arched panels with horizontal members at the top. There is a sliding panel in the table of the cabinet. Date about 1700.

The secretaries of this period are rare.

A feature in the large piece is also seen in some other secretaries, of the mahogany period. The top extends about an inch in the back beyond the line of the frame of the lower part. This extension would suggest that the parts were not designed for one another. But the pieces were designedly so constructed in order that the top might bear against the wall, reaching over the dado of about an inch thickness.

At the top of this page is a piece almost precisely like that on the previous page except for the top. Sometimes as in the instance of the secretary on page 113, the top was made detachable. This piece without cupboard above is in walnut, and the date is the same, about 1700.

At the bottom of the page is a little desk in pine, with maple frame. Its small size suggests a desk box changing by development to a desk box on a frame.

These little desks are often made detachable from the frame. That they are not of the same date or for the same purpose as the little chests on frames is clear. The desks are not in oak.

A TURNED frame desk of the highest merit and rarity which was in the owner's former collection and has now passed into the collection of Mr. Harry Long. The solid and large turnings call for an earlier date than the over-hanging lip of the drawer, but it is necessary to place this piece about 1700 or a little later. The interior is very simple, containing a few pigeon holes, a single range of drawers and in the center a small door without a panel. The point of merit in this piece is the solidity of the frame and the style of the middle and end stretchers.

What seems a defect is the fact that the pulls on which the drawer rests when open are faced with a thin strip to form a lip all about the pull. The wood is walnut and the dimensions are 42 inches long, 38½ inches high and 20 inches wide. The dimension of the square of the legs is 2⅜ inches. The depth of the drawer is 3 inches. The piece is shown practically in the original state.

A LITTLE sturdy desk of pine, in the Rhode Island School of Design. The very heavy lid with its excellent "thumb-nail" molding, the heavy dovetailing, the flush drawer, the heavy turning, bespeak a date inside the Seventeenth Century, probably 1680-1700. The lid suggests a chest top. It is the chagrin of the writer that he once failed to obtain this desk. Economy is often very wasteful.

A SMALL desk in the author's collection. It is of pine above with a maple frame—the usual construction of simple desks of its period. The cabinet is very plain. It has good old butterfly hinges. Desks of this character were only one degree removed from desk boxes. Comparing this desk with that opposite, one at once feels the quainter earlier character of that desk. Date about 1700-20.

A DESK with Turned Frame, the property of Mr. Chauncey C. Nash. While the handles on this piece bespeak a date of at least 1710, which is borne out by double arch molding, the turning leads us to suppose that the date is fully as early. The butterfly hinge and the general character of the desk proper is almost exactly the same as the author's on the preceding pages
Frame 23¾ inches high, 29 inches long, 18½ inches deep.

A WALNUT Desk. Formerly owned by Mr. I. Sack. This handsomely turned specimen, dating about 1690-1710, has handles which of course are too late. The piece is made in two parts, being really a desk box on a table frame, with an extra set of drawers. It is a rather large piece, carefully restored. Obviously a desk so constructed required a special chair of extraordinary hight. Even so one could not sit closely. This fact no doubt led to the development of a series of drawers running to the floor, since there was no possibility of utilizing the space under the desk for the knees.

A PINE Cross-Stretcher Desk. Owner: Mr. W. of Boston. This delightful desk, dating about 1690-1700, is only 31¾ inches long. From front to back it is 19¾ inches. The hight is 33½ inches. It has the early butterfly hinges. It was found not very far from Boston. It is the only desk known to the writer, in pine, in this style.

The dimensions given above are over all. The frame is only 29¾ by 19¼ inches. A desk with cross-stretchers is convenient for the feet of one sitting at the desk. It matches also, if in a chamber, the cross-stretcher lowboy.

A WALNUT Cross-Stretcher Desk. Date: 1690-1700. It has fine old butterfly hinges. The drawer is a restoration, and the writer is not sure it should not have been restored to correspond with the piece on the previous page. The desk came into Boston, in the rough, complete in every detail except the drawer.

The carcass is 36 by 20 inches. The hight, behind, is $32\frac{3}{4}$ inches; and in front $28\frac{3}{4}$ inches. The width of the flat portion of the top is 6 inches, and that of the lid $15\frac{1}{4}$ inches.

The cross-stretcher chair is practically unknown as an American product. One example appears on page 337, and a pair of stools on page 285.

This desk is the property of the author.

A SMALL Desk in Pine. Owner: Mr. I. Sack. The genealogy of this desk is established. The turnings are an imitation of highboy turnings. The date is about 1700-10. It is a piece of no small interest as showing the approach to a smaller type of legs than those in use at the beginning of the 18th Century.

We cannot precisely say when the style of desk hinged in front came in. It is at least a little later than the style hinging in the back. But for years both styles went along side by side. Both begin in 17th Century.

Below appears a desk owned by Mr. H. W. Erving. It has a very prettily scrolled frame, the scrolling being extended around the ends. The legs show the Dutch influence and have button feet. It is constructed of maple and butternut, and the back is of pine. There is a rosette at each side of the upper drawer and the pulls to support the lid are round. The desk is dainty, in advance of its period, which is about 1720-40. It is 28½ inches long, 20 inches from front to back, and 38 inches high.

A PRESS Cupboard in the Metropolitan Museum. The brackets are considered as not belonging to the piece. The carving is very rich, in the early arch style, and strongly suggests the English cupboards. Yet it is supposed to be American. The posts can be, as they are, severely plain. They would otherwise call the eye away from the decoration, which is subtly contrived by an artist. It is very far in advance of the later American carving. It is so early that it was done in the spirit of a previous generation. Date about 1650.

THERE are known to be in existence in America perhaps forty court cupboards, if we reckon under this term also the specialized form called press cupboards. They are a direct inheritance from English styles. The possession of a court cupboard in the early days was a mark of social standing. Only those with pretensions to some dignity in their dwellings had these stately pieces.

The genealogy of the Parmenter Court Cupboard, a picture of which follows on the next page, traces it to the builder of the Parmenter Garrison house. That house was erected about 1683, in South Sudbury, it being the first house in town. When the Wayside Inn was built about 1700, the carpenters passed their nights in the Garrison house, for fear of Indian attack.

Pelatiah Parmenter was born in the early part of the 17th Century and was lost at sea, during the war of the Revolution, in privateer warfare. Abel Parmenter, his grandson, was born in the garrison house in 1754. Joshua Parmenter, who is responsible for preserving the cupboard, was born in Framingham in 1824 and died in 1903. His widow, from whom the writer acquired the cupboard, now survives him. His mother was Lucretia Parmenter, daughter of Abel. Joshua went to live in the garrison house at about 10 years of age.

Sudbury was settled from Watertown and undoubtedly the cupboard was brought with other plenishings for the new garrison house. All the shelves being of pine, together with the backs and drawer bottoms, and the posts being of maple, the cupboard is established as a thoroughly American structure. The great weight of the drawers, their large side runs, and the four-inch posts, have a massive effect. The carving on the doors seems to be deeply recessed, owing to the subtle devise of allowing the molding to overlay the carving slightly.

The lack of a rail below the drawers will be noticed on several chests in this work.

The feet of this cupboard have been pieced by the writer. Joshua Parmenter remembered their being cut off when he was a boy, about 1835. Against all advice he cherished the old cupboard, so that our generation now has this unique example of early American work. Date: 1640-50.

THE Parmenter Court Cupboard, owned by the author. A fuller description appears on the previous page. The author is somewhat embarrassed in placing an estimate on the merits of this remarkable piece, and will therefore confine his statements purely to the historic and structural features. This piece by its bill of sale cannot pass from the author's hands except to a public museum.

A PRESS Cupboard in the Brooklyn Museum of Fine Arts. It should be compared with that on page 139. This example is free from extensive restoration and therefore better. In both the same rather unsatisfactory pillars appear, but in that piece there is the rare feature of carving on the back stile. This piece has lost some three or four inches from the feet. Of course the unavoidable presumption is that these two pieces, with some others like them were made in the same neighborhood of Connecticut. Date: 1670–80.

A COURT Cupboard in the Connecticut Sunflower (or Aster) and Tulip pattern. This cupboard belongs to Yale University and is kept with two others in the president's office, where of course every courtesy is extended to persons desiring to see them. Yet one must keenly regret that it is necessary to intrude on a private office to gain a view of such important objects. Since so few are available for study, the principle of the greatest good for the greatest number—the true educational idea— would seem to be in need of application here.

ON this page is shown a detail of the sunflower press cupboard owned by the Lancaster Public Library. The special interest of this cupboard, aside from its rare intrinsic merit, arises from the fact that it is in its rough state, except that the paint found on it, when it was bought in 1876, has been washed off.

The reason for the purchase of the cupboard, at the early date mentioned, was that it had been a possession of the first minister of the town. There was a question whether ninety dollars was not too much to invest in such an old, queer piece of furniture! So far has public interest and knowledge advanced since 1876!

An object of much interest is the fine drop under the architrave. Many possessors of court cupboards do not know such a drop was used. It is a marvel that so fine a piece should have escaped for so long the knowledge of antiquarians. It is mentioned nowhere in previous literature on antique furniture. It is undoubtedly of Connecticut origin.

THIS Cupboard is described on the previous page. Date: 1660-78.

The Rev. Jos. Rowlandson married Mary White. He was minister in Lancaster, 1654-76. He died in Wetherfield, 1678. His heirs sold the cupboard in 1825 to the Rev. B. R. Woodbridge, of Norwich. He died at South Hadley, in 1846, leaving the cupboard to his nephew, Mr. J. W. Dunlap of that town, who sold it to the library.

A COURT Cupboard owned by Mrs. J. Insley Blair, Tuxedo Park. It
is of rather light construction, but is perhaps more attractive to the taste of
the general public. Its spool turning is quite unusual. It belongs to the
very last part of the 17th Century.

A PRESS Cupboard owned by Mr. Dwight Blaney of Boston. It is very unusual in having three drawers, like one in the possession of Yale University. The repetition of the three sets of triglyphs on the posts and a set corresponding in the center enhances strongly the vertical line effects, often lost in press cupboards, but secured in court cupboards by the repetition of the two tiers of posts. Date: 1660–90.

Obviously the need of drawer space was beginning to impress itself on designers. A cupboard enclosed left very little room for the display of plate, which was beginning to be looked on as a secondary object.

A PRESS Cupboard owned by Mr. Philip L. Spalding of Boston. It came from New Hampshire, being found last in Concord. It of course lacks a portion of the foot, but is otherwise in good condition. The style of the molding is unusual, a series of parallel grooved moldings each interrupted several times in its length, for the imposition of a small boss. Date: 1660–90.

A COURT Cupboard owned by Mr. James N. H. Campbell of Hartford, who also owns that on page 137, and has placed them in a room paneled to honor them. A simple splay-cupboard type, very attractive, owing to its freedom from over ornament. The raking of the small dentils under cap and shelf is very noticeable, and a good decorative feature. This piece was restored a good while since by the father of the owner. Date: 1670–90.

A COURT Cupboard owned by Mrs. Hulings Cowperthwaite Brown of Brookline. An unusual detail of interest, seen in another cupboard only in this work, on page 138, is the engrailing beneath the bottom shelf. It is gratifying to be able to illustrate so many cupboards open below, as the closed or "press" cupboard has hitherto strongly predominated. Date: 1660–90.

A PRESS Cupboard Base, the property of Mr. Arthur W. Wellington. This beautiful cupboard base has some distinctive features which are very pleasing. The columns are boldly and daintily turned. The scheme of recessing the drawers below is interesting. The geometrical moldings on the drawers assimilate this piece to some of the later Seventeenth Century chests and chests of drawers. The piece never had wooden knobs, but was made with the brass drop handles as seen. There are visible on the top the outlines of the splayed cupboard which was imposed upon this base. At the corners little holes have been filled in with new wood where the dowels of the corner posts stood. No trace has been found of the old top. This base, however, presents features of much interest and beauty. It seemed worth while to record it as we have done. We believe that in all cases bases of this character had tops. Several have been found, not as good as this, however, without tops. The wood is of the beautiful old surface in this specimen and is very attractive. This cupboard with four turnings like the two which remain must have been a very beautiful affair. So far as we can discover there have been only the most insignificant restorations to this piece.

Date: 1670–1700.

ON page 130 is a court cupboard formerly in the possession of Mrs. A. W. Mattoon of New Haven, and long on exhibit in the New Haven Historical Society rooms. It is now owned by Mrs. J. Insley Blair of Tuxedo Park. The turnings while very unusual resemble those on the desk, page 119. The piece is thoroughly genuine. Date: 1680-1700.

Court cupboards received more enrichment than any other pieces of furniture. In this particular the sideboard of the mahogany period inherited their importance. The question of livery cupboards has been treated very fully by Lyon. The connection between "livery" and "deliver" should be noted, as the livery cupboard was the point from which the supplies were delivered to the servants by the mistress of the house.

There was a hiatus after 1700, when the court cupboard went out, before the sideboard came in. Meantime a side table did duty.

The English court cupboards, which are being brought to America, seem to have no attractions whatever for the student of antiques. This is partly because there has been a scandalous number of spurious and even poorly constructed cupboards brought to America. Except a cupboard has been here more than two hundred years, collectors will have nothing to do with it. The foreign piece is easily detected, as it has no pine in its construction; the oak is dark. Several American court cupboards have come to light since the great war. Two such pieces have been found in southern New Hampshire and two in Massachusetts. But pieces of such size can hardly hide away in any number. It is not likely that a dozen more will come to light in many years.

In the old inventories cupboards are mentioned very frequently. Sarah Dillingham, of Ipswich, in an inventory of 1636, left "a Cubert, 10s." Later we read of "one great cubberd, 1 li.;" "one cubbortt, 5s. 6d.;" "one cupbord and cloth, 10s.;" "one vallance for a cupbord, 6s.;" "one cuberd and cuberd cloth;" "a cupboard & a cushin;" "one cubboard & cubboard cloath;" "a cubber;" "cobbord;" "a cubbart & cubbart cloth;" "one cubbard & a drawer, 3 li.;" "a cobbord, 8s.;" "a coubourtt;" "curttaings & vallings & cobbartt cloth and cushenghs;" "one coubbard and one leather skin and the things in the coubbard, 13s.;" two cubberds 2 li. 18s.;" "great cobber." There are also mentioned cupboards with the following adjectives prefixed: Court, livery, press, side, standing, wainscot and hanging; the last being in the nature of wardrobes. All these are before 1664. See the valuable records on furniture in *the Probate Records of Essex County, Salem, 1916. Published by the Essex Institute.*

A PRESS Cupboard owned by Mr. James N. H. Campbell. It stands in front of wainscot built to set it off. The design is very unusual and striking. The grain of the oak is very boldly shown. The effect of the five cruciform sets of applied decorations is good. The pillars belong to the simpler type. The date is perhaps later than the average. It may be about 1680–90.

THIS Court Cupboard is now restored, and we venture to show it in its present form. It is in the Metropolitan Museum and from the Bolles Collection. Its design is somewhat ornate for an American cupboard, which it nevertheless is. The center arch molding in these cupboards is a style carried over from early chests and is a reminiscence of the earliest period as always when seen in any furniture. The exuberant quality in taste, a legacy of the Elizabethan time, is amusingly shown here. The ends have cruciform panels; the front diamond shaped panels, and an arch. Corbels, dentils, nail heads, notch carving, molding, applied spindles and scrolled skirt leave nothing out from the discursive mind of the constructor. Date: 1650–80.

A COURT Cupboard in the Stanton House, Clinton, Connecticut, a public collection. The posts supporting the architrave are not as fine as in other types. Several similar pieces have been found in the same part of Connecticut. Date 1660–1690. The nail heads are an erroneous effort at restoration. The moldings lining the panels are also wrongly placed there.

THE Press Cupboard on the next page is in part described there. Its enormous turned posts, reduced at top and bottom to diameters so small, resemble more nearly the earliest cupboards known, the Elizabethan, than any others shown in this volume.

Court cupboards are the most valuable and important pieces of furniture that have come down to us from the Pilgrim time. We doubt if any of the Plymouth people had such cupboards. The ancient inventories mention a good number, beginning in and near Boston and running up along the North Shore to York, Maine, a region where there was greater wealth.

The second region, where they are found, is in the famous oak triangle, if one may so name it, the points of which are Hartford, New Haven, Saybrook. Of course sporadic instances of fine carved specimens may be found outside these limits. And various migrations to newer settlements, carried such furniture inland. Any thrifty New England Settlement of some size before 1660, may be relied on as a producer of oak furniture. The student of history sees at once that he is very restricted, in this investigation. The tradition of oak began to die out before the century was over. Seventeen hundred sees walnut well established, and in England "The Age of Walnut" is a title given to a work on furniture covering the period beginning 1670.

It is eminently true that styles overlap, like shingles on a roof. Thirty years is not too long to reckon as the length of the overlap. America trailed behind England from a score of years to a generation.

But while, in conservative neighborhoods, oak persisted in England, for a century more, the same is not true here. An oak piece of furniture, made in America after 1700 is extremely rare, and after 1720 is practically unknown.

We feel certain from various sorts of evidence that the court cupboards mentioned in old inventories were no better than the articles called merely cupboards. One reason for this certainty is that the court cupboard is not valued any higher than the other cupboards. The same remark applies to livery and press cupboards. The press cupboard is mentioned only once in the Essex records, before 1664, and only once after that. In those cupboards that remain to us the proportion of press cupboards is larger. Side cupboards are mentioned oftener as the date grows later. As a rule there is no descriptive adjective with the word cupboard. We are not always certain what a side cupboard was, or why the term should be used, as we find no corner cupboards in these early times.

A CONNECTICUT Oak Court Cupboard.
Owner: Mr. George Dudley Seymour. The front and cupboard ends are ornamented with corbels and turtle-back bosses, the corners of the top being sustained by boldly-turned, deeply-cut posts.

Hight over all, 54½ inches; hight of upper section, 21½ inches; hight of lower section, 33 inches; depth of lower section, 19½ inches; top of lower section (the cupboard proper) 45 by 20¼ inches. Date 1675–1700.

A PAINTED Whitewood Press Cupboard. Owner: Mrs. G. C. Bryant, Ansonia, Connecticut. On this page appears a diagonal view to give the end board; on the next page is the larger front view; neither picture being made by the author. This is undoubtedly a most important piece of painted furniture, and the only press cupboard, made after the analogy of the court cupboard, of any wood except oak. We have here every feature of the great court cupboards, but in simple, quaint, humble form. Here is a splayed cupboard proper, the corner posts, doors and drawer; only the long drawer is placed below. The decoration belongs to the same class as that shown on page 54 and elsewhere, though we find it here in a simpler form. This unique piece excites our strongest approval. That a designer should have the courage to evoke from a "six board" basis a piece of furniture of so much character, and withal so satisfying, speaks much for the individual artisan of the time.

The date is 1690-1710.

Since the above was written another cupboard, largely pine, of the same general construction as that here mentioned, has been found in New Hampshire. It is decorated in the thistle design.

ON the next page is shown an important wardrobe in pine. It is owned by Mr. W. of Boston, who is to be congratulated, as the piece is perhaps unique. The curved paneling is carved from the solid. The piece stands very high. It is in the rich shade of old pine, natural. The attempt at a bracket foot, which is almost a stile, suggests the early date, about 1700-10.

The small number of early wardrobes arises from the fashion of the time, which favored folding away garments or hanging them in a built-in closet.

On page 146 is a corner cupboard of pine. Owner: Mr. W. of Boston. It belongs to the period when paneling came into fashion, about 1720-30.

On page 147 is an unique cupboard in respect to its canopied top. It was found in Rhode Island. There is no distinctive mark of date, which may be from 1720-50. The shape of the scroll, as it meets the shelf, reminds us of the arm of a settle. The wood is pine. It is owned by Mr. W. of Boston.

The cupboard, built in, or as a movable piece, came into its own in the 18th Century. For the sake of completeness of treatment we shall carry through, beyond our period, the pine cupboard.

Further, as the task we set ourselves was to show native, distinctive furniture, we are fairly compelled to include all pine examples of style even past 1700—thirty years after our period, in other matters, properly ends.

There must always be a question where furniture ends and mere carpentry begins. In the case of cupboards we rule out absolutely plain pieces like boxes with doors. We include whatever has a touch of taste in form, or decoration.

Attention is called to the frequency of side cupboards. The phrase "corner cupboard" is heard everywhere. But before 1730 a cupboard was as likely to be designed for a side wall as for a corner. The material of cupboards, as soon as we leave court cupboards, is usually pine.

If we are to consider the wardrobe on page 145 as what the old inventories designated "a hanging cupboard," we find ourselves obliged to suppose they were very rare. There is a rare mention of presses. Whether they were for press beds or for hanging clothes we cannot be certain. When we remember the extreme rarity or perhaps utter lack of paneled walls in the 17th century, it is easier to understand the lack of "hanging" cupboards.

The word wardrobe, meaning a press for clothing, does not occur in early inventories. In literature of the date it is used of a room where clothing was kept, rather than of a clothes press.

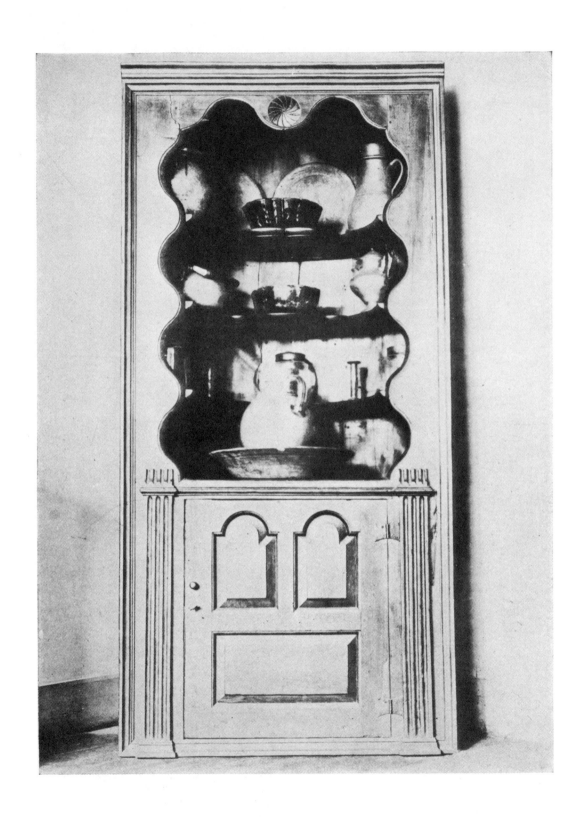

A KNICKERBOCKER Kas. These huge articles were very popular in New York, New Jersey and wherever the Dutch element predominated. The example above belongs to the author. The date is about 1750. There is an immense cornice, two doors, a drawer, and very big ball feet. The wood is walnut and pine; in the finer specimens walnut.

On page 149 is a cupboard of 1720-30, belonging to the author. Such cupboards, with scroll boards flatwise to the beholder, preceded cupboards with doors. The shelves are handsomely shaped. The piece is 73 inches high and 35 inches wide. The bottom shelf is 38 inches high.

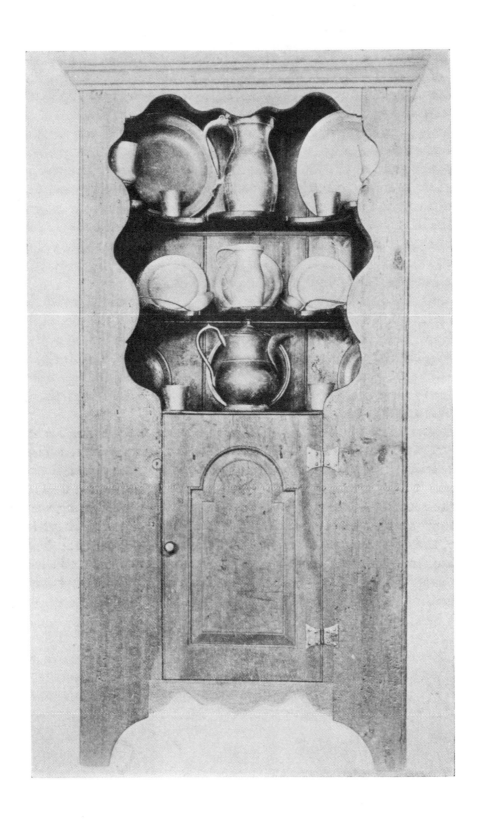

ON the next page is a most attractive side wall cupboard, belonging to Mr. W. of Boston. The scrolled panels are carved from the solid. One notices the early approach to the bracket foot. A very rare cupboard, with but one or two known like it. Date: 1710-20.

On page 152 is the first example we show of an open dresser. The term dresser was in common use up to fifty years ago, applied to any broad shelf in the culinary end of the house. But generally there were, as here, shelves above. The supporting uprights when scrolled as here, dignified the work sufficiently to make it rank as furniture. The specimen on page 152 is peculiar in having the boards in the back scrolled; also the feet. As a rule the backs are solidly boarded, but sometimes they are paneled; and in case the dresser was built into the wall there was often only a plaster backing. The date is 1720-50. Owner: Mr. I. Sack.

On page 153 is a corner cupboard or dresser—on the dividing line because the lack of any facing board above the main shelf brings the piece into close cousinship with the dresser. A feature which gives attraction, and a sense of earliness, is the heavy construction, the boards being a flush inch in thickness. Date: 1720-30.

On page 154 a corner cupboard belonging to Mr. Geo. F. Ives shows some unusual features.

The dresser of page 155 is too generally found with its cornice missing. It is the most attractive large form, following court cupboards, and was the kitchen sideboard. It is now eagerly sought for those fine old kitchens which have been set aside as dining rooms, the cooking being done in a new extension. One reason for the scarcity of such dressers is that, being very large pieces, they were generally built in. Where they have been kept for convenience, they have also been removed to a lower back room and beheaded. Large numbers of such headless cupboards, having no cornice, or tricked out with an extemporized molding, are passed off on the unsuspecting. The writer has never seen an original without a cornice, which sometimes coincides with the room cornice. But as a rule the kitchen had no cornice; that decoration ceasing with the cupboard.

Dressers were almost invariably of pine, in New England, whereas in Pennsylvania they were often of walnut, when at all elaborate.

They continued to be made up to the time of the modern hinge, but lost all interesting features. Their style shows deterioration after 1780.

A DRESSER from I. Sack, Boston. It is in pine, all original, and has some unusual features, as scrolled back board, and scrolled feet. Also it is open to the floor, without the usual cupboards. The cornice which marks the usual dresser was probably not made on this piece, which has a molded face board instead. It stands about five feet and a half high, by about four and a half feet long.

A CORNER Cupboard or Dresser, owned by Mr. Harry Long. It originated in Connecticut and is of pine. An apparently small detail gives it much of its quaintness and feeling of antiquity. The boards instead of being seven-eighths are a flush inch thick, which affords a sense of solidity and stockiness.

A CORNER Cupboard owned by Mr. George F. Ives of Danbury. It is wider than the usual style, and carries the original strap-and-wedge hinges. Such cupboards were as a rule made to fill the entire space from floor to ceiling, the cornice being continuous with that of the room.

A DRESSER with scroll boards. We enter here upon a class of subjects which has lately stirred a furor of desire. These pieces are generally pine throughout, and the open sort, without spoon racks, are mostly New England examples. They date variously from 1720 to 1790. They are mostly found on the East Coast of Massachusetts.

THE paneled wall is in the possession of the Metropolitan Museum. The cross combined with the arch in the lower section of the wainscot is characteristic of Connecticut, although the arch with the panel is a very rare feature even there.

It is a matter of continual regret that so little panel work was used in America when there was such abundant wood for the purpose. One of the noblest rooms in this country has cloth very carefully pasted over the tongues of the panels, so as to give a smooth surface and then the whole is carefully papered over. People became ashamed of paneling, because their neighbors did not have it. The cupboard on the left was saved from the Marsh house, Wethersfield, date about 1730.

It has the demi-dome top, in plaster, plain. Some cupboards were plastered, to the floor, on the curved back.

THE Kitchen of the very ancient Fairbanks house at Dedham. In this case the dresser is built against a remarkable sheathed wall, the boards of which run horizontally and are beautifully molded. The end boards of the dresser are very boldly and handsomely scrolled. These dressers, as here, often ran across the entire available wall space on a side of the room. The effect, when all the family utensils were arranged in state, was very good. One lived in the atmosphere of wholesome utilities, and household treasures.

This cupboard may be seen by the public, with the delightful old house. We may doubt if the cupboard was originally here. That would give us a date around 1635. We presume its addition occurred about 1720-40.

A BUILT-IN Cupboard in the famous Benning Wentworth house, at Little Harbor, New Hampshire. Date: about 1745. The cupboard is recessed into the wall of the house, the corner post showing, and being decorated with a turned piece. It is a most ingenuous and pleasing conceit.

A CONNECTICUT Press Cupboard from Fairfield County. An heirloom in the Wheeler family. Owner: Mr. Winthrop Edwards Dwight.
This cupboard shows interesting variations from the other two shown,
principally in the rosettes, or repeated sunflowers on drawer and architrave.

IN the lower cupboard the panel construction of the door is squared behind and mitered-in part in front, on the same board—a strong and ingenious device.

The upper cupboard has a corner mold. Hence the base mold is cut off before reaching the corner. Dates of both pieces: 1720-40.

A PENNSYLVANIAN Dresser, owned by Mr. Arthur W. Wellington, who has also two more very handsome specimens. This piece shows the rat-tail hinge which is characteristic of the region.

A WALNUT Wardrobe, in the later Pennsylvania style. Owned by Mr. C. C. Littlefield of Newfields, New Hampshire. It is a large piece, nearly reaching a low ceiling. The construction of these cupboards, like that of the kas, is contrived with wedges and slots. Date: 1740-70.

A FINE Dresser, belonging to Shreve, Crump & Low, of Boston. The scrolling of the end boards is the best we have seen. The scrolled cornice is very good. Date: the former part of the 18th Century. By an ingenious offset of the hinges they are made secure by rivets through the body.

THE side of the parlor in the Robinson house, Wethersfield, built about 1737. This is said to be the oldest house now standing, in the village, but the Michael Griswold house may dispute the claim.

The arrangement shows the usual panel effect of the period, whereby an opening at one or both sides of the fireplace was made to do duty, the one for the door of a shell, or domed, top cupboard, the other for a passage to a rear room.

A curious feature of many of the finest domed cupboards is that their best details, the pilasters, are hidden back of these large doors in the wall paneling. One would say the paneling came later, but the date of the houses themselves is that of the paneled period.

ON the left is an excellent small cupboard, designed to be fastened up on a side wall. There are arched doors, with glass in the upper part, and panels with long bevels below. There is one shelf. The wood is all pine. It is one of the best and the rarest specimen of the kind. The date is about 1700. The walls are at right angles.

On the right is a little corner wall cupboard dating perhaps before 1700. It is all original. Owner: the author. It has one of the earliest types of hinge. The wood is oak. The cupboard was found in a very weathered condition, in 1921. It is American.

The smaller pieces of 17th Century furniture passed out of sight almost entirely. There must have been a good many fascinating cupboards like the above, but they are very rare now. An amusing feature about the lower cupboard here shown is that no one knows which end up it should hang. "There is much to be said" in favor of both ends! The absence of any molding leaves us without a guide. For variety's sake, and to please all, it may be well to reverse it April 1st, annually.

THE quaintest little cupboard which has fallen under the author's eye is this hat box with drawers under. The piece may possibly have been intended to rest upon a table or a chest of drawers, but as now it could also have been attached to a wall.

The three cornered box at the top with its H hinges, dates the piece somewhere about Revolutionary times when the three-cornered hats were in vogue. The hat box is closed with its original button. Below, the owner would have kept his bands and other linen. This piece is of pine like all other cupboards unless otherwise specified. It originated in New England.

On the right, at the bottom of this page is a little cupboard to fasten on a wall. Pieces like this in pine are extremely rare. This is probably to be accounted for by the fact that a recessed cupboard was ordinarily used. Date: 1700–1720. Owner: Mr. George F. Ives.

The corner cupboard on the opposite page is perhaps the most important that has come to light. It stood in the Jaffrey House in Portsmouth. Owned by the Boston Fine Arts Museum. Date: 1730.

The cupboard is remarkable for its great hight and for the elaborate carving of the capitals and the cornice. There is a slide under the large door.

THE little recessed cupboard above is built over a fireplace in the Williams Place in South Easton, dating from 1717. It shows the method of utilizing the space formed by the slanting of the chimney as it drew in above the fireplace, and is one of the earliest examples of this use. In the same house there still was in place in 1920 a diamond-pane leaded window, showing that such windows were in use to a later period than is generally supposed.

There are also simple corner cupboards in the same house which originally had no doors above.

The habit of recessing cupboards was very popular in the early years of the Eighteenth Century. There is everything to be said in favor of the fashion, as it gives economy of space, and adds charm to an interior. In some homes such cupboards took the place of desks for the preservation of valuable papers.

A quaint little set of hanging shelves is shown here. The sideboards end in simple pigtail scrolls. It is of pine. We can only judge by the rarity of such simple little things of the slight estimation in which they were held, but nothing adds more than pieces like these to the quaint charm of an old home. We endeavor, in this particular, to preserve not only the notably important articles but simpler objects like this. The date is uncertain, perhaps 18th Century. The large walnut cupboard on the opposite page is a fine example, dating about 1740–60.

THE closed door of the demi-domed shell top cupboard in the Webb-Welles house, Wethersfield, shows the characteristic feature of Connecticut panels, with the cross at the base. The date is 1752. Washington was regaled on china from this cupboard, and accorded the distinguished privilege of entering the parlor where it is situated—a privilege reserved otherwise to attendants at weddings and funerals only; attest the perfect and unworn condition of the wide pine floor. This cupboard is supplied, like all the doors in the front rooms below, with the brass box-lock, which attained, between 1730 and 1790, a high place as a decorative feature. It was at that period made with the drop swing handle, never with a knob.

ABOVE is the interior of the cupboard described in the previous page. While it extends to the ceiling, the cornice is at different level owing to the framing.

THE Dining Room of the Quincy Homestead at Quincy has a charming corner cupboard or more properly a side cupboard, here shown. The hidden appearance of the pilasters is noticed. The panel work may have followed the cupboard in date. The date is about 1740. It has been observed that corner cupboards ceased to be built into houses between 1750 and 1760. On the later date none was built in the very elegant Wentworth-Gardner House. Nor does one appear in the beautiful Lee Mansion, Marblehead. This leads us to feel that while many refinements in architecture and furniture came in after the middle of the century, it is a question whether the losses were not more than the gains, in architecture after 1760, and in furniture after 1770. Certainly paneled walls were more numerous before 1760.

THERE appears above a distinct surprise for searchers after cupboards, if they have not seen the parlor of the Sparhawk house at Kittery.

Here are two demi-domed shell-topped cupboards, opening diagonally from each side of the fireplace. Only one such cupboard appears here, but the second is identical. The combination is distinctly beautiful. We cannot but feel however that the projection of the fireplace into the room is a loss to the sense of unity. It seems to divide the room. It cuts off the length of the vista, from any point into the fireplace—the focus of any room. If we compare this method of construction with the recessed fireplace style, we shall at once feel the greater beauty, and especially the greater charm— the cosy home sense, of the latter. The structural features here call for the date 1745-55.

[174]

A MOST remarkable chair appears in the large on the preceding page and a side view of the same on this page. It is owned by Mr. Paul A. deSilva of Boston and is or was on exhibition in the Old State House, Boston. It bears this inscription: "This chair was brought from Lyons, France, in 1685, by the father of Nathan Waldo. Nathan, who was born in Boston, settled in Windham, Connecticut, taking this chair. By one of the direct descendants it was given to Rev. John P. Cleveland, D.D., of Providence, R. I. It afterward came into possession of the late Mrs. Jane C. Austen, the novelist, and is now loaned the Bostonian Society by her daughter, [Mrs. Albert deSilva]."

Now there are two odd facts connected with this chair: the arms and a stretcher are American cherry, so pronounced by Mr. Morris Schwartz. The rest of the chair is said to be American oak. Then, if American, it must have been made at least a hundred years after its period, and is the only American chair of the sort. The English corner chair of oak, which Walpole sought, and examples of which are brought to America, was never made here. Of course, if there has been a slip in the tradition and the chair is American, it is far more important.

There have been brought to America not a few buffet chairs, as the three-cornered chairs are called. They are turned throughout, and the turned pilgrim chairs seem to have been their descendants some generations removed. Such a transition chair is in the rooms of the Connecticut Historical Society at Hartford. The chair above should be of date 1500–1600, if built in its period. If it is an American chair it can hardly be denied the highest importance. The shape of its arm is that of the oldest American Wainscot chairs.

ON THE previous page is a wainscot chair with tape-loom back, owned by the author. Chairs like that on the previous page and made in America are extremely rare. There may be half a dozen known. This is the stranger, since they are quite common in England, and were continued up to a late period. It is probable that their bulkiness forbade any general importation to America.

The chair in question belonged to Thomas Robinson who removed from Hartford to Guilford in the year 1639.

"The Robinsons and their Kin Folk," a book printed for the Robinson Family Association, contains a cut of this chair and some description of Thomas Robinson. There is great similarity of moldings used in this chair to those of the American oak chests. The sharp scroll of the under arm is a characteristic feature. A delightful detail is the tape-loom back. This chair was undoubtedly built with a solid back, and some time after the weaver of the family conceived the idea of cutting her tape-loom in a solid plain panel. Thus she had always a loom set up which was stable and actually added to the comfort of the chair. It gave the back some springiness. The holes for the yarn were burnt through with a hot iron. The reeding is somewhat crudely done showing less attention for precision than in the original chair.

An effort has been made to connect the original owner of this chair with the Pilgrim Robinsons, but without substantial results. The original John Robinson, pastor of the Pilgrims in Leyden, remained behind in the old world for a very excellent reason, to pay his debts, the reason which perhaps has driven some immigrants to the new world, instead of keeping them at home.

Date: 1620–40.

The chair opposite is in the possession of Yale University and is in the President's room. It belonged to Rector Pierson of the College, and bears an inscription to that effect. It will be observed that in this example the scroll on the under side of the arm is developed and carried out under the frame of the seat. The simplicity of this chair as compared with the English types is marked.

Date: 1640–1660.

There are supposed to be less than six wainscot chairs of American origin, of which we show three. This remark may call out the knowledge of other specimens.

THE Wainscot Chair gets its name from the original meaning of wainscot, which is one of the most fascinating studies in etymology. There is hidden a great deal of history in the word. The common English word for a large wagon, a wain, is the forepart of the word; the *schot* (English *shot*), meaning partition. That is, wainscot was the best kind of oak for panel work, such as was used in wagons. We say oak, because those who used the term first, always thought of the construction as in oak, and in England today wainscot means oak panels suitable for wall partitions. Elderly Americans who lived in New England can well remember when the sides of wagons were paneled, in long curves, on boat-shaped sides. So persistent is the tradition of cabinet makers.

The word wainscot as generally used today is sought to be confined in meaning to a wall completely paneled to the ceiling, as distinct from a dado, or low panel-work. But the distinction can hardly be made good, in early usage.

The wainscot chair therefore was an oak chair with panel work, and so of course with solid back. It is little wonder we have so few of them, as a new country had little time or place for such cumbersome furniture. The three shown here, the Gov. Leete chair on the next page, the Rector Pierson chair, and the Thos. Robinson chair on pages 177 and 179 are about one-half of the American wainscot chairs known. The desire for a light chair of course consigned many early solid back chairs to the fire. Among this number we do not find any that are carved, so far as known. Some carved specimens are obviously over-restored. The wainscot chair was not built for a surface to ornament, but as a matter of custom and dignity. There are some six, then, uncarved. This is not remarkable, as out of a half dozen one would hardly look for carving, which would not be likely to occur often. We can only presume, since we do not know, that there were carved wainscot chairs of American manufacture. The inventories seldom use the word "carved" in descriptions of furniture. Of course, if the De Silva chair is counted as a wainscot, which would be straining a point, we have carving there. But the case is sporadic, as the particular piece was out of period.

The Gov. Leete chair opposite, in the Stone House, Guilford, like the other wainscot chairs shown has its top rail mortised between the posts, rather than capping the posts, as so often seen in England. This is a better construction. The arched back afforded a head rest. The turnings are the oldest type.

THE BREWSTER CHAIR. The piece opposite is possibly the finest example that has ever come to light, being altogether original. It was purchased of Mr. John Tufts, formerly of Sherborn, Massachusetts, by the author. Mr. Tufts stated that the chair had been in his family eight generations of record. The posts are two and a half inches in diameter, and the chair has lost nothing but the balls on the front posts which have been restored since this picture was made. All the spindles are, we believe, original. It has now passed out of the author's hands.

Comparing this chair with the Elder Brewster chair from which such types derived their name, and which is in Pilgrim Hall in Plymouth, it appears that the original is in a far less perfect state of preservation than the one here shown, a good part of the spindles of the Plymouth example being missing and its posts being of lighter construction. Also it lacks the upper turned rail in the back. It is to be noted that the Brewster chair is found with a wooden seat whereas the Carver chairs which follow are usually rushed. Of course, the wood seat is the older type.

The finials of the piece before us are especially noteworthy and it is remarkable also that it seems to have lost almost nothing of its hight beyond the slight necessary wear.

Regarding the origin of such pieces it should be pointed out that Benn in his "Style in Furniture," a very full and careful work, was obliged to send to America for pictures of the Brewster and the Carver chairs. The conclusion is inevitable that such pieces were either made in America or that they came from Holland. The writer does not believe that either the Elder Brewster or the Governor Carver chair came in the Mayflower, or indeed any other known pieces of furniture.

Date: 1620–40.

The chairs of both types are almost invariably in ash, a very poor material, as it splits too easily and in all specimens there is shown a tendency to chip away at the bottom or elsewhere. Further, it doesn't lend itself to delicate turning as the wood is too coarse in grain.

We have to help us in solving this riddle the fact that at first all lumber was riven. Ash was used in England; it split smoothly and easily, and John Alden was the skilled man among the Pilgrims to attend to this work. It was the best available wood for preparing quickly material for turning.

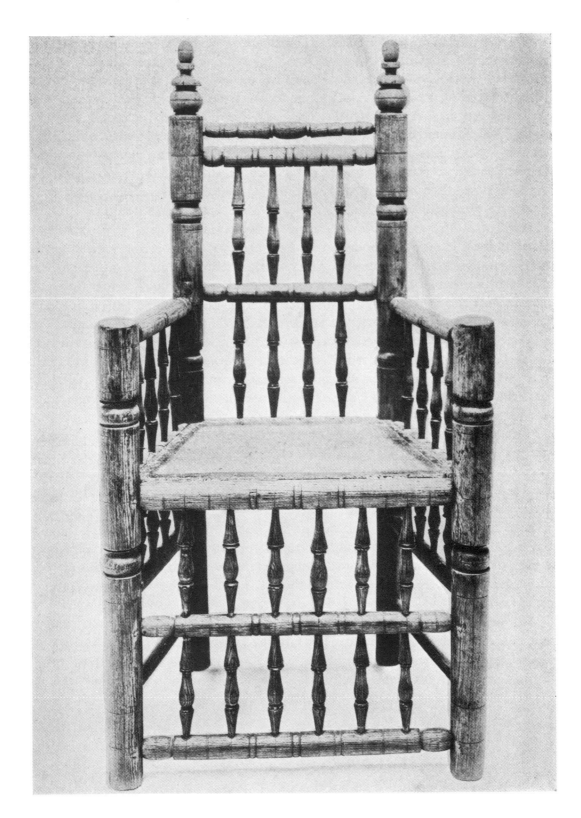

ON the next page is a Brewster chair owned by Mrs. Francis H. Lincoln of Hingham. Its date is 1620-40. There are some records and traditions regarding this chair which should perhaps lead us to call it a Myles Standish chair. It is said the chair belonged to that doughty Pilgrim father; was inherited by his grand-daughter, and so came down to the present. The record is that Isaac Sampson married Lydia Standish, daughter of Miles and Sarah (Alden) Standish. The son of Lydia was Jonathan, born 1687, who married Joanna Lucas. George (3) Sampson married Hannah Soule. Caleb (2) Standish married Mercy Standish. (*Boston Transcript*, 4031.)

A Mr. Huggins from Maine married Miss Sampson, daughter of the Sampson who married Lydia Standish. The chair remained in the Huggins family till the marriage of his grand-daughter to A. C. Hill, from whom it came into the possession of Miss Mary S. Baker, and from her was inherited by the present owner. The expert in evidence will drive a coach and four between some of these lines. But there is a better proof in the chair itself. Its posts reach a diameter of 2 11-16 inches in places. Its type carries it well into the first Pilgrim generation. As such great chairs were rare, always, one feels strongly that with Carver and Brewster represented by their chairs, it is more than probable, since we have a Standish tradition, that it is correct. He was the third or the fourth in importance among the Pilgrims, and Edward Winslow had a wainscot chair of state.

The chair had lost its spindles under the arms. When the Ship Church, Hingham, was deprived of some of its old fittings, spindles from the pews (late 17th Century) were used to repair the chair. They fell short of the seat rail, into which they should go; hence the square rail introduced to receive them. The bottom of the chair has been cut off. It had two rungs in front and on each side, and one at the back. The spindles were turned like those on page 183, and then flattened. The front balls are a restoration.

Two or three more Brewsters, though known, cannot yet be secured for museums. The greater pity as no museum has one except Pilgrim Hall at Plymouth.

The Metropolitan Museum and various other museums had an opportunity to acquire the chair on page 183 but did not exercise it. May a grain of love for our early history sometime sprout in the powers that be, that, from millions expended on museum material, a wee fraction may be allotted to the unique belongings of the settlers of America.

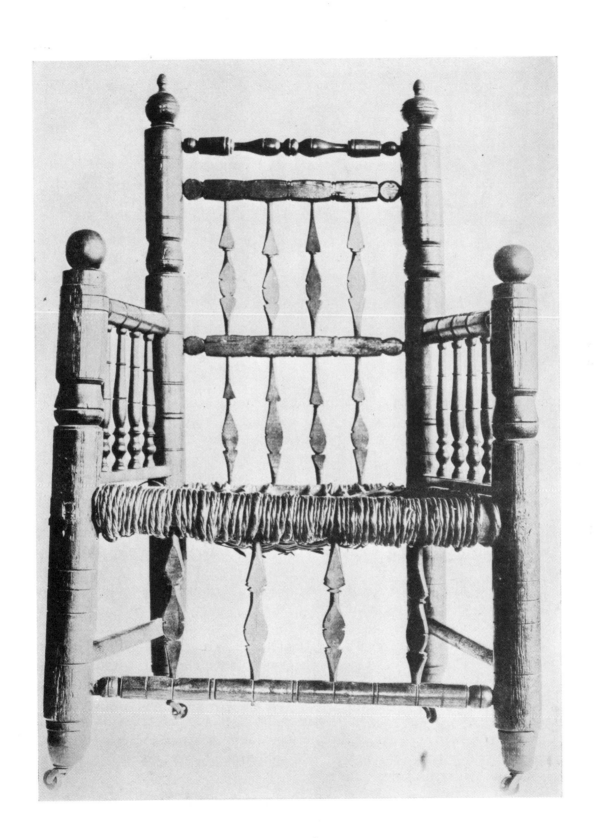

THE picture above represents the supposed front of a livery cupboard in oak. It was found in the Capen House at Topsfield. The frame is in oak. We do not know of any other very ancient American specimen.

Of great interest are the turnings as they very closely resemble those on the ancient chairs in this work. It is not beyond the realm of the possible that the backs of the Brewster and the Carver chairs were suggested by the spindle work on livery cupboards.

It is supposed the cupboard on which this front was used hung on the wall, though why that conclusion has been reached the author does not know.

There is also in the Capen House a hutch which was found in an old farmhouse about three miles away. This is the only ancient specimen which we know of the English type found in this country. The door differentiates it from our chest and the result is what might be called either a hutch or a cupboard. One of the best points about it is the fact that the back legs are made shorter than those in front. The ancient sills of the houses projected into the rooms and no doubt the short legs rested on the sill as now in the Capen House. The specimen has a restored lid and inside shelf but the rest is absolutely as found. Mr. George Francis Dow has furnished the author with the photograph of the livery cupboard front and with this information.

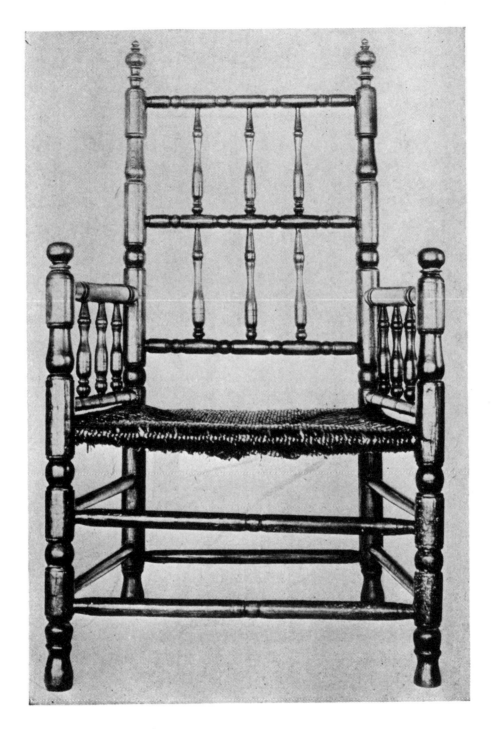

A BREWSTER-TRANSITION Chair in the Geo. F. Ives Collection.
Description on the opposite page.

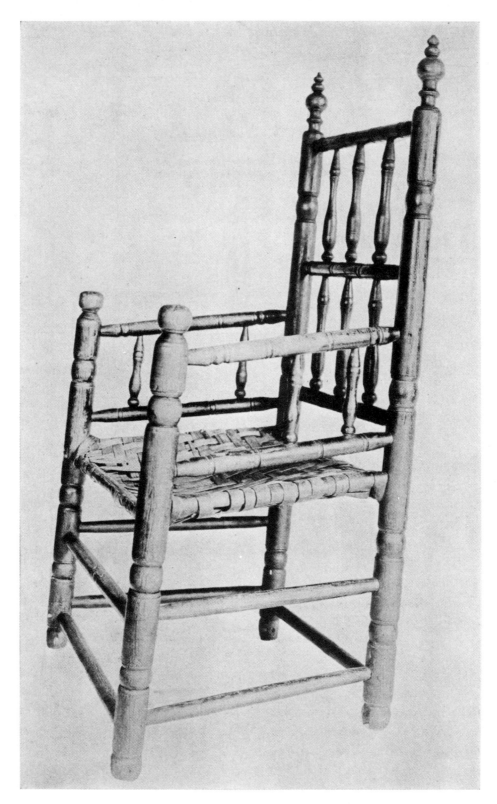

[188]

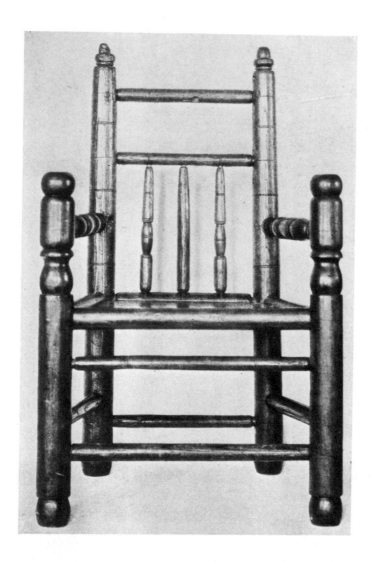

ON the preceding page is a remarkably heavy fine Carver, owned by Mr. Chauncey C. Nash. The back spindles are very short, The finials are very large and elaborately carved. The date is 1620-60.

On this page is a sport, an interesting chair owned by Mr. Geo. F. Ives. Its spindles go directly into the seat rail. It is somewhat smaller than the usual Carver, but, the turnings being heavy, it loses nothing by its reduced size. The seat is slipped in, panel-wise, and is of wood. Its date may be 1630–60.

In many cases the last, most delicate member of a finial is broken off; the wood remaining is then smoothed, and only attention to this detail reveals the loss. The front ball, heading the arm posts, is more often missing than present.

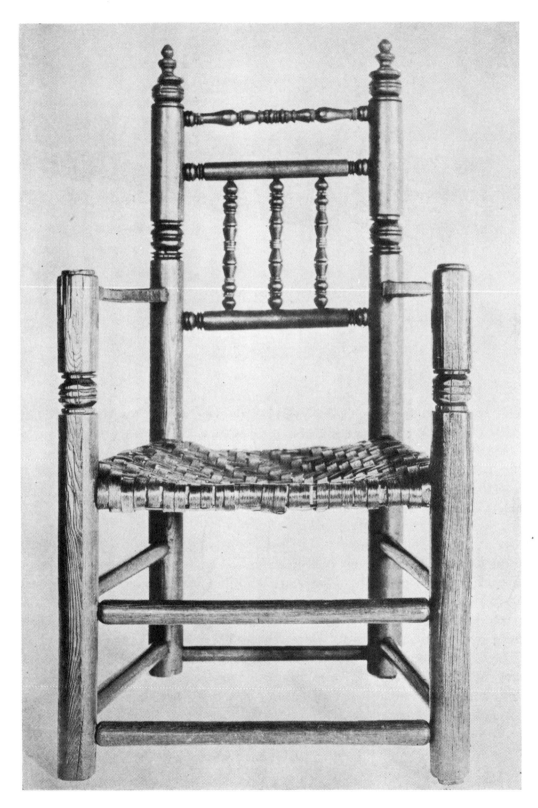

[191]

ON the preceding page is the beautiful Carver, owned by Mr. B. A. Behrend. The triple spindles are elaborately turned. The posts are 2½ inches in diameter. The limit of massiveness so far discovered, and about the same as the chair on page 189. Date: 1620–50.

On this page are two Carvers owned by the author. They are rather light, 1⅞ and 2 inches in diameter of the posts. That on the left is rather dainty for a Carver. Dates: about 1650–80.

On the next page is a very fine specimen of a leaning-back Carver. It is said to have been found in Fall River. The turnery is very handsome; the back finials are distinguished. It is built with rake backward for comfort. The posts are heavy, and the chair is as good as any specimen we have seen. It belongs to Mr. George Dudley Seymour, and is in the Wadsworth Atheneum, Hartford. Date: 1630–60.

There are several Carvers coming to light annually. When Dr. Lyon wrote he knew of only fifteen. The author estimates ten times as many are now known, but only a half dozen of the very heavy sort.

[193]

AT the left is a heavy side Carver Chair. It has probably lost something from the finials. The ball turning of the top spindle is quite unusual in Carvers. This chair is high. It is painted black. Owner: Mr. B. A. Behrend. Date: 1630–60.

It had, until quite lately, been presumed that side Carver chairs were always light, or what are called in Connecticut, "lady" chairs. But recently three heavy examples have come to the attention of collectors, as heavy as fine early specimens of arm Carvers. The writer inclines to believe that these chairs have only recently been recognized by searchers. If this view is correct, we are likely to have a considerable addition made to our list of such chairs.

On the next page is, perhaps, an unique child's high Carver. The turnings are very heavy, and it has the "panel" seat. It adds to the regular features of the Carver a fine intermediate turning between the arm and the seat. These turnings,—arm and intermediate, are elaborate. The chair seems to be of walnut and is very heavy. It belongs to the author. Date: 1660–80.

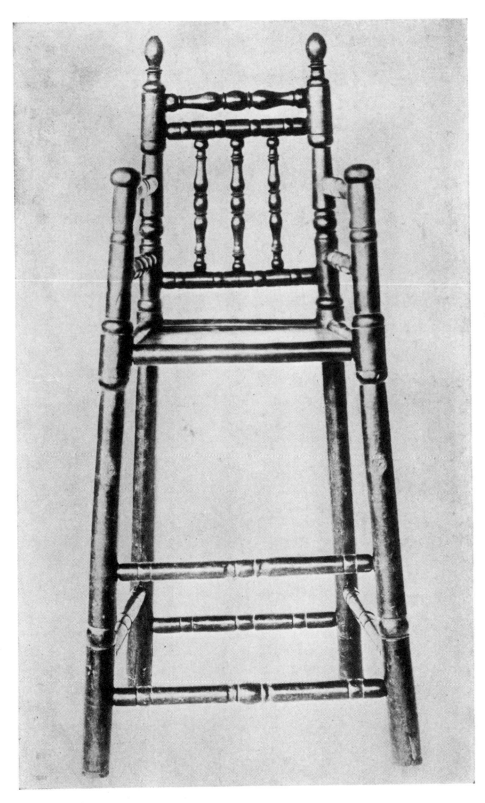

 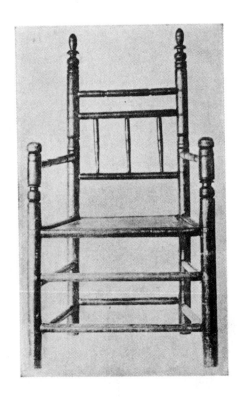

ABOVE on the left is a Carver chair, owned by the author. It has a very fine arm turning. On the right is another Carver, owned by the author. It has a panel seat thinned at the edges and inserted in grooves of the frame rungs. Dates: 1660–1690.

On the opposite page is a remarkable high chair in the possession of the Worcester Antiquarian Society. Although this piece has been repeatedly shown before, it being one of very few of which that is true, in this book, we cannot refrain from reproducing it again and more carefully. It is said to have belonged to Cotton Mather.

The finials are almost precisely the same as that of the Brewster chair shown on page 183.

It also has some other Brewster features. Date: 1630–50.

A CHILD'S Carver Chair, owned by the author. There are only two low chairs of this style that the writer has seen, but of course others may exist. This chair may have had small finials at the back. It is now absolutely unrestored, and while the picture of it is sizable the chair itself is very small, the seat being only seven inches from the floor. It is especially pleasing to be able to trace these Carver chairs through their various adaptations. Thus we have a low and a high baby Carver chair, side Carvers, and large arm Carvers of different sizes.

In the example before us there is very extreme wear on the fronts of the posts where the chair has been dragged about by children. This mark of use is especially appealing as it indicates that the piece has been concerned as a comrade in the joys of childhood. It was bought in Connecticut and is of ash.

The habitat of the Carver chair is defined fairly well. While many of the earliest and finest specimens are found near the Massachusetts shore, a considerable number have appeared in the Connecticut Valley and a few in Rhode Island.

The delightful variants in type cannot be correlated to locations with any degree of satisfaction. No two of these chairs are alike, nor are they so similar as to be confused with each other for a moment. Nevertheless, there is a mark of unmistakable family likeness. The date may be 1630–70.

THE bringing to light of several fine side Carvers of late, has added much to our interesting specimens. The example here, belonging to the author, was found on the South Shore. Its date is early, because the posts are heavy, being 2 inches in diameter. Perhaps 1630–50 would be a fair date. The object of very great interest regarding it is the remarkable similarity between the finials and those of the great standard Brewster, page 185. The feet of this chair are pieced, and correctly. The rungs are too low to take another set below them. Compare the chairs on the next page.

Another side Carver has been heard of better than this, it having never lost its feet. The specimen is not now available for a picture. A pair of such chairs would certainly supply a fine setting with a great arm Carver.

When we use the name Brewster we do not intend to convey any idea that a recognized style, like that we call a Brewster, existed. The three or four known examples of Brewsters, all different, do not give sufficient data for a style.

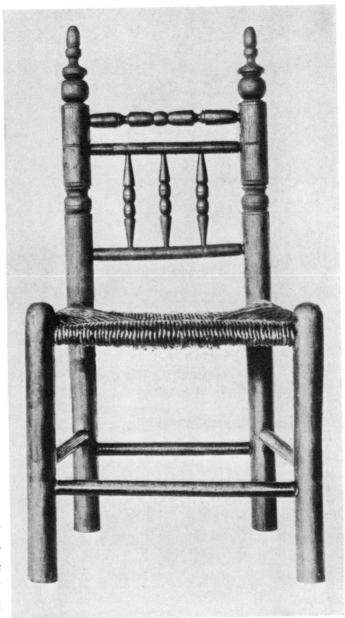

A PAIR of Side Carver Chairs, the property of Mr. Chauncey C. Nash. The arm chair in a Carver style is the usual thing, so much so that some do not know of the existence of the side chair. We have before us a pair made to match, and though somewhat worn down, still having their original finials. There is very rapid declension in size from the arm chair. Perhaps a dozen to a score of side Carvers have been discovered and all but three are of this light type. It will be seen that the turning of the three vertical spindles is an almost precise counterpart of that in the arm chairs.

Date: 1640–80.

These two chairs were found in Southern New Hampshire. The seats of the Carver side chairs were generally low, which indicates that they were probably made for sewing chairs and all their dimensions point to their being designed for the feminine portion of the family.

A CARVER Chair, owned by the author. This piece is somewhat stocky, the diameter of the legs being two and a quarter inches. It is original except the balls on the front posts. It is painted black. The simplicity and generous size of the turnings indicate a date from 1630–1650.

In this case the arm is turned simply. The three vertical spindles are unusual, being rather fat, and apparently made from a vague memory. It was found on the South Shore of Massachusetts, where perhaps Carvers are most numerous, as would naturally be the case. Fine furniture, in the sense of expensive and ornate, is not found to any considerable extent in the Plymouth colony as the

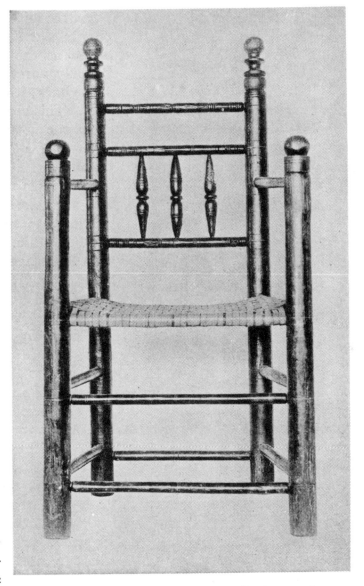

poorness of the land and the original condition of the colonists, who were seldom men of substance, leads us to look for simple furniture in the vicinity of their settlements. At the same time, we gain a native flavor, and examples of early Yankee ingenuity, in the provision of our forefathers for themselves of articles which they were unable to buy either from lack of a market or a purse.

Often the Carver is found converted into a rocker and cut down from one to three inches, and the balls of the front posts are usually lacking. It is hardly probable that the original seat remains in any of these chairs. At least it is absurd to maintain that the seat is original as there is no possible way of proving it.

ON the left is what we have named a pilgrim slat back. It is of the same period as the Carver and Brewster. Its only variation from the Carver is in the back, which has from two to four slats. This specimen dates about 1650.

On the next page is a truly superb example of a "four back" pilgrim chair. Owner: Mr. Dwight Blaney. It is the finest of this type that we have seen. The arms are flat. It has a massive intermediate spindle. The finials are almost Gothic. The turnings are somewhat later than the earliest chairs, which never show any decorative turning below the seat. The slats are most fascinating. The chair is very large. The date, from massiveness should be 1640, but judged by the turning we place it 1670–80.

It is more difficult, to the surprise of most collectors, to find fine examples of pilgrim slat backs, than good Carvers. The light types, with four or five slats, dating 1700, are common. Of course one would be unwise to presume that more than a score of the first pilgrim generation of these chairs exist.

One should very carefully distinguish in the use of the term "pilgrim slat-back." It is often confined to three slats, sometimes to only two, and never more than four. The simplicity of the turning and the great weight of the chair, mark it as of an earlier period than the New England slat-back. It is only necessary to see the two sorts together, for they vary greatly in massiveness. For instance, the examples on pages 204 and 205 are obvious 17th Century pieces.

A HEAVY Pilgrim Slat-back Chair. This example is probably unique as to its massiveness. The total hight is 38 inches and the seat is 22½ by 15½. It seems not to have been cut down more than an inch, yet the seat is but 13 inches high. It is owned by the author. Date: 1620–50.

ABOVE are a pair of pilgrim "three back" side chairs. Of course the seats should be rush. Their stocky appearance leads us to determine the date at about 1670–90. They belong to the author.

On the next page is a large chair with arched slats, molded. Owner: Mr. Geo F. Ives. Date: 1630–60. The general appearance of the chair suggests Italian influence. The chair, however, came from the remote country district—Vermont.

The seat of this chair is 18x21 inches and 20 inches high. The back is 48 inches high.

On the preceding page is a heavy pilgrim slat-back. Owner: Mr. Chauncey C. Nash. Date: 1630–50. This stocky chair, with the fine flavor of the first pilgrim generation, has recently come to light. Except that the tips of the finials are missing, we can give the strongest endorsement to this pleasing appealing example. It is in the soft natural color, with excellent surface.

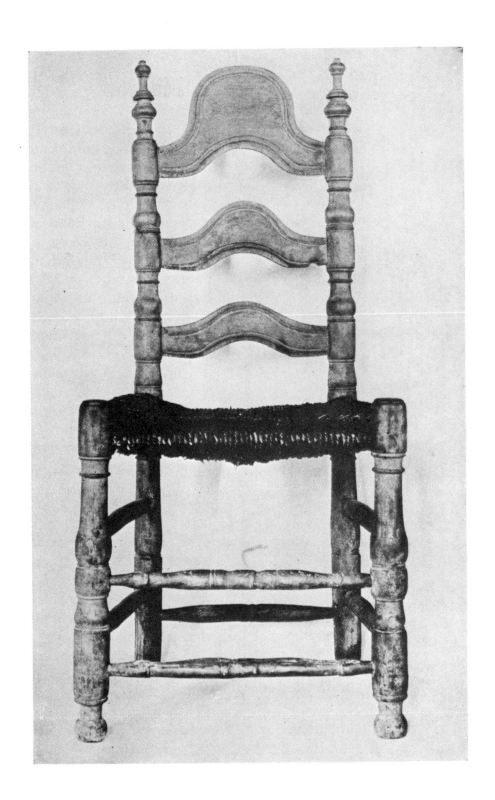

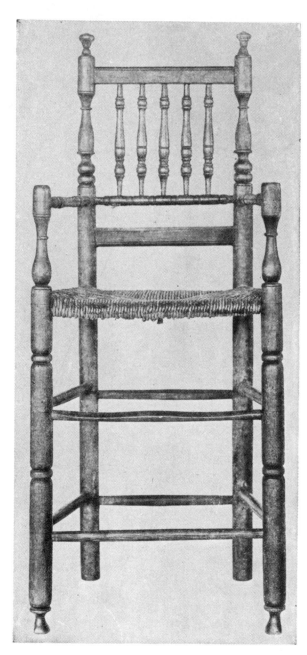

THE Child's High Chair here shown, with five back spindles is an interesting variant. The owner is Mr. Geo. F. Ives, and the date is perhaps 1700–20. The top and bottom rails of the back are flat pieces. The turning of the arm suggests the 17th century. The balls, or pear terminations of the front legs have suffered somewhat.

The lore of high chairs is an amusing study. The author has photographs of about fifty, of low and high degree. The question whether a foot rest is correct for an early chair must be answered in the affirmative. Likewise we may say many early high chairs had no foot rest. This one has a worn rung which served as a foot rest. Whether the love for children has grown cold, or for whatever reason no fine child's chairs are made now-a-days.

In case there was no bar across in front of a child, a leathern thong could be strapped across attached to the posts. In this case they show wear as if from such use. The equilibrium of the chair was better maintained without the projecting foot rest. In the best examples it has been lost.

There is no trace of the use of a tray attached to a high chair. In modern use such trays are thought necessary, but the early use was confined to meal time only, and children were obliged to behave with decorum—if we believe all we read. Besides, the feeding of babes by Eve's method was the rule in those days.

A BANISTER-BACK Child's High Chair. Owner: Mr. George Dudley Seymour. Date: 1700–20. The chair was found at Milford, Connecticut. The banisters are reeded. The cresting or top rail is profiled and pierced to produce the "crown and heart" design. A part of the top rail is missing. The turned intermediate spindle under the arm is excellent. The chair is maple, was never painted or restored. It has lost something in hight. It was given to Elizabeth Davidson of Milford by her father. She married Abner Perry in 1795, and the chair has been held by their descendants till the owner bought it in 1921.

On page 210 we begin to show a fine collection of mushroom chairs, a variant and successor of the pilgrim slat back.

One readily sees that the horizontal spindle, under the arm, served to strengthen the chair, to keep its occupant in place, and to enhance the appearance of the chair.

The transition from an all-turned chair to a banister back was in the interest of comfort, as the flat banisters were agreeable to lean against, whereas turned spindles were not. Further, no bending was required as in the Pilgrim slat-backs.

Compare with chairs on pages 259 to 262, where we find the inspiration for this chair.

We are compelled by the exigencies of assembling the volume to place this chair out of its proper position.

[211]

ON page 210 is a small mushroom chair. It is owned by Mrs. W. B. Long of Boston. We cannot too often impress the reader with the fact that nothing is, or can be, shown in scale. This is of course true of all furniture books, but especially true here, because we are trying to show details, and often give a large cut for a small piece. Date: about 1700.

On page 211 is a very fine mushroom chair owned by Mr. B. A. Behrend. It was in the Lyon volume. Date: about 1690.

On this page are two mushroom chairs owned by the author. The banister-back helps us date these chairs. The style of enlarging the top of the front post came in, occasionally in the 17th Century, and continued into the early 18th Century. The chair on the right has the slanting arm, an early and good style. It dates about 1700; the other possibly a trifle later. They were found near Boston. The slant arm chair is in ash. The other is maple, and a more suitable, but later, wood.

On the opposite page is a humorously huge mushroom chair in the author's collection. The chair also rakes sharply backwards, seven inches from the perpendicular. The mushrooms, in seasoning, have flattened nearly a quarter inch. It was found in Southern Connecticut.

Size: Top slat, 5¾ inches wide; each slat below diminishing a quarter inch. Width, over all, 32¼ inches; seat 28½ x 22 inches; back posts, 46½ inches; front posts 30½ inches. Date: 1680–1720.

A GREAT Double Mushroom Chair; further described on opposite page.
It was evidently designed to be the father of chairs of this type.

[213]

THE room shown is the fine reproduction of antique framing in the parlor of Mr. B. A. Behrend's house. It is a suggestion to those who have, as he has, fine examples of Seventeenth Century furniture and who wish to form a proper setting for it. It is true that old materials may often be secured and worked into such a room with a greater quaintness of effect and a closer approximation to the mellowing influence of the past. The room shows pieces most of which are elsewhere described in this volume, though the quaint little stool with only one leg in the back is not elsewhere seen. It seems an adaptation of a milking stool, with a back rest. Here I propound the subtle inquiry, why was a milking stool made with three legs while of all seats made in the world it needed to be better based than the ordinary chair? So far as our views are concerned we want to say that from experience with the portion of the cow suggested, we enter a proposal that all milking stools should have five legs, like one in the collection of Mr. Geo. F. Ives.

THE Chair at the right has very large mushrooms. The large chair at the bottom of page 217 is a combination of a pilgrim slat back, a mushroom, and a Brewster suggestion. The little child's chair by its side is the only mushroom in that size known to the author, who owns the three chairs. Date, on the "combination," about 1680; on the others 1690–1710.

At the top of page 216 are two mushroom chairs of excellent type. The "sausage" turnings on the chair at the left, together with the slant arm, give it merit. Owner: Mr. Arthur W. Wellington.

On the right on page 216 is a mushroom chair with a finely scrolled set of slats.

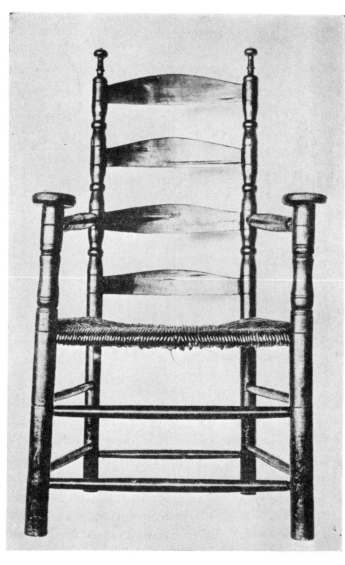

The sizes of posts of chairs are generally above two inches if they reach back to the first pilgrim generation. The largest posts are hardly two and three quarter inches. After 1660 we begin to find posts of two inches diameter the rule. After 1680 the posts are often only an inch and three quarters. Something must be allowed for the style of the chair, and its size, in general. Side chairs have posts averaging about a quarter inch smaller than those of arm chairs, of the same style. How the term side chair, for a chair without arms, originated, we do not know. In some regions side chairs are called "lady" chairs. That is, they were intended for woman's use.

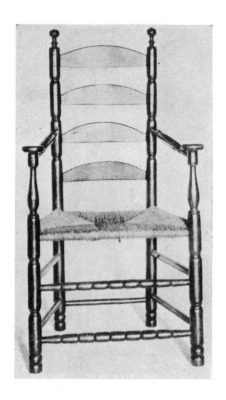 

ON the next page, at the top, from the author's collection, a Pilgrim slat back with three slats rounded in the most usual fashion but with very good finials. The front balls are missing. The arms are in what we may call the flat turning; that is to say, turned pieces which are substantially flattened for comfort and convenience, and which preceded the so-called shaped arm. The slat back chair persisted to a late date, well into the Eighteenth Century, in fact, whereas the Carver and the Brewster ceased to be made.

The rather common side chair with slats which was used in kitchens throughout the Eighteenth Century was merely a lighter type of the Pilgrim slat back, and was made in very small turnings. On the other hand the arm slat back seems to have gone out of use earlier than the side chair, which is one more mystery connected with antique furniture.

Size: Hight 42 inches; seat hight 15 inches; seat size 23¾ by 16 inches.

A "Near" Carver appears on the right, from the author's collection. It is heavily turned.

Returning to the large chair on page 217 at the bottom: It is in all respects original except a bit of slat, and the large fist-like balls which are turned as a part of the posts are extraordinary. An inch or two has, however, been lost at the bottom. We can conceive no use in the row of spindles in front except to strengthen the chair. Thus, while this truss work prevented side rack, the spindles under the arms prevented racking fore and aft.

TWO Cromwellian Chairs, owned by the author. Date: 1640–60. The chair on the left has more turning than the other, but is not therefore any earlier.

These chairs are marked by low backs, with a somewhat narrow rest, vertically. They are called Cromwellian, because the era of simplicity under the Commonwealth revolted from the more luxurious furniture of the earlier part of the century. With the restoration comes in the florid, rich school of Charles II. Of course these chairs are American, being maple. The coverings for this sort of chairs were in a great variety of materials, but preferably leather.

These chairs are to be distinguished sharply from the Spanish style which prolongs the back post above the frame, and ends it with molded face. Such chairs were perhaps made in America, but we refrain, lest we err, from introducing them into this book.

A CHAIR generally called Jacobean. It is more accurate to give the date merely, as this chair persisted many years, and most of those found in this country were of the time of Cromwell or of Charles II. The date of this chair may be 1660-1700. The chairs of this type have been set forward in date somewhat by the discovery of a date as late as 1699 on a very fine specimen.

The leather covering of chairs is very satisfactory, conducing to cleanliness, durability and a sense of the mellow past. They are inviting—the best compliment we can pay to a chair. This example belongs to the author. It was found in New Hampshire, and is of maple and birch. The nails are those usually found; the very large oval nail head is more likely to be Spanish.

All the original leather seats are thoroughly studded with nails, so much so that it sometimes seems as if an effort was made to insert a nail wherever space could be found for it.

The ovaling of the top and bottom of the back panel, on a surface so arranged that the surface of the doubled leather is flush with the wood, gives an excellent effect.

Chairs of this style in England are sometimes very high. The American examples known are usually of the hight of an ordinary chair. We have elsewhere commented on the almost total lack of American cross-stretcher chairs.

A LEATHER Back Chair. The simplicity is restful and in very good taste. The chair is all original except the leather, which is restored in the natural color taken from another old chair. Leather backs, such as are shown here and on the preceding and following pages, are more rare than banister-backs; and if we regard style, perhaps we should count them just as good, if not better, than the banister-backs.

The date of this chair is about 1670–90. It shows the quieting influence of the Commonwealth time. The wood is maple.

The method of construction of chairs was unfortunately governed by style more than by sound cabinet principles. Most of the chairs of this and the cane type are frail in the back. This is especially true, when, as usual, the back slants at an angle beginning at the seat, so that a cross-grain strain occurs. Not all old furniture was good. Only the best survived.

Luxury was not lacking in the homes of the 17th century where there were means to indulge it. The inventory of the chair coverings in a 17th Century house startles us by the rich material it reveals.

Table linen also in ordinary households was common. Indeed, one would infer it was more common, in good patterns, than it is now. Napkins in large numbers are enumerated. The bed linen also was often real. Where a housewife was forehanded she often had a store of linen for many years ahead.

The homes were not wholly without silver and glass, with some china, though the last named was not made in England. The bulk of the table ware was in pewter, with much wooden ware in the poorer families.

A LEATHER-BACK Chair. Date: 1670–90. The high stretcher is a desirable feature. This chair is a variant from the cane chair, and is of the same period. It belongs to the author. It is maple, and practically all original, except the leather, which is old.

It is regarded as a very serious loss if the feet of a chair are missing, but even more important are the finials, nevertheless any relic of a dignified article of furniture two hundred years old is worth possessing, and if a chair has lost both finials and feet it must be, if so old, wept over.

In the re-upholstering of old chairs care should be taken to keep the padding low. The effect is spoiled by plump padding. It is true all old chairs have had so much use that we cannot say just how the seats originally looked. But they certainly are not in keeping with their age unless the seat is pretty well flattened. The backs sometimes did and sometimes did not have padding. In case the back was padded the leather was often doubled and padding placed between so as to show leather at the back of the chair.

AT the left is an Original Seventeenth Century Rocker, in the author's collection. We use the phrase here "Seventeenth Century" more as an indication of style than of precise date. The piece has all the characteristics of the Pilgrim slat-back, except that the bottoms of the posts have enlarged turnings unmistakably designed to receive rockers. The writer owns another chair of the same type. They are extremely rare, yet seem to have come to light in three or four instances lately. They lack massiveness, this piece being about 40 inches high; the seat 15½ inches high with an area of 20¾ by 16 inches. The rockers are shaped to prevent an overturn.

On the right, a high desk chair. This piece at first appears to be a high chair for a child, but the size is that of an ordinary chair, namely 17½ by 12¾ inches on the seat, which, however, is 22 inches high; the back being 37½ inches high. It is very substantial, though the posts are rather light. It is all original, except the rush.

Date problematical, perhaps 1700–1740.

ABOVE are two high chairs of the finest style each in its kind. The left chair belongs to Mr. G. Winthrop Brown. The right chair is delightful from its flaring base.

One never knows where to stop on children's chairs. They are too delightful to leave behind us. They add more to the home sense than any other furniture.

A high chair, similar to Mr. Brown's above, but with three slats, is owned by Mr. Chauncey C. Nash. Had the makers taken a little more pains, as in the right hand chair on page 278, we should have had a remarkable Pennsylvania arched slat-back.

Turned chairs, which to us appear most desirable, were at first made as substitutes for wainscot chairs, and were not highly regarded. The turning lathe, run by the foot, with all parts made of wood, was without question the earliest wood-working machine in America. John Alden was amply competent to make a lathe and no doubt did make one. The labor was far less than was required for any other sort of chair. An ax was sufficient to prepare the rough sticks for the turner.

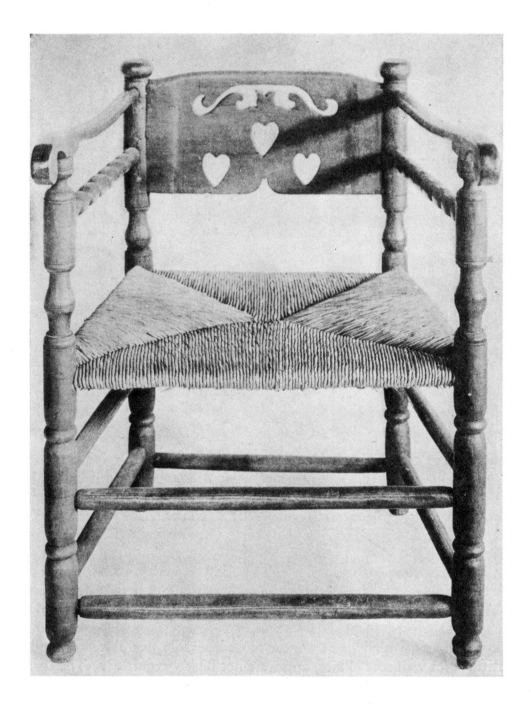

AN unique arm chair which was found in Connecticut. The back is hollowed from a single board and shows, besides the three hearts, a peculiar scroll which are together called the "heart and crown." The piece has been very much admired. It was in the former Wallace Nutting collection.
Date: 1690–1720.

TWO Turned Slat-Back Chairs. Owner: Mr. George Dudley Seymour.
Date: 1710–40.

They are from the Capt. Chas. Churchill house, Newington, Connecticut,
built 1762–63. They are now in the Wadsworth Atheneum, Hartford.

These chairs bear the name of New England Slat-Backs. This distin-
guishes them from the arched slat forms whose habitat is Pennsylvania.
Also it means, though the name does not show it, a New England chair
succeeding the pilgrim type. The earliest of them dates about 1700. From
that time they were popular, always growing lighter, through the century,
as every day chairs.

ON the left appears a five-back New England chair. It is in the author's collection. The hight is 34½ inches and the seat 15½ inches, the size of the seat is extreme being 25 inches wide by 19 inches deep. This generosity is attractive. The hight of arm chairs used to be considered to be properly 18 inches, as well as the side chairs, but many measurements of ancient arm chairs disclose the fact that not a few were made lower than the side chairs, which later usually have a good hight to be used at a table.

The arm chair, however, which in this case shows the elongated ball or pear-shaped foot, has not been cut down, which indicates that it was built for comfort by the fireside. The so-called sausage turning so often seen on a New England slat back is here very prominent. The roll-shaped arm suggests a simple plain variant from the more elegant Jacobean type and helps us in the date of such a piece, making it 1690–1710.

On the right appears a turned four-back arm chair in the author's collection. It is all original, is painted black with some late decoration. The finials are good for the period. The leather seat has been added, but it is so substantial that it may well remain.

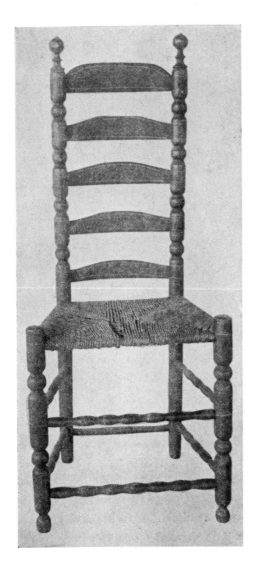

TWO fine high backed New England turned chairs, the left hand example being a very perfect type, having five backs; complete in its turned scheme, and with sausage rungs not only in front, but at the sides.

The other chair is remarkable for its wealth of rungs, all alike, twelve in number. The spacing of the back is a characteristic feature, the slats increasing in width and in spacing, from the seat upward. What it is in this chair that is so attractive one hardly knows, but all eyes linger on it. The dates are about 1710–30.

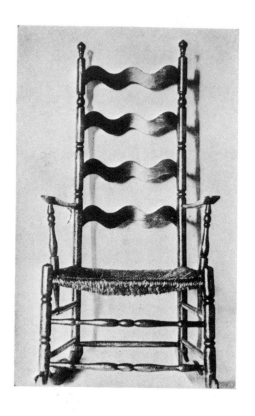 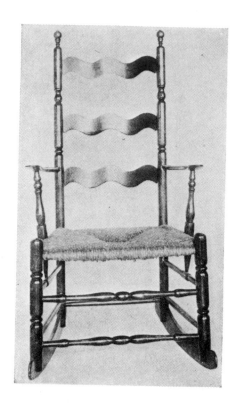

THE Chair above with four waved or serpentine slats is owned by J. Milton Coburn, M.D. It is very rare. Chairs of this general type were made, sometimes, with rockers. We are not certain in this case, whether the rockers are original.

The other chair, a three-back, is owned by Mr. G. Winthrop Brown. It appears that the turnings of the two chairs are identical, so that they were made by the same craftsman, or one was copied from the other. The date may be 1730–50. These lighter turnings were not used much before that date.

The arms are short, and are reinforced for strength by running down to the first rung. The style must have been popular.

Comparison of these chairs with the baby's chair on page 277, at the top, on the right, indicates that the little chair is of an earlier date, as the arms belong to the 17th century. Another example of a reinforced arm, with two bearings, appears on page 230. In the earlier style the front post of the chair would have sustained the arm. The change was not wise. It also interfered with the rushing.

ON the left is a rare, possibly an unique Chair, owned by Mr. B. A. Behrend. It has on the rear legs small rollers like those used on trundle beds, though of course much smaller. We have here then the genesis of the caster. The chair is apparently a 17th Century piece—just coming inside that limit. The ends of the arms are sawed off.

The other chair, owned by Mr. W. of Boston, is a Pennsylvanian or Knickerbocker product. It is called a name chair, from the inscription of the lady's name, to whom it was doubtless presented. The turnings and finials are in accord with its origin—two little balls, and a central finial being applied at the top rail. The chair has the "panel" seat.

On the back above the name is a flying cherub, carved. The piece is altogether very quaint.

The chair at the right has that much to be desired, six-slat back. The type is Pennsylvanian. It introduces the arched slat. It is characterized also by ball-feet, turned larger than the post, though in this case a restoration failed to take note of that fact. We admit chairs are found without the enlarged foot.

This chair is light and attractive. It is common with four slats, not rare with five, much sought for with six, and found in one or two known instances with seven slats. Another mark of these chairs, when made with arms, is the cutting away of wood under the arm, for lightness. We know of no exception to this rule, in the best style.

This chair, those on page 233, and the chair at top of page 234, belong to Mr. Francis D. Brinton, West Chester, Pennsylvania.

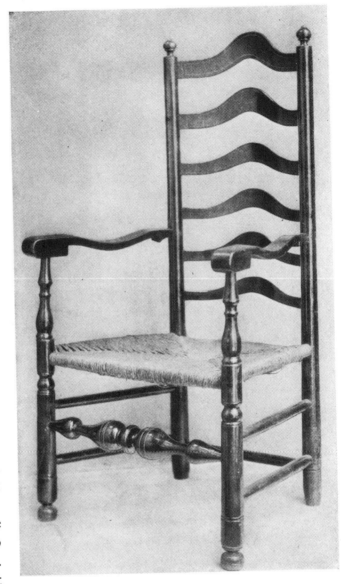

ON the left at the top of page 230, there is a curious chair. The turnings have enlarged shoulders. The obvious object was to secure greater solidity. The posts are left square, except the finials behind and the section under the arm in front. One or two other examples have been seen with this sort of turning. We do not count it at all important; it is merely an oddity. Date uncertain; perhaps 1710–50.

Another chair on that page has "sausage" turnings not only in front, but on the intermediate spindles below the arms. The date may be 1700. The left chair, bottom page 230, is a good example of 1710–30.

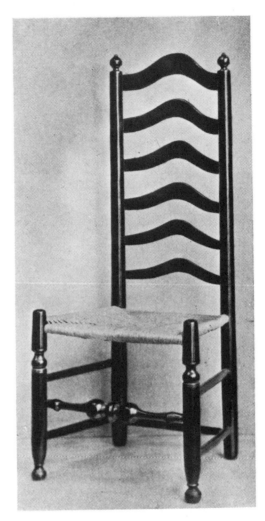

The chair on page 232 was bought in Albany. It is one of the most delicate imaginable. The finials run to a needle point. The slats are very thin. The piece is maple.

The right hand chair above is a fine example of the Pennsylvania side chair, with six slats.

The left hand chair above, corresponding with the arm chair on the next page, has fancifully scrolled slats. They were evidently made as part of a set. The chair above shows the "blunt arrow" formation of the front right-hand foot. This is also a feature of the earliest Philadelphia Windsors. The front spindles of these chairs are generally very handsomely turned, in the Queen Anne style.

These chairs date from 1720 to 1750.

The chair on the left is mentioned on the preceding page. The chair at the bottom of this page, while its rockers are an addition, is of a massive fine design.

The Flemish chair, on which we here enter, became popular among the well-to-do in America at the end of the 17th Century. It was the age of walnut, but native woods that were convenient claimed attention. Virginia walnut was not found where these chairs were made.

The feature of the Flemish chair that most impresses one is the famous Flemish scroll, seen to good advantage on the beautiful chair on the next page.

The chair there shown is owned by Mr. H. W. Erving and the one on the next page following, slightly different, by Mr. G. Winthrop Brown.

A fine feature of each is the so-called ram's horn arm, which gains this name when it curves outward as well as downward.

The back legs are never carved. There is sometimes a sharp—too sharp, backward angle of the rear leg beginning at the seat. The chair is weak at that point. In the case of the arm chair the arm acts as a brace. On the side chair there is a frequent fatal weakness.

These chairs are a far cry from the simplicity of the turned chair. They represent very well the reaction against Puritanism. While they were never common in America, owing in part to their expense and their too ornamental character for a new country and a simple generation, they are found

in considerable numbers. The caning of these chairs is of the finest character, and some of it remains in the examples we show. The finish is preferably natural, but many specimens are painted black.

AN Arm Chair with turned base and Flemish back, and a Flemish side chair. Owner: Mr. W. of Boston. In the backs of both of these fine chairs the Flemish scrolls are strikingly prominent. The wood is "fruit" wood—a term indicating apple or pear.

On the preceding page a chair with a strong English appearance, but said to be American, is shown. Owner: Mr. Stanley A. Sweet of New York.

On page 239 appears the most perfect example I have seen of a pair of Flemish side chairs. They are owned by Mr. W. of Boston. They are painted black.

 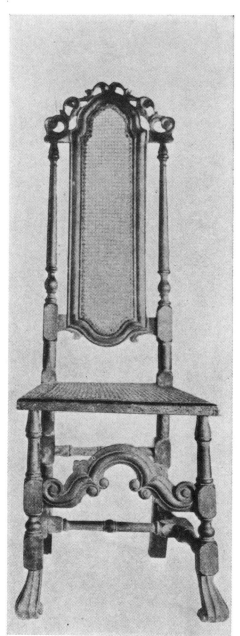

AT the left is a beautiful Flemish chair. Owner: Mr. W. of Boston. A rare and winning feature is the shape of the molded panel. The color is black; the wood we cannot certainly name.

On the right is a chair, present owner unknown, with rarely fine Spanish feet. Such feet bear study, as there are so many inferior ones. Spanish in this sense means the Spanish Netherlands. The date of Mr. W.'s chair is 1670–90. The other is about 1700.

AN Arm and Side Chair, Flemish style. In fruit wood. Owner: Mr. W. of Boston. One should note that the arm chair, as often occurs in this style, is lower in the seat than the side chair. The boldness of the scrolls, combined with the delicacy of the connecting carving, and the beauty of the carving on the arm are notable. The inward spiral of the foot is called the English scroll. The date is 1670–1700.

ON the left is a Flemish chair owned by Mr. W. of Boston, on which the carving of the side stiles of the panel is inside a reeded member. The wood is very hard—possibly beech.

The other chair, present owner unknown, has a handsomely scrolled panel. The plush back is a bad addition which does not fit the panel. The carved stretchers sometimes, but by no means always, match the top rail, as in this case.

THE left hand chair belongs to Mr. Stanley A. Sweet. It is very elaborate, showing every feature of the Flemish style. Date of this and the other chair: about 1690.

The reader will have noticed two distinct types of top rail on Flemish chairs. The earlier in date, and the handsomer, is that in which the rail projects beyond the posts, such as the chairs on page 240. The other sort is much less frail; for the rail is wholly between the posts into which it is entered by mortise and tenon, as in the chairs on this page.

The chair on the right is the property of Mr. W. of Boston.

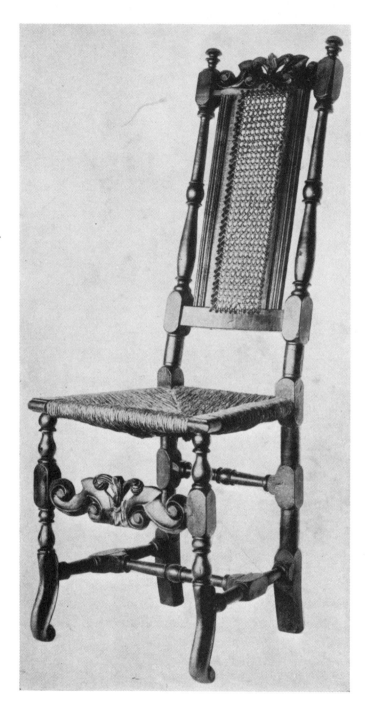

A SIMPLE Flemish chair belonging to the author, and accorded rather more prominence than it deserves. Still as a type it affords opportunity to point out that the elaborate chairs heretofore shown are too rare to be within the reach of the average collector.

This chair, with the simple reeded sides of the back panel, and an absolutely plain bottom rail beneath the panel, is more like what we see as a rule. The work on the two carved members is worthy so far as it goes. It will be seen also that all preceding Flemish chairs have had cane seats as well as backs. This chair has a rush seat which in old days was counted not so good as cane.

This chair of maple dates about 1690–1700.

It will be noted that the cane chair has a middle stretcher. The rear stretcher, therefore, is placed very high.

A BEAUTIFULLY carved Flemish chair, belonging to Mr. W. of Boston. It is reported to have been the property of William Penn. The date is about 1670–1700.

The reader should be warned that in large photographs made close to the object there is no little distortion, so that as here the base of the chair looks too heavy in proportion to the back. This blemish is inevitable, under the conditions necessary for procuring these pictures.

The small scroll on the legs into which the carved stretcher is mortised, is a fine touch of design, as if intended to receive the stretcher. Many Flemish chairs, even those of the very highest character otherwise, lack this detail.

There is generally a "shoe" or knob on which the foot of a Flemish leg rests. But in the English scroll, this shoe is regularly lacking.

Attention is called to the extremely narrow band of caning in the back, in this chair. This "gesture," as the French say, is very effective. Never mind about the comfort. The seats of Flemish chairs, in the better styles are strongly molded on the outer side, as here.

Note how the scrolls on the top rail cunningly intercept one another!

[245]

A DOUBLE-PANEL Cane Spanish Foot Chair. Owner: the author. This example has a great deal of stylish feeling. The back follows all the curves of a Grecian bend, with a few to spare. The outward rake of the foot behind is particularly "fetching." The skirt is a thin piece of applied wood. Owing to the lighting, the Spanish foot shows in a different color from the leg above, but it is all original. The rolling scroll of the top rail is delicate. The stretchers also are effectively scrolled. Altogether the chair presents many features different from the ordinary. The chair is painted and decorations in gold were discovered when a modern upholstered seat was removed. It was originally caned. The habit of beginning the cabriole curve of the leg, not at the frame but after an intervening spool-like ornament is the regular style. Date: 1690–1700.

On the next page is a very delicately carved pair of Flemish chairs belonging to Mr. Francis Hill Bigelow of Cambridge. The carvings above and below are a more perfect counterpart of one another than we have elsewhere noticed. Of course the upholstery on one of the chairs is a later addition. Date: 1670–90.

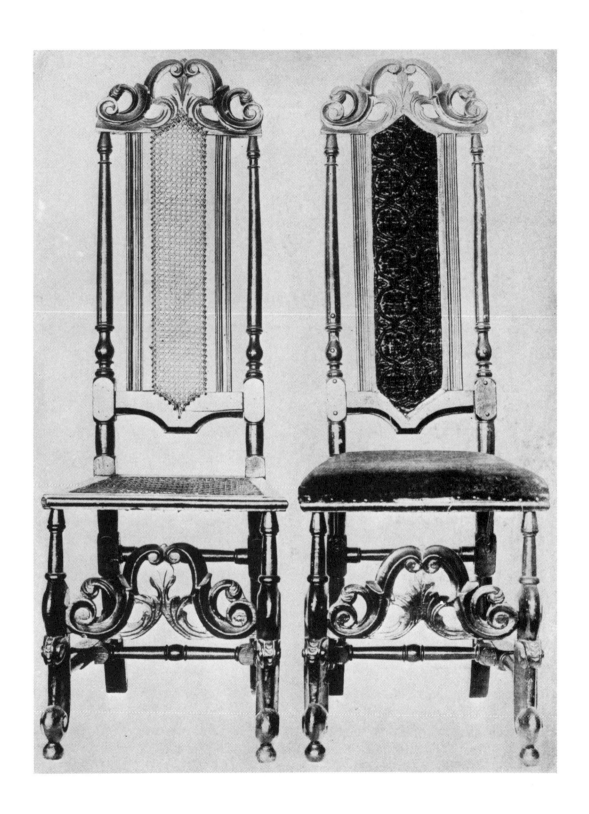

A PAIR of Carved Cane Chairs, with Spanish feet. Owner: Mr. Francis Hill Bigelow. The feet are in very good style. The roll at the top of the rail suggests comparison with that on page 246. The turned stretchers are very bold. A touch of carving running about the molded back and on the squares of the legs, is interesting. Date: 1700.

A PAIR of Panel-Back Chairs. Owner: Mr. W. of Boston. The small
skirt resembles that on page 246. The painting is decorated with bands of
gold. These chairs were found at Salem and are said to have belonged
to Nathanael Hawthorne from whose former residence they came. There
is a very striking resemblance between these chairs and those on the opposite page. There the decoration on the squares of the turnings in the
legs is carved. Date about 1700.

We approach, in the form of the molded back frame, the early Dutch
style which shortly followed these chairs.

[249]

THE Chair on the left, belonging to Mr. Brooks Reed of Boston is in a style immediately following the Flemish, and far more generally seen in America. Date: 1700–10. All the stretchers are ornamentally turned. The style of the arm, while a declination from the more elegant Flemish, is the proper type for this chair. The only carving is on the cresting.

The chair on the right has five banisters, a feature counted worth while. While the chair is supposed to be later than the Flemish, it has the imposed not the built in, top rail, an early feature. Date: 1690–1700. Owner: Mr. B. A. Behrend.

Banister-backs are the usual "old fashioned" chairs in America, having been immensely popular. They divided this supremacy with the simpler "New England" slat back. The dates were coincident. But the slat backs began sooner and lasted later.

The method of turning the banisters was to glue two pieces of wood together, with a paper between. After the turning was done, the pieces could be separated by inserting the point of a knife, and a smooth surface without loss of shape through planing, was obtained.

SPANISH Foot Banister Backs. Owner: the author. These chairs while not precisely alike in every detail, were evidently made to match. The stretcher of the arm chair is huge. The turner loved to show what he could do when he tried. The arm is better shaped than usual. It is seldom one sees such large ball turning in the side stretchers. Date: 1700–1710.

The growth of the turner's art from the Egyptian bow string lathe to the present, presents many aspects of interest. All early work in America was done on foot-power lathes. Having made this statement we await a statement from some one that water power was sometimes used. It is possible in sporadic cases. It was not possible to turn very small articles because the back rest was not invented until long after our period.

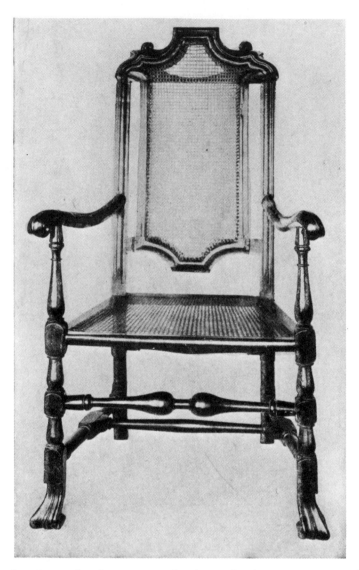

A CANE Chair with Spanish Feet. This somewhat simple but effective design has good ram's horn arms, and like the Flemish style, a middle stretcher. The back is done in the molded style of the Dutch chairs. The stretcher is not as satisfactory as one could wish.

In tracing the development of style, much attention should be paid to physical geography. While a furniture maker might bring his materials from far, in special instances, yet the cost of transportation was great. Hence, after a little, an artisan would look about him, and learn to adapt the materials that lay ready to his hand. If no cane was available, he used rushes. If he had no walnut he had a fine wood in maple. The banister back gave springiness lacking in a slat back. Style is developed more through necessity than through deliberate design. The abundant pine, found in America, furnished the logical wood for the interior of cabinet pieces, and to take the place of the oak wainscot of Europe. The pine was so wide as to overcome, to a large degree, the necessity of small panels. Anyone with a little ingenuity could construct a crude lathe. The all-turned furniture of the earliest period was more easily produced than any other kind. The only tools used in putting a turned chair together were auger and mallet. And the work stood.

ON the preceding page is an unusual chair owned by Mr. Stanley S. Sweet. It is peculiar in that the arm post is not a continuation of the leg, but is set back on the frame of the chair. The broken line is pleasing to the eye, but probably no improvement from a structural point of view. There is a fine arm and back, and altogether, after the Flemish period, the chair is as handsome as could be desired. Date: 1690-1700.

Above, on this page, on the left, is a fine Spanish foot banister back side chair owned by Mr. B. A. Behrend. It is one of a pair. It was not feasible to present both of them. Date: about 1700.

On the right is a rich Flemish chair treated on the following page.

[254]

ON the preceding page: the Flemish chair is owned by Mrs. John Marshall Holcombe of Hartford. It is very close in its lines to that on page 241. It belonged to a clergyman in Warren, Connecticut. Date: 1680–1700. Its details are very rich.

Above on the left is a chair which carries in its top rail a crown, repeated below in the stretcher, and having spiral turnings. This chair is in maple, and is stoutly defended as American. We have failed to find the owner of the fine chair on the right.

It very strongly resembles the chair at the top of page 243. The manner of marking in the carving of the legs, the place for the stretcher is good.

A NEW ENGLAND Slat Back. A large chair. The seat is 21¼ inches wide, and 19 inches deep—an extraordinary depth. Its hight is 17¼; and one may see, by the wear, that it was 18 inches. The back is no less than 46½ inches high. It leans 3 inches. The chair had been used with candles on the front posts. Several such chairs have been seen. The candle holders were usually constructed with hollow cone bases to fit over points on the posts. The wood of this chair is maple. It is owned by the author. Date: about 1700.

The remarkable chair on the next page is owned by Mr. Mark M. Henderson of Norwich. It is the extreme specimen of turnery, as we know it. The fine scrolls of the back should not— and they will not—escape us.

The arrangement of the balls and rings looks easy, but is in reality very difficult if the symmetry be maintained. Date: about 1710.

The play of fancy in a maker's mind whenever it is allowed to materialize as when one works for one's own use, is a valuable as well as an interesting embodiment. By such exuberance a worker makes a flourish which proves that neither he nor nature have exhausted themselves.

It is a question whether the turning in such a chair is not slightly overdone. For instance, the chisel has cut so deeply that the strength is imperiled. Yet it has stood the test. But if these posts were turned down evenly to their smallest diameters very little would be left.

The shape of the slats suggests paired salamanders. They are very effective. Had the maker gone still farther and given us five slats!

Altogether the effect is sufficiently striking. But when one starts out to see what he can do we are just human enough to inquire why he did not go on?

A BANISTER-BACK Spanish Foot Side Chair. It was in the Webb-Welles house, Wethersfield; and its present ownership is unknown. It has a sense of restraint although it bears no little embellishment. The writer was always fond of the chair. Date: 1690–1700.

ON the next page is a turned arm chair, with heart and crown back, and an intermediate spindle under the arm. It is owned by Mr. George Dudley Seymour. Date: 1720–30. Wood, maple. A large chair, combining lightness, grace and strength. It was found in Milford, Connecticut, and is now in the Wadsworth Atheneum, Hartford. The reader is again warned that, in chairs of this size, the camera greatly enlarges the front at the expense of the back. When viewed with the eye the proportions are more harmonious. The posts are really of moderate size, but they look very small. One sees a molded or rather beaded line on the arm. The Spanish feet of the chair on this page are cut from the solid, and are not glued on as is often the case.

ON the preceding page is an arm chair, with heart and crown crest, intermediate spindle under the arm, and with ornamental turning on all the rungs—an unusually full degree of decoration. The chair is all original, including perhaps the seat. It was probably brought from Connecticut, but it was bought in Boston in 1921. Owner: the author. Date: 1720–30.

On this page is a New England five banister-back chair, owned by James Davidson of New London, Connecticut. The three hearts in the back are similar to a low back on page 224. An effort was made at some ornateness in this piece, as the top and bottom rails of the back are both scrolled. The arms are done with a hollowed surface. However, the special peculiarity of the piece is the apparent mixture of styles. We would like to see the secondary spindle under the arm lower down and in a horizontal position. Finding it, however, where it is, we would not expect the scrolled arm with it. A casual glance would suggest that the arm had been added, but a careful examination seems to indicate that the piece is all original. Date: about 1720–30.

A REVERSED Banister-Back Chair. Owner: Mrs. John Marshall Holcombe. The intermediate spindle under the arm is very rare in a chair of this style.

The fashion of reversing the banisters, showing the rounded side in front, we used to regard as a mark of lack of knowledge in the cabinet maker. We are now compelled to believe that the action was deliberate, taken with a view to conforming the spindles, or banisters, with the posts, which in this instance is perfectly accomplished. Date: about 1700.

On the following page is a wonderful high chair owned by Mr. Hollis French. It is the only instance known of a spiraled, open-work rung in an American chair. The Spanish feet and the fine arm add to its attraction. The first introduction of a Dutch back into this volume, as here, indicates the dawning of that fine style; while the under body has still the features of an earlier time. Date: about 1700. The upper rung was used as a foot rest. Special foot rests were very early.

The writer has never personally examined this chair.

turned stretchers and tasteful finials, and especially with its uniquely turned front posts, it stands well up in its class. Date: 1700–20. It seems to have lost perhaps an inch at the bottom, but the balls there are still visible.

This chair carries out strictly the proper agreement between the spindles and the posts, thus securing an effect often lost by failure to attend to this detail.

A REVERSED Banister-Back Side Chair. Photograph furnished by Mr. Geo. S. McKearin of Hoosick Falls, N. Y., the owner. It has a rather striking crest, and the lower rail of the back is shaped. The feet are remarkably long and light.

At the bottom of this page is a remarkably well-done chair, belonging to Mr. J. H. Stiles, of York, Pennsylvania. It has the mushroom arm, such as are shown on pages 210-216. With its six "sausage"

THE Left-Hand Banister-Back Chair is owned by Mr. Arthur W. Wellington. The great turned rung and the semi-circular molded crest, reminding us of the backs of day-beds, are the striking features. Date: 1700.

The right-hand chair is the property of Mr. G. Winthrop Brown. The long bevel on the top and bottom back rails makes more of a feature than one would think a slight thing could make. The great rung is remarkably effective. Date: 1700.

A CHILD'S Turned High Chair. The "sausage turnings" are rare on high chairs. A still more rare feature, however, is the original turned foot rest, the only one known to the writer. The general contour of the back is like that of a very early slat back. The chair was found, and is left, in red. Date: about 1700. Owner: the author.

It would appear as if some one had substituted for the original arms two pieces adapted from rush seat rungs. It is possible, but barely so, that the arms were originally as now.

The ascertaining of the age of a chair from the wood of which it is made is hardly possible. We know, it is true, that oak is the oldest material, but the oldest chairs we have, except perhaps a half dozen wainscots, are of ash. Both Carvers, Brewsters and Pilgrim Slat Backs are usually of that wood. But one of the finest and earliest known is of maple. Birch is not unknown in 17th Century chairs, and is frequently found in tables of that date. We have seen one Walnut all-turned 17th Century chair. Beach is also known. Cabinet makers regarded it more brittle than maple.

A CANE Ram's Horn Arm Chair. Owner: Mr. Dwight Blaney. In the cabriole leg the coming of the Dutch style casts its light before it. The stretcher is well scrolled. The back has unusually fine lines. Date: 1700–20.

We earnestly desire to impress on the reader that wherever in this work any human figure appears in a room of furniture, it is because there is no other available picture. We have eliminated as many such pictures as possible, but after taking expert advice, have followed it in allowing the few such pictures shown, to remain. In almost every case they are subjects that never come to the attention of the public. The writer is no longer engaged in exploiting such pictures. He would vastly prefer to eliminate them were not the loss to the book too great. He has discarded hundreds of negatives for this reason and has gone to no end of pains to find other subjects to take their places.

We do not wish in this volume to show the cabriole leg. Its genesis may, however, be traced back to a suggestion in some Flemish chair. The piece before us is an interesting mixture of styles, the back agreeing with earlier types.

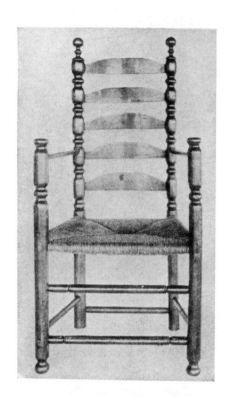

ON the left is a fine specimen of a New England five-back arm chair. It has the flat arm. The effort at uniformity in the back slats is different from the usual varied spacing. Owner: Mr. Arthur W. Wellington.

The chair on the right is a rare piece owing to the slanted and shaped arm, terminating in a spiral. The strong crest is scalloped. Owner: Mr. Geo. S. McKearin.

In the estimation of furniture, too much attention is given to the matter of age. If a specimen is in fine condition, and is worthy in itself, it is better than a wreck of any period. Again, mere rarity is thought too much of. Sometimes an appeal is made to a collector, regarding an article, that "it is the only one of its kind." He may sometimes answer that he wishes there were none of its kind. While all that is good is old, not all that is old is good.

A BANISTER-BACK High Chair. The turning is very graceful. Date: about 1700–10. Formerly at Hazen Garrison house, Haverhill. Owner: unknown.

At the bottom of the page is a low baby chair, in which the regular order of Carver backs is reversed, and the third rail introduced at the bottom instead of at the top of the back. Such good turning is rare in baby chairs. It has lost most of the feet, as is usually the case. The primary object of a baby chair, from the baby's stand-point, is something to move. It is on the go most of the time, and more a cart than a chair. The posts, front and back, are worn flat, and the feet disappear. An unworn chair would not be worth carrying away. Owner: Mr. B. A. Behrend. Date: 1680–1700.

The existence of various types of chairs is probably forgotten. They have no doubt become as extinct as the dodo. It is all the more important to record every worthy variety we can discover. In this way nothing more will be lost. That is one of the principal objects in issuing a work of this kind, by the art which preverves all art.

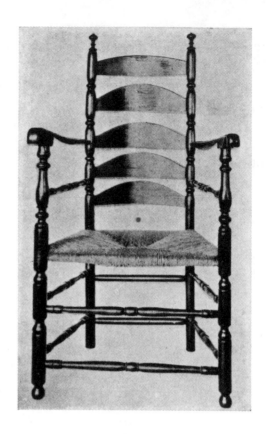

ON the left is a fine five-back chair with a very high back. Owner: J. Milton Coburn, M. D. Date: 1700–20.

On the right is a delicately turned New England chair, belonging to Mr. Henry S. Stearns, of New Hartford, Connecticut. These chairs are the first we have shown which use an arm cut away back of the post, as is more plainly seen on the next page.

On the next page we have the glorified specimen of a New England chair, to show what it may be like. Every feature of the best style is present. The intermediate arm spindle is especially delicate. Yet the chair is rugged where it needs to be so. It belongs to Mr. George Dudley Seymour, and was found in the Capt. Chas. Churchill house, Newington, Connecticut. It is now in the Wadsworth Atheneum, Hartford.

We have seen somewhere a similar chair, except that the arm is turned and overruns the post. The turning was sufficiently heavy, and the result was an all turned chair.

A HEAVY early example of the corner chair. Later the chair would have been made with splats in the back instead of slats.

Happily the feet are not wanting here. The heavy turnings are, strangely, not symmetrical, but the two bottom rungs are alike, and the two upper rungs are alike. The chair belongs to Mr. Mark M. Henderson of Norwalk. The corner chair possesses so many merits that we are always surprised at their comparative rarity. The date is about 1700–20.

MR. Arthur W. Wellington is the owner of the possibly unique corner chair above. It is called a courting chair. Why it is any more so than any corner chair does not appear, but let the name stand. We like it. It varies the usual low back and round back of the corner chair by carrying the back to a great hight, at right angles to one another. The date may be 1710–30.

On the right is an odd chair belonging to Mr. Geo. S. McKearin. It should be relieved of its rockers. The peculiar feature is the method of attaching the arms. It results in requiring spindles, under the arms, of varying hight, and so of affording a pleasing outline. Date: 1720–40. The style of the back coincides with that of a number of 18th Century braced arm rockers. The owner questions the authenticity of the arms. They are at any rate interesting. The mania for adding rockers is shown on this chair, to an extreme degree.

MR. JAMES N. H. CAMPBELL is the owner of the banister-back arm chair above. The roll-over of the arm is pierced by a circular opening. The usual straight top back rail is varied by a contour like early panel tops. Date: 1710–30.

The round-about chair is owned by Mr. G. Winthrop Brown. Such types are more frequently seen in England. The secondary imposed back or comb turns the piece into what is often called abroad a barber's chair. A chair like this was the precursor of the Windsor chair, though in this case of heavy construction the spindles did not continue, in one piece, through the main back rail. Many are of opinion that the sack-like back secured by numerous spindles was to support a temporary upholstery, as a shawl, to ward off drafts.

THE Low Backed Chair is for a spinner's seat, or high stool like a monk's stool. It was used to rest a spinner while she continued at her work. Date: 1700–1750.

The five-banister back is marked by a huge stretcher and a concave back rail.

The rockers are a later addition. Date: 1720-30.

On the chair below the rockers are added. It belonged to the Rev. Samuel Newell, Yale, 1739; first minister of the First Church, Bristol. There is a touch of Friesian carving on the arm end. Owner: Mrs. Niles Lewis Peck, of Bristol. Date: 1700–30.

Hight, 45½ inches. Posts maple, rungs oak.

 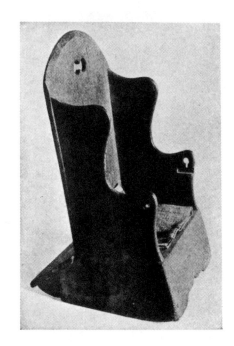

THE Child's Chair on the left is the property of Mr. Chauncey C. Nash. It is of graceful outline and larger than is usual. It has the rare merit of having preserved its feet, or enough of them to keep its rungs well up from the floor. Date: 1700–30.

The baby's wing chair was formerly supposed to be English, but now on investigation is counted American. It has a good hand-hole at the top of the back.

On the next page are four chairs for children, all remarkable, all distinctive. On the left is an early Dutch chair.

On the right is a three-back with reversed wave. It is a treasure. Mr. Geo. F. Ives, the owner of all these chairs, has a room, probably unique, furnished entirely with baby furniture and very complete in all details. There are several rare pieces in the room which are a little too late for this work.

In addition to the two at the top, described on the preceding page, we have below a rush stool and a corner chair. All but the Dutch chair probably come within the 17th Century.

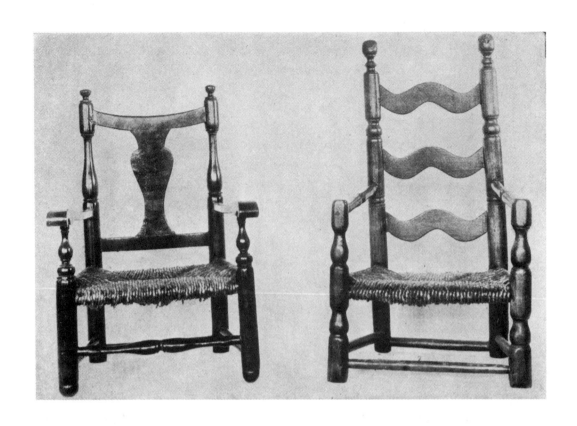

TWO low baby chairs in the author's collection. The left-hand piece has a prettily turned front post. The over-running arm, projecting beyond the post and capping it, is later than the arm which is dowelled into the post, which latter extends above it and has a finial. This piece, therefore, would be an early 18th Century production. The right-hand chair is an interesting example of the Pennsylvania arched slat back, with a scrolled arm, of about the same date as the other, but perhaps superior to it in style.

They are about 8 inches and 6 inches respectively, in hight, of the seat. Baby chairs dispense with one row of rungs, as the space is so short.

They exist in almost all the styles in which adults' chairs are found, but are not common in good forms. Several shown in this work are unique. As a rule the arm chair is found. The theory that a child needed holding in was strongly intrenched in the parental mind. Cords or bars across the front were common.

WE present three more chairs for little people. That on the left is the only one we have seen with a slant arm, and is therefore cherished. The middle chair is provided with rather pretentiously high finials. This sort is found in a number of instances. The right hand chair has flat turning in the back. The chairs date respectively, about 1700; 1690-1700; and 1740. They are owned by the author.

We are very happy in the recent great progress of nomenclature in furniture. Terms are now common enough, descriptive of antique pieces which were unknown a few years back. The jargon of the collector may sooner than anything else disclose the fullness and accuracy of his information. Later in this work we supply a list of names applicable to the pieces or parts of pieces shown.

No doubt the process will proceed, and we shall shortly have a name for everything. Names add humanity to furniture. And they obviate the need of diffuse explanation.

THE left hand baby chair, with wings, is covered with decorative painting. It is an effort, rather unsuccessful and amateurish, to imitate the more pretentious decorated pieces.

The middle chair is not the usual "elbow" chair. The finials mark it as somewhat late. The stool may be of almost any period in the 18th or early 19th centuries. The dates respectively may be: 1740-70; 1720-50; 1710-70. Owner: the author.

Many rare baby chairs have passed out of sight, but very early footstools, of which vast numbers existed, are practically unknown. The very high chairs were all provided with foot-stools, to escape the cold of the floor. Low stools were called crickets, in some sections of New England. Of course our word stool is practically the same as the German word for chair. This etymology suggests that at one time chairs with low backs were called stools.

The middle piece above has a seat ten inches high, and was therefore intended for a late stage of babyhood. Stools vary from five to eight inches, those intended to be used as seats of course exceeding the latter figure.

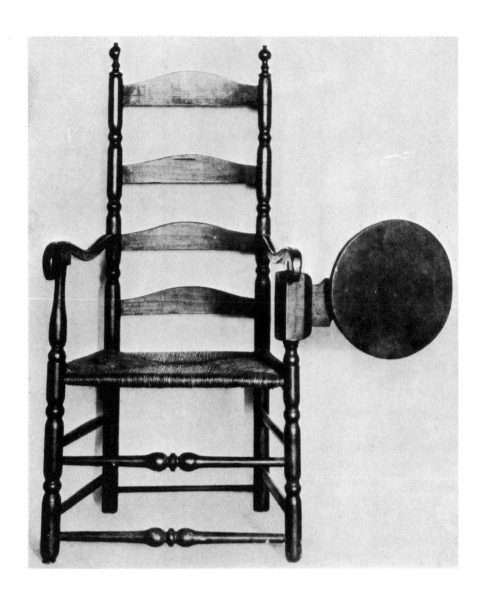

A CHAIR recently seen, belonging to Mr. I. Sack, which has a swinging tilting table that may or may not be original with the chair. The contrivance is a two-part box-bearing fitted to the post by fastening the two parts together. An arm was then attached and the little round table, rather small for writing, was hinged to it. The affair is interesting by comparison with the Windsor writing chair, which came in very shortly after the time of this chair, perhaps 1720–30.

A DECORATIVE Spanish Foot Dutch Side Chair. Owner: Mr. W. of Boston. We seem obliged, within the limit of 1720, to show a very few Dutch backs—so long as they have the Spanish feet. This piece, with the rush seat, dates perhaps 1720. It is well decorated on black paint with gold lines, constituting an intricate scroll on the splat and curve of the top rail. The decoration extends to the very feet, a part of which are missing. The center of the splat is done in colors. If we recollect that the date named was the time of lacquered furniture, the art of which scarcely existed in America, we can understand the American effort to do with paint what was being done in the more pretentious medium abroad. We are not sorry that America was driven to that effort because many of the pieces of painted furniture were truly artistic.

The question is sometimes raised whether the decoration on a piece of furniture was added at a later period. It is not always possible to determine this matter. In the case before us we regard the decoration original because it agrees with the period. The decoration of furniture in America, in the early period we treat, was very rare. Knowing their inability to reproduce the exquisite foreign lacquers, makers as a rule left their work plain.

THE Arm Chair is an early transition Dutch model, which instead of a splat has four reeded banisters. The Spanish feet, rather worn down, and the style of arm, suggest as a date, 1710–20. It is from a picture furnished by Mr. Henry V. Weil.

The leather chair is owned by Mr. George Dudley Seymour. It is of maple, with stretchers of beech. It was bought in Hartford and is supposed to be of local origin. We look for a chair with this outline to have a splat back. This earlier piece was a feeling out of the style to follow. The date is perhaps 1710–20.

The richer, more artistic Dutch chairs, beyond our scope, are not, to our thinking, any more attractive than the earlier furniture. They were the best artistic furniture of any period. But the chairs we have shown mostly have the flavor of a new country.

WITH the single example of a Windsor chair before us we leave the subject of chairs, which is most engrossing. In the author's work, "A Handbook of Windsor Chairs," that important subject is given careful attention. The high chair here shown was brought to light after that little volume was issued. Since that time one or two others like it have been found. It was brought from Philadelphia by a woman who died at Exeter at 95 years of age. The sturdy, humorous spread of the legs, the holes in the front arm posts for a bar, the massive comb and especially the fine Queen Anne stretcher, all bespeak the earliest type of the Windsor. It may go back to 1720, certainly within a decade of that date. One easily sees how the chair arose. The English type perhaps derived its name from the fact that such chairs were made in Bucks, centering at High Wycombe, and often went to London by boat from Windsor.

Attention has already been called to the "blunt arrow" turning on the front of the Pennsylvania slat back chairs. The same terminals mark the earliest Philadelphia Windsors, and the same stretchers. These chairs, therefore, beginning just as our century closes, about 1720, mark the opening of a new epoch in style of the wooden seated chair, at first made ostensibly for gardens, but shortly commending itself by its many merits so that it usurped all other styles for ordinary uses. For the parlor the Dutch style made its place good. For all other rooms the Windsor was popular. But this popularity was shared in the Middle States by the arched slat back, and in New England by its plain slat back.

A PAIR of unique cross-stretcher stools with beautifully curved stretchers. The legs are in the style of the six-legged highboy. This pair of stools was found in Newburyport. They are the hight of an ordinary chair, and are apparently all original. For similar American subjects see pages 336 and any of the six-legged highboys and dressing tables.

The wood of these stools is very light, probably bass. The style is scarcely adapted for strength, and if more of them existed, one can easily see that they would have gone to pieces before this date. Nevertheless, they are of exceeding interest.

The covers were worked many years ago and are in fine condition. They are not, however, original, though very well adapted for their purpose.

It will be noted that no two of the turnings on these stools are of the same size, a very common occurrence. The date would be the same as that of cabinet furniture in this style, namely 1690-1720. Owner: the author, who prizes them more than anything else of a similar sort in his collection.

AN Oak Joint Stool, with vertical legs.   Date: 1640-60.   This possibly unique, quaint low stool, is only 14½ inches high.   It has lost about a half inch of the legs.   Thus it lacks but that half inch of equalling the hight of the Robinson chair on page 177.   The frame is a scant 13 inches square, at the feet and at the seat. It thus follows the chair in another particular, as joint stools generally have legs raking one way.   The turnings also are identical with those on the chair, not only as to style but as to length.   The stretcher is the same, so also is the frame.   For these reasons we assign it a date so early, and are further driven to conclude that the stool and the chair were made at the same time, by the same person.   The finding of the chair and the stool, at different times and places was a remarkable coincidence, for the stool is probably one of several made to go with the chair, at a time when one chair was supposed to answer for the head of the house, the other members of the family being accommodated on stools.   It is owned by the author.

A MAPLE Splay-legged Stool with a pine drawer, owned by Mr. Chauncey C. Nash. This piece is apparently a stool, although it has, of course, lost something at the bottom. It may have been two or three inches higher, but even so could have been used as a stool. There is no possible reason why a high stool should not have done service as a stand just as at the present time we often place articles in a chair that more properly, in the view of a precise housewife, should go on a table. A piece of this sort is so rare that it gets much more attention than would otherwise be the case. There is charm in small pieces, commonly expressed by the well understood, but inaccurate term "cunning." Top, 11¾ by 18¼; hight, 16¾.

ON the right is a joint stool from which the feet have been worn off or disintegrated by decay. While we are on this subject of the feet of pieces of furniture, we may say that the wear was not as great as the decay. If the pieces stood on damp floors as they often did, or were put into back rooms, they were often decayed from one to three inches.

The joint stool, as a rule, splays in one direction, and has a frame in that respect quite like that of the butterfly ta-  ble except in size. A good number of joint stools have come to light in very recent years. The author knows of at least a dozen in Boston alone which have been found since the Great War. Yet they are among the most prized pieces in any collection. The seat itself is usually rather thin—about three-quarters of an inch. It projects at the ends several times as much as at the sides and in most of the earliest specimens had the thumb-nail moulding on all sides. The frames are sometimes oak, though maple is more usual. The seat is pine or maple. The hight is the same as that of a chair or a little higher. There is a dividing line where it becomes doubtful in some cases whether a piece is a joint stool or a low table. The use of the joint stool was very common in the ancient times; probably every house possessed a considerable number. The specimen here shown dates 1670-1690, and is owned by the author.

The term "joint" is only a variant of "joined." "Joint" or joined is used to distinguish furniture from that which was turned, and which had no mortise and tenon. The joined furniture being more valuable, the specification was made in inventories, to indicate its character.

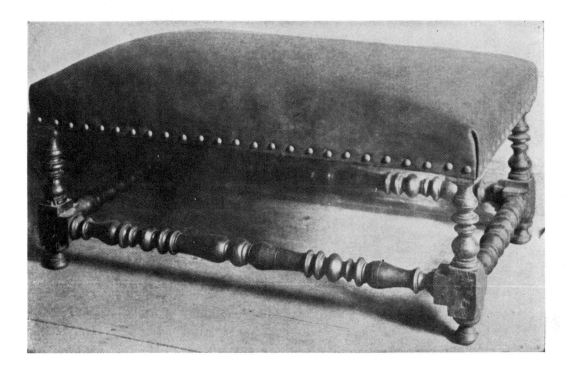

A LONG, turned, upholstered stool. Stools of this character always challenge our careful attention, as more likely to be English than American. Many poorly joined English pieces are being brought to this country; and as they are made from old wood, they deceive the novice. The joint is the point at which the spurious nature of the article may be determined. An old joint, if it is solid, has an appearance which cannot easily be counterfeited. These pieces were upholstered in various materials, but leather is the most suitable. In the piece above all is original except the cover.

Below appears a smaller upholstered joint stool. The ownership of these articles at present is unknown. Of course such pieces were turned to match turned chairs.

It will be noted that the turning on the piece at the top closely resembles that on gate leg tables. The turning of the piece below is quainter and earlier.

The distinction between English and American joint stools is in the greater simplicity of the pieces found here, especially in the stretchers.

TWO joint stools belonging to Mr. Dwight Blaney. The piece on the left is the more usual style of the American stool.

The piece on the right is of the heavier, more antique pattern, scarcely distinguishable from the English stools. The simple carved ornaments on the bottoms of the frame-rails also assimilate this piece to the English style, but both pieces are regarded as American. The only manner of distinguishing the English from the American, in the case of oak, is the color of the wood. While many claim that they can at once detect the difference, the author frankly admits that he has not only been deceived, but has seen much more expert judges deceived. It is the same old question of the color of American oak. If the English oak is darker than our own it may easily be age, or creosoting by the smoke of hundreds of years. The author knows that he will be challenged in this statement. What, however, is to be said when one of the lightest pieces of oak ever seen is pronounced English, and when pieces which we know came from England, recently, are pronounced American? There is, of course, in the mind of a man who has a genius for such things, and who has handled them for years, what he calls a feeling which warns him if an article is English. If, however, this feeling is unreliable, it would appear that it is a matter of judgment, and judgment errs.

The date of the left hand piece may be 1670–1690; that of the right hand piece may be 1640–1670.

A SQUAB which was in the possession of Mr. Brooks Reed. This very remarkable piece is not as large as it looks since no attempt is made at scaling the furniture here shown. It is about the hight of a chair. The marks of style which attract the collector here are the high stretcher, the middle stretcher, the ball turnings, and the hollowed top made for a cushion from which the name squab is taken. The author has never seen another American piece like this. Its date may be 1670–1690.

An interesting question arises with the high stretcher so placed on one side and not on the other. This construction is not unique. It was easier, of course, to draw the feet under the stool on the side unobstructed by the high stretcher. The cushions placed on furniture were, as they are now, made of every conceivable material. They were often stuffed with flock or hair and their covering was sometimes of a very elegant character.

ON the left is a joint stool belonging to Miss C. M. Traver of New York. It shows better than most stools the nature of the seat and its molding. The date is 1670-1690.

At the bottom of the page appears a heavily turned joint stool on which the top is not original. The turning of this piece has an English look, but we are persuaded that it is American. The stool is smaller than usual. The average length may be placed perhaps at 20 inches. Gate leg tables are sometimes found with turnings like this stool. We know that some of these tables are American. This piece is fortunate in showing nearly all the feet, which are original.

A fashion is noted of showing ostensibly old stools and tables with the leg coming square to the floor as if this was a mark of age or of original condition. In no case have we ever seen an early American piece that was turned above the stretcher, and was not also turned below it.

Date: 1650–1680.

We cannot reconcile ourselves to the disappearance of articles so useful as joint stools. There is nothing in modern furniture to take their places. Once they were looked down upon, their day was over.

A DAY-BED belonging to Mr. Geo. F. Ives. It is of a simple but satisfactory style. In this instance the posts at the head are turned to match the other legs, rather than in the usual curved style of a chair leg of the period. The head in this couch is very plain. Nearly all couches were made with swinging heads, supported by chains. Many heads have now been fixed in an immovable position. Upholstery was not originally attached to any old couch we have seen. There was a movable cushion.

The material of couches was, if the turnings were simple, likely to be maple; if elaborate or carved, walnut was more usual. Oak had passed out of use for such purpose—unless in extremely rare instances.

Couches were very light, and readily moved, more so than the later sofa.

They exist in small numbers. Perhaps there may be forty fair examples known aside from the Pennsylvania day-bed. They are limited to the walnut period, even when made of maple, that is to say, 1670-1730. This example is perhaps to be dated, 1690-1710.

The day-bed may be either the most graceful or the most ugly piece of furniture. But whatever its appearance it was most useful. Without any mechanism to change it was always available in emergency as a very comfortable bed. It is gratifying that the great merit of its shape is now being recognized. It is, however, a misnomer to use the term day-bed if a couch has both head and foot rest.

A CHAISE Longue, belonging to the estate of Mrs. Reinhold Faelten of Boston. Seventeenth century sofas were extremely rare and the writer is not aware of any existing specimens of American origin. The piece in the Essex Institute is avowedly of foreign origin. The chaise longue, as it is called in France, the couch in English and the day-bed in America, seems to have supplied the place of a sofa. The specimens made with eight legs are, other things being equal, regarded superior to the six-leg style. The piece before us has curious Spanish feet, being carved on three sides, on the second and third pair of legs; and at the bottom being carved on four sides, an otherwise unknown variety. Probably it was restored wrongly. The theory of the style of the chaise longue is that it is a truly long chair, made as if the seat of a chair were drawn out to couch length, while the head is left without change. Date: 1690-1710.

THE Parlor Chamber in the Concord Antiquarian Society House, being the Captain Brown House. The couch at the left is a well known and exquisite example of a Flemish type and has been shown hitherto, but we illustrate it here in combination with chairs of the same period. The lowering of the head was doubtless intended to extend somewhat the length of the couch. Date: 1670-1700.

The couch above with the chair to match, belonged to the Reverend Peter Bulkeley, the first minister of Concord, and the ancestor of Governor Bulkeley of Hartford. This specimen is one of the finest found. Another very elegant example is that formerly in the Dwight Prouty collection. There are perhaps not more than a dozen known of this grade of merit.

The collection of the Concord Antiquarian Society is very notably good, being composed of some unique pieces. We know of no other Museum collection in a town the size of Concord of equal merit with this, or indeed in any public collection aside from the two or three greatest.

A TURNED Couch, the property of Dr. William G. Erving of Washington. It will be noted that while the legs follow the typical good Jacobean style, the head has the Dutch style of splat. Also the comparison is worth while between the methods of attaching cross stretchers in this example and in other couches. They are near the bottom of the piece and differ from those in the first chaise longue shown in this book. This construction is better, since to bore from three directions into a post as in some examples, at the same elevation, must very greatly weaken it. Also the leg is better braced by the method shown here. Size: Length, 72 inches; width, 26¾ inches; hight of frame, 16¾ inches; hight of head, 36¾ inches.

In an example shown on the previous page, and all others in this book, except the Pennsylvanian types, the stretchers are kept low and are far more effectual in that position.

As an example of turning this couch is attractive. The maker was called on to devise a very long yet graceful stretcher for the sides. Date: 1700–1710.

The method of forming the seat was the same as that followed in many beds of the period. Sail cloth was laced across. This made necessary the covering of the couch with some sort of cushion. The more finished cane couch did not strictly require a cover. But to use a cane couch without a cover would speedily destroy the cane. And when the cane was covered there was no need for a seat so elaborate, or fragile.

The custom of using a short couch, in the French style, bringing up to its foot a lengthening stool, obtained no particular recognition in America.

A DAY-BED belonging to the Metropolitan Museum. The arched and scrolled stretchers give us a date practically the same as that of the pieces whose legs are carved in the Flemish style, namely 1670-1700. The varieties which we find, some with turned legs and some with carved legs, are merely a matter of local taste or expediency. It will be noted that the foot of the day-bed does not carry a scrolled stretcher in any instance. It is usual for these pieces to be made with both sides alike. This photograph does not fully show the back, but it is like the front. It is possible that the caning is original, in some of these ancient pieces; but if so, it must have been preserved with unusual care. It is always fine, and does not have a finishing strip on the outside.

We have no record of the first designer of the day-bed. The style is being revived at present. It is certainly far better than the Empire "lounge," to which we bid good-bye with pleasure. It no more needs a back than does a bed.

Incidentally a bed with a *front* like a head-board recently came to our attention. Placed at the side of a room, it compelled the occupant to climb to the head from the foot and was without foot-board.

THE simple day-bed above is so nearly like that on the opposite page that its insertion here is, in part, to show the method of lacing, or trussing the canvas. This couch is the property of the Metropolitan Museum. Date: 1690-1710.

Among the woods used in early American furniture the most important after the period of carving, is maple. That is a statement applying to the frequency of its use. If we regard furniture from the decorated aspect, the next wood after oak, in importance, is walnut.

The Virginia Walnut largely used even as far north as middle Pennsylvania was perhaps not found in the North as a native wood. The black walnut is not very uncommon in Northern furniture. The so-called white walnut was hickory and its use was confined to bent work or places where great strength was required. Hickory was formerly plentiful in New England. Growing in forests it was free from knots. "The cattle shake their walnut bows," wrote Whittier on the edge of New Hampshire.

AN all turned day-bed, the property of Mr. Hollis French. It shows such a cushion as was added to the foundation on the couch on the preceding page. There are at the head two stretchers, a possibly unique feature. One sees here that the rails are framed into a foot post, whereas in the last example, we have legs identical with the other pairs. Date: 1690-1710.

Hickory did not enter appreciably into fine furniture. Even in the 17th century we seldom found it in the spindles of chairs.

It is probable that the colonists did not at first feel its admirable qualities. Once the Windsor Chair had come in, hickory found its place.

Beech was less common here than in England. Maple, therefore, for the most part took its place. Enough beech was available had it been really preferable. The woods while of similar grain, can be distinguished with ease. Ash was the material for great turned chairs. Oak held its place for framing and carving to the end of the 17th century in cabinet pieces.

A WALNUT Day-bed with Spanish feet on the last pair of legs, the others being plain turned. It is the property of the author. There was an ancient inscription attached to the under side declaring that the piece belonged to Clarissa Griswold, of Killingworth, Connecticut. The date is about 1690–1710. There is on the piece as shown an upholstered frame laid on top of the original frame. The author has now removed this excrescence. In every case that has come to our attention so far there was a loose cushion above the reeding, or the caning, or the canvas of the seat. The use of the chaise longue, so far as fashion is concerned, seems to have gone out in the first quarter of the 18th century or a little later. It was supplanted in popular favor by the Queen Anne and Chippendale sofas with the back on the long side. Those pieces are practically all too short for use as day-beds. It is too bad that an article so convenient should, at the dicate of fashion, be disused. In the piece before us the splat at the head would indicate a somewhat later date since it is purely Dutch. The merging of styles in this manner is not by any means disagreeable, as the connection is always between two adjacent styles, and marks a growth rather than an abrupt change. This piece is longer than usual, being 74 inches over all. The width is 21¾ inches; the height of the head is 37¼ inches. The frame is 14 inches high.

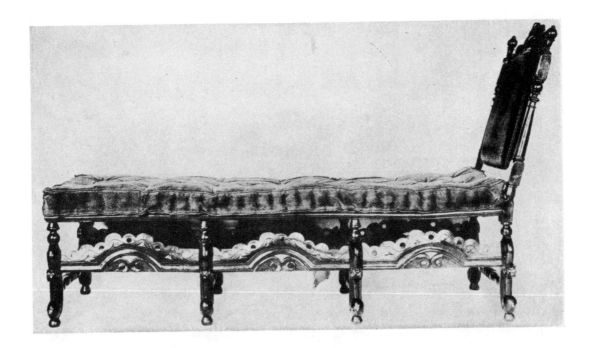

A FLEMISH Day-bed, owner Mrs. Rogers of Hingham. This piece has often been seen at the annual exhibit of the Arts and Crafts Society at Hingham. It is a very elegant specimen and in good condition. It will be noted that the arch of the stretchers is filled in with a scrolled member; also that the feet or more properly, shoes beneath the feet, are not very much worn. The head of this piece is especially good, being carved very well indeed, though its upholstery should be removed. The wood is walnut. Date: 1670-1700.

The finish of early furniture is a subject concerning which discussion has grown warm. An English author of much prominence refers to the "nasty French polish," as if varnishes had not been known and used for many hundred years, and as if there were something intrinsically bad about them. Varnish has its place on very old furniture, but not on the class of furniture shown in this volume.

There is a strong presumption that the earliest turned furniture had no finish at all. Many chairs of pilgrim date show no trace of finish. The old surface of such a piece of furniture is very desirable. It cannot be counterfeited.

A HANDSOME Spanish foot day-bed, the property of Mr. Martin Gay of Hingham. So far as we have noted this piece is different from others in that it has no less than four strings of stretchers. The two lower sets of stretchers, it will be noted, are totally lacking from all the other pieces which we have shown. The excellent effect, combined with the greater strength secured, render these sets of stretchers very commendable. The shaping of the Spanish feet is excellent and the head is elegant. Date: 1690-1710. The wood is walnut.

Walnut was the principal furniture wood of Italy at the time of the Renaissance and afterwards. The rich, ornate productions, with much carving and gilding, on walnut, which came from Italy to France and England, brought in the fashion of walnut. The wood, in its lighter colorings, is well adapted for carvings. The black walnut was somewhat too sombre, and the grain rather inferior to the Southern walnut, which in old, often washed table tops, has bleached very greatly. The color can be restored somewhat by oil as the wood is hungry, as cabinet makers say.

A PENNSYLVANIA Day-bed, the property of Mr. Hollis French. This style seems to have been popular in Pennsylvania. The legs are turned in a very heavy form, averaging about two and a half inches in diameter. The same heavy ball and ring stretcher is used as appears in Queen Anne furniture and other turned furniture of its date. In the particular specimen before us the head posts, instead of being shaped, as they are in the example on the page following, are turned and slanted. It is a curious and interesting attempt at getting the feeling of chairs without using the usual square post.

The heads of the Pennsylvania day-beds are made of reeded banisters. The student should notice the difference between this head and that on the next page which is made solid in the half moon shape, whereas this one is arched below as well as above. The horizontal end member of these heads was made to strike against the post when the chains were drawn up, to prevent the piece falling forward on the couch.

In some examples of the Pennsylvania day-bed the middle stretcher is placed higher than the end stretchers in order to avoid cutting away so much wood at one point. While the scheme is meritorious from the standpoint of construction, the effect is not as harmonious. Borrowing an expression from automobile parlance, one loses the stream line, by varying the hight of the stretchers. The seats or frame of these Pennsylvania pieces were always reeded so far as we have noted in the dozen examples which have come to our attention. They are very comfortable, substantial and quaint articles of furniture. Date: 1710-1730.

A DAY-BED, similar to the one on the preceding page. This piece shows the usual square leg at the head post, which is here roughly notched to give the semblance of an analogy to the turned legs. The present ownership is unknown.

Attention is here called to the marked similarity between the Pennsylvania day-bed and the earliest type of Windsor chairs, which were made in Philadelphia. The stretchers on some of these chairs are identical with those on the day-bed before us. The leg also is of practically the same contour, except that it is smaller on the chairs. This analogy helps us to arrive at a date. Of course the stretcher is borrowed from the Queen Anne style and the only difference in style between the day-bed before us and the Philadelphia Windsor chair base, is that the Windsor legs are raked. Of course the Windsor stretcher is medial. An example is shown on page 284.

Date: 1710-1730.

This day-bed avoids the weakness at the head shown on the more stylish Flemish couches, which always have a strongly marked angle in the head posts beginning at the level of the frame. In the Pennsylvania pieces that angle is attempted by a kind of half-hearted bend or slight bevel on the front, in some instances; and in other instances, like that on the preceding page, there is no attempt at curvature. The effect, of course, is to gain strength at the expense of grace.

A DAY-BED belonging to J. Milton Coburn, M.D. This interesting piece may be classed among country-made furniture; that is not to say that it is any the less meritorious, but that it was made at a point where the artisan was removed from the direct influence of an established style. He therefore worked out from memory or from his own ideas the various details of his construction. In this instance he has placed seven splats or spindles on the head and has made it fixed, in the form of the earlier Flemish chair crest in which the posts are doweled into the top rail.

The same interesting evidence of the influence of individuality is shown in the stretchers. The legs are of a somewhat lighter character than in the specimens heretofore shown in this work. Such examples as that before us have the quality of American work, which is always marked by greater variety than that of the English.

When we attempt to date this piece we are at somewhat of a loss for the very reason that it is individual. We shall not be far astray in giving as wide a spread to the date as 1710-1740.

In ending our treatment of day-beds we cannot avoid concluding: Their existence is another proof that our ancestors had not the iron constitutions with which they have been credited. They found it important to recline even in the day time when they could afford it—like their children's children.

A CHILD'S settle and a wing chair to match. These charming little evidences of attention paid to child life are the property of J. Milton Coburn, M.D. They are the only pieces of that character, made to match, that the author has seen. Each has the same finger holes at the top by which the piece may be handled. The object of making the holes rather than cutting out a large piece was to conserve the strength of the wood. This little settle has its counterparts. The owner once had such a settle which bore marks on the end showing that it was used as a pung seat, to take the place in winter of the usual wagon seat so common in New York State and Western Massachusetts. It was almost identical with the piece before us. There is no evidence that Dr. Coburn's piece here was ever used for any other purpose than a settle. We arrive in these pieces at the pine period and the simpler construction of the humble home. The date is 1730-1780. We give a long range of years because these articles continued to be made thirty or forty years each side of the middle of the 18th Century.

The settle was the sofa of the poor, or of the well-to-do, for kitchen use. In English forms, with carving, it is a pretentious piece. We have not seen an American carved settle.

IN this picture the figures are seated on a pine settle, with their feet upon a mat made of corn husks. It is said that the knowledge of mats of this character was derived from the Indians. The material was unlimited. We have no picture without the figures, although they do not obscure the outline of the settle at the end. It is the usual, and formerly common, pine style, made with the solid back without paneling. The seat, as a rule, is hinged so as to form beneath it a chest which was a receptacle for wood, for Indian meal or for any other articles.

The pine settle was moved about a good deal, as in the nature of the case, it was needed to draw up to the fireplace to shield the back from the cold draughts which made in toward the fireplace from every quarter of the room.

The use of pine in settles was especially important because the pieces needed to be light in proportion to their size for easy removal. The contour of the end board varies very greatly in the different specimens. That before us is counted a very good shape. The length of such pieces varied from four to six feet; about four and a half to five feet being the usual length.

Beds and Couches in the Scheme of Civilization

IT appears that the northern nations have dignified the bed far more than the classical nations. The farther south we go the less attention we find paid to beds. Among the simpler peoples of the Orient, and especially among the nomads the bed as an article of furniture did not exist. Nations dwelling in permanent houses of some architectural pretensions, as the Romans, had very small sleeping apartments, like monk's cells, and their beds were couches.

Architectural beds among the Flemings are wonderful creations. The Bretons have elaborate bunks, with a screen in front, and a step before them. A bed in the Quincy Homestead, Quincy, just fills a space built for it, and is enclosed by two doors. Its date is after our period, but it shows the tendency to place a bed in a retired position.

On the other hand when, as in Queen Elizabeth's time, great beds, some of them twenty feet high, were constructed, they became the most important articles of furniture, and in wills beds with their furniture are often devised when no other furniture is mentioned. It is known that a few great carved beds were brought to America. The settlers however found they could get on without such beds, and they reserved their energies for furniture more in evidence. To them, up to 1720 or 1730, a bedstead was little more than a plain frame for the bed and the curtain around it. Far more attention was given to the materials for covering the frame than to the structure itself. We find many records of heavy, elaborate and expensive bed draperies. As the fashion came in of allowing the posts to show, more care was given to beauty of construction, as in the middle and latter parts of the 18th Century.

The Restoration of Antique Furniture

IF furniture is restored so that its age is not readily apparent the advantage of the old over the new furniture is lost. This is more obvious in furniture of the Pilgrim Century than in later instances. Anything new added to a very early piece contrasts glaringly with the old. If the old is made to agree with such additions it must be practically made over. This is a great disaster. Many ancient pieces of great value are ruined by this means. The taste for collecting old furniture sometimes becomes educated in advance of the best taste in restoring it. The false taste has often gone so far as to varnish the interiors of drawers on 17th Century pieces! The sense of wear and use on early furniture is its greatest charm, and its highest commercial value. Both of these are destroyed by restoration. Many fine tops of tables have been thrown away because they were old. For what then was the old piece wanted?

A PINE settle belonging to Mr. Geo. F. Ives. It is 64 inches long. The arms are 35 inches high, and the back 52 inches high. The seat is 16 inches deep, and the height is the same. The candle shown is struck by its spiked base, into the wood. It is not a part of the settle. Sometimes a settle had a folding central arm, as a candle rest.

The ten panels here, and in the specimen shown on page 311, are raised, in the early style.

The advantage of paneling the backs of settles was slight, so far as use was concerned. Hence most of those found are not paneled. When found as here, they were the successors of English tradition, or were paneled for the sake of appearance.

We seem not to find cushions for settles, but no doubt they were sometimes used. The seats are never shaped and are rather uncomfortable. They certainly do not permit a slouchy posture. Tall candle stands, hanging Betty lamps, or a candle held in the hand were the means for reading.

A BUILT-IN Settle with one end only. This settle is part of the structure in a 17th Century house in Wrentham. A board, close to the left door, would have obstructed the passage so that this short settle was built in. It rests upon the protruding sill of the house which is cut into to afford an opening for the door. The doors of this house still, for the greater part, have their original wooden latches. This is the only instance of a built-in settle within doors, that has come to the author's attention, though they were common on the porches of American Dutch houses. Date: 1670-1690, possibly the oldest known.

Below is a quaint settle rocker. It will be observed that the foot rest is concaved to match the ends of the rockers. It was doubtless designed to raise the feet from the floor so as to avoid chilblains. The piece is owned by Mr. B. A. Behrend. It seems to have been "built for two" as its length will not admit more. Date very doubtful, perhaps 1740-90.

A PINE Paneled Settle, the property of the Rhode Island School of Design. This piece is marked by very bold knobs on the fronts of the end boards and by a strong scroll at the base of those boards. The hood as usual slants backward slightly. The seat is not designed to lift. It is scrolled near the ends to avoid awkwardness. Size: 74 inches long; 53½ high and 20 deep. Date: 1700–1750.

In the same Museum is a second settle very similar. Paneled settles were much more rare than the plain board backs, and are eagerly sought for. Even the ordinary board settle is now uncommon. Of course the object of the hood was the same as that of the wind-ends, and the hight of the back— to afford protection from drafts at the fireplace—where one otherwise must turn as on spit unless willing to roast on one side and freeze on the other. It is, of course, for the same reason that the back of the settle almost invariably ran to the floor. A practical aspect of the use of the settle is often lost sight of. When it was placed in front of the fire, it obviously spoiled the unity or attractiveness of the room, except for those who were seated upon it; it was an entirely utilitarian object. The only manner in which it can be placed in a modern house is along a wall near the fireplace.

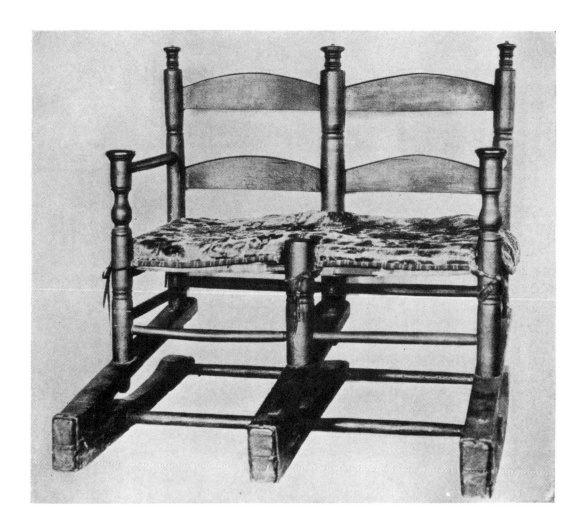

ON the top of the preceding page is a New York wagon seat. These splint bottom seats seem to have been very common in New York State. They are designed to be placed in a market wagon with sides, which kept the piece in place. When the vehicle was not in use for persons it was important to discard the seat to make room for freight. Hence the happy idea was conceived of using the seat as a kind of small settee in the house. Owner: Mr. Rudolph P. Pauly, of Boston.

The lower specimen on the preceding page is owned by Mr. Chauncey C. Nash. It is 29 inches high; the seat is 13 inches high, and 14 by 33½ inches in area.

The odd specimen on this page is owned by Mr. Geo. F. Ives. Its base forms a crude wooden spring. The wagon seats date from any time in the 18th Century.

WE are told that the cradle as an institution has been abandoned. We lament it. We believe that someone who purports to be wise has said that rocking a child is bad for its brains. Had hygienic objections arisen against the papoose board on which the aborigines are strapped we could easily have allowed that impeachment, but how any child could fail to grow up strong from so rugged a piece of architecture as that on the opposite page we cannot understand.

In passing this aspect of our subject we may say that all the English speaking race up to the last generation were rocked in cradles.

There is a more practical reason for the use of the cradle in the early days. The housewife who attended her own child in the simple years of American settlement could not, obviously, be encumbered with a bed in the fire room, and it was necessary for her, in order to attend to her duties and to keep her babe comfortably warm, to have a cradle in the room where she worked. Her foot was applied to the rocker, while her hands were busy with spinning and her tongue with singing. Her heart beat high with love and hope, surrounded thus as she was by all the household goods and gear. The cradle here set forth has a remarkable history. The owner is Mr. Chauncey C. Nash.

The writer can vouch for the fact that he obtained it from the Cushman family, who in their turn had it through inter-marriage with the Fuller family of Mayflower fame. It is an undisputed tradition that it came down from Dr. Samuel Fuller who was the physician of the Mayflower.

The tale told is that Peregrine White, born in Provincetown Harbor on the Mayflower, before the landing, was first rocked in this cradle, which belonged to Dr. Samuel Fuller, the brother of Mrs. White and the officiating physician. This cradle was available in the lading of the Mayflower, where-as the wicker cradle now on exhibition at Pilgrim Hall, Plymouth, which belonged to the Whites, could not be reached. The reader may take all these tales for what they are worth.

Before the day when Americana in furniture was so much sought, the tradition concerning this cradle would probably have been very dear to the owner and the public, but now that English furniture is a decidedly second choice with the collector, not so much is being said about the English origin of our furniture. The author has doubts concerning this cradle. An odd circumstance is that the four great panels in the sides are of pine, whereas the end panels are oak. Experts in wood claim that the oak of which the piece is chiefly composed is American. In this connection we may call attention to an odd fact that the reader may not have observed; unfinished oak will in process of time show darker on the quartering marks, whereas a finished piece of oak will show lighter on the quartering marks and darker

in the body of the wood, thus reversing the coloring. The piece before us bears no evidence of any application of finish nor has it ever been cleaned. It is satisfyingly heavy and substantial.

It is perhaps unique in having a gallery, not only at the sides of the hood, but also at the back. The spindles are of beech. A delightful feature is a half spindle applied vertically at each side of the face of the hood just such as one sees on chests. This applied spindle is considered among antiquarians not to have been used before 1650 so that this feature is a further argument against an English origin.

IN the Fuller cradle on the previous page the rockers were missing and were supplied by the author from surface wood of the timbers of the Marsh House, Wethersfield, the oldest house in that town. The color of the wood without treatment is precisely like that of the rest of the cradle, a circumstance hardly likely had the cradle been English.

The board of the hood is of pine with gouge carving all about and a double line of diamond hatcheling.

A cradle shown in a glass case in Pilgrim Hall, Plymouth, which also bears the tradition of Mayflower ancestry, is not composed of panels but is a plain pine cradle on which thin narrow boards were nailed to mark false paneling and one of these divisions is wanting at the foot of the cradle, thus showing a plain unpaneled board. We must, therefore, consider the Fuller cradle here shown a finer piece, although the hood of the cradle in Plymouth is slightly arched and composed of spindles on the top, an extremely rare and charming feature. The body of the Plymouth cradle is not of oak, which would speak against an English origin. So far as known four or five of these great paneled American cradles have been found. The distinction between them and the ordinary cradle is that these older pieces have vertical sides, never splayed. They are also heavier and have larger posts. An odd fact is that all these ancient cradles have been found within very narrow limits, three of them within five or ten miles of one another on the South Shore.

Until within five or six years there has been no great interest in Pilgrim cradles, but all the specimens, except that at Plymouth, have been discovered within that time and there has been the highest degree of avidity in seeking other examples.

At the top of this page there is another example of a similar cradle which is in the Metropolitan Museum of New York. Date: 1630–70. It apparently never had a top to its hood, otherwise there would be no meaning in the finials at the head. It is supposed that the foot posts of these cradles were designed for convenience of the hand in rocking but the writer has such a high idea of the diligence of the Pilgrim mother that he inclines to the belief that finials were purely decorative; that she might knit while her foot rocked the cradle.

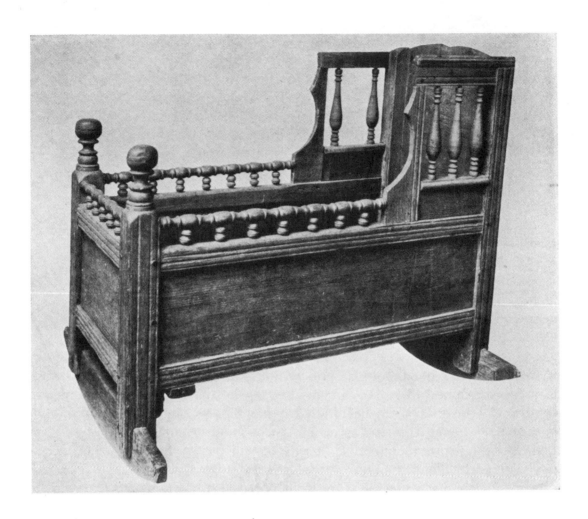

A PANELED Cradle of Oak, owned by the Rhode Island School of Design. This cradle is marked by a low gallery of turned work about the sides and the foot. It lacks the top of the hood. The bracket-like supports of the sides of the hood remind one somewhat of the cradle in Pilgrim Hall where there is a brace something like a modillion, but in horizontal position. It will be noted that the grooving on the rails and stiles here, is different from that in the Fuller cradle, on the second page back, where it is a true shadow molding, quite like that in use on the Connecticut chests of oak. The finials on the piece before us, however, are very good and the rockers are apparently original. The panels are of pine and the rails are narrower than those on the Fuller cradle. It is to be regretted and wondered at that not more of these oak cradles were preserved. Date: 1640–70.

One would naturally presume that a piece of furniture carrying so much of tender tradition would have been jealously guarded as an heirloom. We are confident that one more will come to light.

[317]

A PANELED Cradle of Oak and Walnut, owned by the author. In this example we come to the flaring type, larger, that is, at the top, than at the bottom. The interesting heart shaped hand holes on the head and foot boards were also a convenience. The piece is all original and probably of Pennsylvanian origin, like that on the second page following. The small knobs on each side of the cradle were used to button the quilt. The scrolled brackets at the head are a feature to be noted also. The panels are seen to be shaped like the sheathed paneling found on walls of rooms.

It will be observed that the spindle galleries about the earlier cradles were designed to admit vision from all sides, certainly not for air.

Below is a pine cradle, a quaint early type—which, while rare, is far oftener seen than the paneled cradles. Date: 1680–1720.

A HANGING cradle of maple. It is difficult to fix a date for a cradle of this type since very early examples are known, while on the other hand there are dainty late examples in mahogany, notably at the Essex Institute, Salem. The one here shown is of somewhat crude though substantial build, and certainly has advantages over the usual form of a cradle in that it is more easily kept in motion. Date: 1700–30.

Some very elaborate ancient examples of this sort exist in Europe. Perhaps more than any other family piece the cradle was the handiwork of the prospective father, who lavished upon it his ingenuity in the long winter evenings.

Cradles in this country are like beds in that they never attain to the rich elaboration seen in England, a condition to be expected in a new country. It is known that in some instances nine generations have been rocked in the same cradle. Not only so, but many successive infants, in one generation. It is probably not too much to suppose that forty babes may have slumbered in the Fuller cradle we have pictured on page 315.

A PENNSYLVANIAN Stenciled Cradle, owned by Mr. I. Sack. This stenciling is done on the ends and sides in rosettes of parti-colors. Other examples in considerable numbers are known. This cradle has holes pierced in the base of the frame through which ropes are drawn in the manner of the corded bed. The author noticed in the basement of the Metropolitan Museum a wainscot chair, the bottom of which had been similarly roped. It was an ancient and popular device in common use within forty years, but the origin of it is not known, as it probably reaches back to a very ancient time.

The cradle before us is of pine as are most of the simple cradles. Date: 1710–50.

The older the cradle the deeper the sides, presumably for greater protection against cold gusts. The cradle was drawn near the fireplace, its foot to the fire. Some examples show slight charring.

The connection between rocking chairs and cradles is suggestive of the origin of the rocking chair. An Englishman of our acquaintance stated that his mother bounced back and forth as she fondled him in a chair without rockers, whose posts were worn in a rounded form as a consequence. Rockers seem to have obtained popularity in America only, and it is very probable that they were introduced in connection with the care of children. To this day such chairs in England are spoken of as American rockers.

[320]

A PANELED Cradle of Beech. It is in the Branford, Connecticut, Public Library. The cradle belongs to the Plant family, from the Mill Plain District of the town. It has been traced back to Jonathan Barker, born 1705. The sides are not quite vertical, and the head, in this form, is not so early as that on the Fuller cradle, page 315. The careful paneling of the head, as well as all other parts, mark a distinguished article of furniture. The paneling of the head is perhaps not known in another American cradle of this date, about 1690-1710. The condition is rather dilapidated, but by small repairs could be much improved. The rockers seem not to be original. In the turned and extended corner posts we have a reminiscence of earlier 17th Century work.

THE Room above is the parlor chamber in the Saugus Iron Works House. This house, together with all the chain of houses once in the possession of the writer, has been dismantled and the furniture dissipated and the houses are no longer in the possession of the author, nor is iron work now carried on at this center.

The bed shown here is of uncertain date, belonging to that class of styleless beds such as were made throughout the 18th and pretty well into the 19th Century. An amusing and pleasing feature is the division of the head board into two arches, as much as to say, "Here slept grandfather and here slept grandmother." The method of pushing the trundle bed below the large bed is here shown.

This room is very large, having about four hundred square feet on its floor, a size very uncommon in the 17th Century.

A set of hanging shelves on the right wall is dateless. The writer has seen such shelves still in use and knows that they have been in use for generations. They are plain boards with holes bored in four corners and small ropes carried through and knotted to sustain the shelves.

A piece of chintz hangs over the edge of the table; it carries a figure of Washington. We have noted a standing figure of the Father of his Country, driving a pair of leopards which come perhaps to his knee. The leopards on wall paper are also shown, attached to a chariot, drawing Bacchus.

A FOUR Poster and a trundle bed, formerly in the Hazen Garrison House. There is no article of furniture of the 17th Century in which we are so poor as in beds. The massive examples have altogether disappeared, and the huge English beds are all lost. A piece of furniture so bulky would naturally not be brought to America, except by the wealthy. When we have before us a simple bed like the one above, with small octagon tapered posts, alike at the head and foot, we are at a loss to name a date, because such a bed could have been used by the original generation of Pilgrims and also as late as 1820. The earliest beds, however, seem to lack bed screws, and were held together merely by the tautness of the ropes. This bed has its original simple white canopy, and the tester is of one piece drawn over a frame, built on all sides like the old-fashioned curtain with rods run into the hem. This canopy was carefully laundered and laid away by the dear lady who had used it. The general method of using a canopy bed is here plainly seen. The curtains were drawn away in the day time but could be completely closed in at night.

ABOVE is a slaw bed, otherwise called a press bed; that is to say, it was sometimes set into a shallow cupboard which was of the depth of the portion that was intended to stand permanently on the floor. The lower part of the bed closed somewhat like a modern folding bed on the joints seen in the picture. When the doors were closed, the bed was entirely out of the way. Below is a trundle bed with a pine paneled head board. Such panels are rare. Both of these beds are owned by the author. The date of the upper one is any time in the 18th Century. That of the lower one probably the latter part of the 17th Century or early part of the 18th Century.

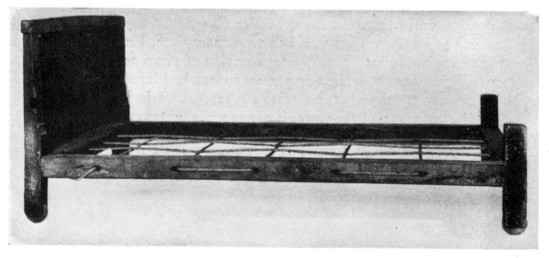

ON the preceding page is the famous bed in the old jail now in the exhibition rooms of the Historical Society at York, Maine. This is one of the dozen pieces in this book previously shown in books of furniture, but it is believed that this is the first photograph which renders the quaint inscriptions legible. They are in the form of poems such as were worked upon samplers.

The colorings of the foliage are very rich, especially the greens and the reds, and the counterpane and valance are a part of the rich and complete set. Date: 1745.

At the top of this page is a bed belonging to the author. Its width is unusual, being 60 inches. Date: 18th century.

A BED with a canopy on which appears a repeated figure of peacocks in blue with foliage. The phrase, "tent bed" often used is perhaps derived from the rounded tops of some canopy beds. Others derive their name from the fact that the posts are made in two sections. The upper sections were called poles, hence the term tent bed. No other photograph of the above bed, except this with the figures, is available. Date: late in the 18th Century.

ABOVE is a canopied bed with an early printed pattern. One may see from this picture the slender character of the eight-sided poles which support the top. We cannot too strongly stress the fact that no 17th Century beds and no early 18th Century beds have been found in America with carved posts. They are always small as shown. This bed was in the fire room chamber of the Iron Works House at Saugus, which has now been dismantled.

The earliest beds did not show an arched top but were flat, and the composition of the frame work at the top was called laths. They were usually two cross pieces beside that at the head and the foot, and the whole was pinned on at the corners by iron spikes.

Why a bed is called a four poster is a puzzle as we can hardly imagine a bed to be without four posts. Possibly the answer lies in the same cause which gave the thousand-leg table its name.

Obviously the reason for the simplicity of early bed posts was the fact that they were housed in by the draperies so as to be useful merely as supports.

We do not know when mosquito netting came into use, but the East Indian protection of netting had not in the 17th Century become a customary thing in America.

A HIGH Bed belonging to Mr. Geo. F. Ives. It is said not to have had hangings at the foot. At this date the statement could scarcely be verified, but obviously there is no use of the posts without hangings. The bed is a handsome figured maple, which came into use early in the 18th Century, when we date this specimen.

A BED of Maple, in the Geo. F. Ives Collection, Danbury, Connecticut.
This bed is made with a joint in the frame near the head, for folding under
the canopy, the drapery of which may then be drawn down over it. Below
the head was a small cabinet for holding linen. Date: 18th Century.

ABOVE is an oak four poster. This bed is so far as the writer knows the only example of an American high poster in oak. He had the good fortune to find it in Wethersfield, Connecticut. The owner of the last generation had cut off one of the posts for a ball bat! There is no manner of estimating its age. It might easily have been in use in the 17th Century.

The Connecticut settler clung as now to his traditions and to the fondness for past customs which has given his state the name of the land of steady habits and to which we owe the preservation of more than half of the finest pieces of 17th Century American furniture. The motive for destroying high posters, however, was fashion. We know of two ambitious young sisters who went throughout their house, a great New England mansion, and sawed off every high post bed, and there were many!

The stuffiness incident to draperies about a high poster can be overcome by the use of the airy, netted canopy, so that we may retain in modern use the stately and romantic bed of our forefathers.

We regret not being able to show on the preceding page the bed frame, which is braced by a base piece.

THE Picture is of a small bed with a handsome fish-net stitch canopy, in which there is a doubled border so that the points of the fringe show in two lines. It was the early fashion to place such netted pieces over a muslin ground, to exhibit the net more plainly. A bed draped like the one above is therefore not complete, but answers the modern requirement of airiness.

Bed spreads were in an endless variety of materials and patterns. The patch work style was later. Copperplate preceded it, or tufted white counterpanes. The heavy woven and colored spreads were in numerous styles. A fine floral or tree pattern, in color, sewed in a white base, is a rare and beautiful design.

The lower valance was sometimes separate from the spread, and sometimes attached to it. When separate it usually matched the canopy. This bed is owned by the author. Date: 1720 or later.

A COUNTERPANE owned by Mrs. Wallace Nutting. The material is hand woven linen, and the decoration is in heavy cotton, which in this case is not cut. The size is eight feet square. The color of the foundation and of the wicking is all white as always in this style.

Sometimes the material is cut to show the blossoming of flowers. The purely geometrical patterns are not as desirable. Frequently the design is cut out at the lower corners for the bed posts.

The date of these pieces is indeterminate as in many sorts of fancy work which have survived through many generations. They seem to have been in use at an early date and are being made today, but the modern copies are more likely to be found in cotton.

A HIGH Post Bed in the John Alden House, Duxbury. John and Priscilla died in a small down-stairs bedroom, where a later bed now is, off the kitchen. It is too bad that a place built by the son of these typical ancient worthies, cannot be restored and kept within and without as a permanent memorial.

The house at Duxbury is at last available to be seen by the public, and sometime the proper attention will be paid to its restoration.

The construction of the house frame, with its great braced posts and beams, is clearly shown, and no doubt follows the plan, and may even be the handiwork of John Alden, who was the most skilled in tools of any man of the original settlers.

[334]

ON this and the next page are two aspects of an American oak chair-table, which is in style unique so far as at present known. The uniqueness consists in the combination of the cross-stretcher, scrolled, with a chair-table. The piece was found in New Jersey, a most extraordinary breaking of the Connecticut oak traditions. The drawer is flush. We therefore date the piece about 1690-1700. The table top is not only scrolled but has the "thumb-nail" molding. The feet have lost the lower half of the balls, but in the portion remaining show their full diameter. The hight is 28¾ inches, and was probably 29½ or a trifle more. The frame is 18¼ by 23½ inches. The seat is now 17¼ inches high. The top is 27 by 34 inches. The enigmatical lettering on the under side of the top has no reference to a date of manufacture. The drawer has not the grooved runs but has the wide dove tails at both ends, and is oak. The chair is heavy, strong, in fine condition and a striking instance of oak continued to a late date, similar to the case of the highboy on page 73. Owner: the author.

It is not to be thought strange that so little oak is found out of New England. Wherever an industry becomes established there it tends to remain. Mechanics happened to be numerous in the Connecticut colonies, who had worked in oak at home in England. Then the parts of Connecticut where oak is found are very old.

The use of the chair table as a dining table has even now much to commend it. Evidently this table has been moved from the middle to the side of the room a vast number of times to lose any part of its very heavy feet. The hugeness of these feet suggest an earlier style than the table would otherwise call for. It is entirely possible the date has been placed twenty years too late. The finial is a restoration but there existed a picture with the old finial to serve as a copy. Every other part is original.

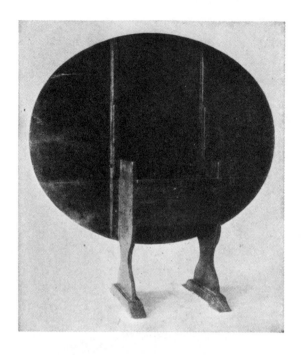

A HUTCH Table with a pine top, here shown, is almost precisely like a dozen known to the author and similar to twice as many more. Chair tables are rather easy to find in Eastern New England. This specimen has the usual notches cut on the feet. The date may be 1700-20.

On the next page is a fine sturdy old table of the same description, except that it bears signs of greater age, and has more attractive features. The various quaint scrolls on the boards of the frame and the cleats harmonize in an appealing whole. The cross member of the box, or frame, is as usual dovetailed at its edges. The table belongs to Mr. Geo. F. Ives. The wood is pine.

Chair tables are rather oftener round than oval. They are oftener of sufficient size to seat six, and sometimes eight persons. They require to be moved, if advantage is taken of economy of room. For this reason probably they went out of use. As rooms grew larger standing tables succeeded. But they possess too many good features to be discarded. We use the term chair table to include hutch tables, because they resemble one another closely, and the hutch supplied a high-seated chair.

The writer has never heard hutch pronounced correctly. Chair tables are very seldom mentioned in old inventories, only four times in Essex County records before 1674. A stool-table is mentioned once, whatever it may have been. A hutch-table is not mentioned at all. In Mandeville it occurs spelled hucche—as it is pronounced. It was synonymous with chest. Macquoid applies the name to the church chest, with doors, that is a cupboard, but never to a chest, in his *Age of Oak*. It has now become a common word in furniture discussion, but the meaning is still unsettled. Some apply to a small chest, others to a small cubby or cupboard.

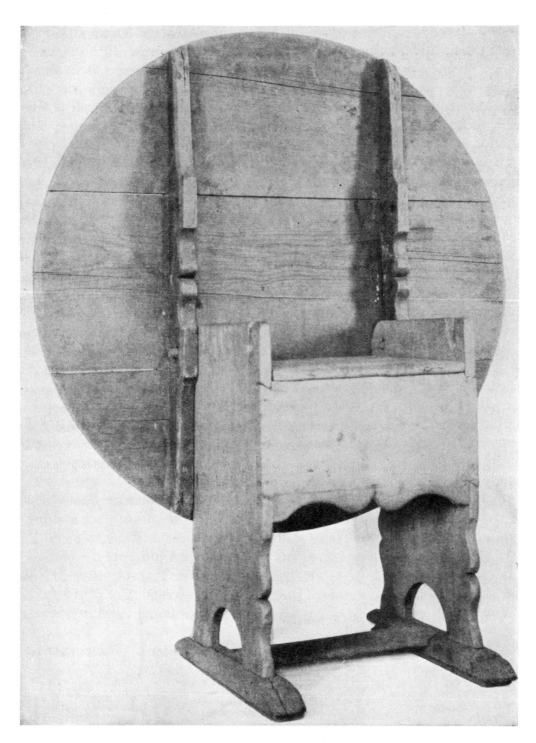

A HUTCH Table in the Geo. F. Ives Collection. It has much merit in the scrolled sides of its trestles and cleats. The hutch tops of such tables could be used as high seats by the use of stools. Date: 1680-1700.

TABLES in a fixed form belong to an established civilization. A very large table means a great house. Great tables were primarily designed for dining. They got their form in communities like monasteries or in the retainers' halls of nobles. The word table is pure Latin in origin, and thus etymology enforces the foreign origin of the table itself. Oriental peoples, especially those who sat on the floor, felt little need of tables. Great tables were not, so far as old examples show, brought to this country from Europe. Materials were too abundant here. Given a pit saw and a great tree, a couple of men could soon provide a board which only needed supports, of any temporary sort, and hence we have the trestles and board.

The permanent table afforded little room for carving. In a very few survivals there is carving on the frame. Perhaps in no instance is there a carved leg on a table of the period before 1670, of American design. The richly carved bulbous legs of the 16th Century tables found no encouragement here. The feeling for solidity and permanence was naturally not as great in a new as in an old country. The settler did not feel as certain of his abode, and particularly, when he did build permanently he could not afford great rooms.

For this reason tables with leaves, and with folding contrivances, or movable features like those possessed by boards and trestles, by chairtables, and by gate-leg tables, were very popular. A large family in a room of moderate size—the one great fire room, found a great fixed table most inconvenient. Hence when we arrive at standing tables we find them not large as they are in England. The few with six legs were mostly for public purposes, such as church communion tables.

Trestles survived in small gate legs, but the tops were not removable. Also trestles survived in a few tavern tables. Illustrations of both instances are found on pages 381 and 448. The use of oak tops in American tables is practically unknown. Pine commended itself for this purpose as well as for the finest chest lids. It is in the latter part of the 17th Century that we begin to find maple and walnut in table tops, to correspond with the bases. Even so the maple was generally badly warped, though walnut kept its form better.

No early table top is ever nailed or screwed in place. Sometimes nails were inserted later to fix more firmly an old top.

KITCHEN of the Webb House, otherwise called Hospitality Hall or the Yorktown House, formerly the property of the author, at Wethersfield. This fine house of 1752 is now in the hands of the Society of Colonial Dames and we may gladly anticipate its continuance as a permanent public heirloom. A feature of much interest is the bracing of the chimney girt frankly showing in the room. This style has also been noticed in a room of the Benning Wentworth Mansion at Little Harbor, New Hampshire.

The hutch table on the left in this picture is interesting from the scrolled upper side of the shoe or base; a similar scroll also shows on the base of the front board.

On the right appears another chair table with beautifully bleached maple top, held together with butterfly dowels. The frame is oak, a very rare feature. The flush drawer also indicates an early date. Both of these tables may be placed around 1690.

The little child's chair in the center of the room is of pine and has a very high back; its quaint effect is rarely good.

THE Earliest Tables known in America were boards on trestles. The two mentioned on the next page are the only large fine examples yet found. The one there shown is the property of Mr. B. A. Behrend. Date: 1620–50.

The exciting hunt for this table, when the scent grew warm, sheds a humorous light on the collector's experience. The author directed the hunt by telephone a thousand miles from the field. This example is peculiar from its two spindles, resting on the heavy stretcher, to give the top stability.

The rarity of the board and trestle is such that only within a decade has attention been given to it, and searchers have probably passed by such mediaeval styles merely because they did not know what they had found. The one pictured was sold at auction for a nominal sum. Indeed when the author wired to pay what was necessary to obtain the rarity his agent wrote back that he could make a better one for three dollars! And the original buyer at auction valued the piece merely as a Washington relic.

No other article of furniture speaks so strongly of the ancient time. The Last Supper of Leonardo shows a board and trestles.

The construction of the trestle is simply a double headed T.

In Scott's novels more than one reference is made to these progenitors of the modern table. The third chapter of Ivanhoe opens with a description of them, and of their arrangement.

Boards with frames or trestles have recently been brought from England.

The Shaker colonies made such tables within a century. One such sixteen feet long, with three trestles, was recently in the hands of Mr. I. Sack.

A somewhat inferior board with trestles was not long since discovered and a well grounded rumor has reached the author that another example, a counterpart of the one shown on the next page, has recently been found and sold to someone in Cleveland. As this style comes to the knowledge of collectors we may hope that other specimens will come to light.

Boards were easily available in America for single-piece tops of tables. The author has recently seen in New England old forest pines which might have furnished single board tops five inches wider than that here shown. A piece of pine 48 inches wide is in one of our New England panels. But apparently no effort was made to find for tables the widest board possible. The trenchers used on such boards, in a simple home, were of wood, as also the great bowls. Each man had his own private clasp knife. Spoons were wooden, and forks were probably not used.

The trestles and board in the Metropolitan Museum were found by Mr. Eugene Bolles in Essex, Massachusetts, in an attic.

MORE than half the world eats without tables. Even the early English, from whom most of our furniture styles were derived, brought in a temporary table for dining, such as that here shown. It was called a trestle board and frame, a table board, a long table, a table and frame, etc. A good many are mentioned in the old probate inventories, though such pieces were already falling out of fashion when America—or our part of it—was settled. Yet some families had two such tables, and in a great household, one for the family was placed on a dais, while two or more, on a lower level, at right angles to the first, accommodated the servants. Mr. Bolles found the one in the Metropolitan Museum, while the author stumbled upon the one which heads this chapter. It was preserved in the attic of the Richardson tavern at Medway, because Washington had sat at it. One more debt to Washington! Its base is maple or beech. The long truss rod was, in use, lightly fixed by large wooden pins. The top was unattached. The length is more than ten feet, but probably a little has been cut off at one end. The top is an inch board of pine 25 inches wide.

Owner : Mr. B. A. Behrend.

A Pair of Trestles, and a board about six feet in length owned by Mr. Harry Long, The ingenious stiffening brace is located at a point where it is wholly out of the way, and effective, it being let down into a slot in the trestles. The two stools are half moons in shape. The writer does not know their origin. Date: 1670-1700.

Below is an X-trestle table, belonging to Mr. Willoughby Farr, of Edgewater, New Jersey. A considerable number like this but with plain X-trestles have been found. Date: 1690-1730. It is braced at the center with a four-sided strut. The manner of pinning the truss or stretcher rod is plainly seen.

SINCE the trestles and their board must be moved daily, the invention of the drawing table was induced. No complete American specimen is now known. That in the rooms of the Connecticut Historical Society at Hartford, which is very massive, its legs being nearly five inches in diameter, is the best of its kind, but it has lost its draw boards. It has already been illustrated.

The natural successor of the drawing table, whose leaves pushed under the main board, at the ends, was a table with hinged leaves. That shown above, at the Wadsworth Atheneum, Hartford, belongs to Mr. George Dudley Seymour, and is the only one now known in this style. It is most valuable as a connecting link between the drawing table and the gate leg, The obvious thing, for us, would be to add leaves at the side. With only a trestle or a drawing table before us we should place the leaves as here. Date: 1690-1710.

AFTER the trestles naturally come the standing tables. Whether any of those having an extreme length were ever used in dwellings may be questioned. Most of the great standing tables now known of American origin were like the example above, communion tables. The frame is too high for domestic use, it having been about 34 inches. No large table above 31 inches high, except a side table, can escape the challenge that it may have been a communion table. The top here is composed of two pine planks. The posts we believe are maple or birch. It was owned by Mr. I. Sack. It is large, but the dimensions are not available. The great size of the posts and its marks of age, date it about 1660-1690.

About the only use for such tables now, outside museums, is in libraries. They serve admirably in large rooms to spread many books, but are not available, owing to hight, for reading.

A table six feet long with carving on the front side of the frame, and otherwise very like the table above was recently found near Exeter, and is shown elsewhere. The plea that the very high tables might have been for domestic use, with high chairs, is hardly allowable. If the fashion was for high tables in the earliest period, why are not the trestles high? Refectory tables are not known by that name in the old inventories. "Long, standing, joined," were the terms used. The name refectory refers to the frequent use of such tables in college commons. It is a stilted word. Long would be a better name, though there are scarcely enough of American origin to require a name.

AN American Oak Refectory Table. Length, originally about 92 inches; now about 86 inches, owing to the loss of the end cleats, the dowel holes of which are to be seen. Width 30 inches, all of one pine plank, originally, which has now split into three parts. Frame, about 26 by 72 inches. Hight, about 34 inches. This remarkably preserved and no less remarkably turned communion table, at one time was discarded and the top seems to have been used in chopping meat. It was finally restored to the church from which it came. The parish organization was formed in 1638, and the church edifice shortly after erected. This original communion table therefore, without reasonable doubt, dates as early as 1638-40. The author does not know of another American oak table at once so old and so meritorious. The turnings are seen to be the same as those on the Robinson chair, page 177. The size of the posts is about 3½ inches. The pine top is about 1⅝ inches. Owing to fear of endless solicitations, the precise location in Massachusetts is withheld.

A ROOM with furniture of the 17th Century and with a wall in old natural pine should have a charm for any one, but especially for the lover of harmony. There was much variety in the furniture of the same period, because the artificer was not shut around with many artificial limitations. He loved and wrought according to his loves. He saw a light and followed without hearing a voice commanding him to finish, in so many hours, a certain piece of work. Yet like the best artisans he worked rapidly, because he was eager to see the embodiment of his ideas. When he finished he had dispensed with a part of himself, yet he was richer in conceptions than before. No man can make a good thing, without at once becoming able to make a better thing.

As to the wall decorations of 17th Century homes, old charts or early ship models are good, and oil portraits would be better. But such portraits are altogether too rare even to be thought of hopefully. No doubt few are retained as family heirlooms. What the collector finds is of the early 18th Century at best. Of course the old masters are still available but can scarcely enter into our view here.

Exterior slat shutters admitting light but shutting out vision came into use somewhat at the close of the 18th Century. In our period there were possible a few inside shutters, but we doubt if the fact is established.

AN Oak Refectory Table with light turnings. Owner: the author. The top is 29½ by 67¾ inches. The hight is 25½ inches. The frame is 20½ by 47 inches. This is a lighter and later type than that shown on page 347, and was of course made for domestic purposes. It is obvious that such a table was much more easily moved about than the heavy sort which we associate with the word refectory. At the same time the wide everhang all around this table made it convenient to sit at. Frames of oak usually point to an earlier date than maple frames. Date: 1690-1710. Origin: Connecticut.

The so-called "gate-leg turnings" were rather more elaborate than those on tavern or refectory tables. In the table above one sees the beginning of the gate-leg style of turning, but with the plain stretchers which gate-leg tables of handsome types discarded in favor of turned stretchers. The plain stretcher was stronger than the turned stretcher, an important matter if the stretcher is long.

The large early English table can usually be distinguished from the American table of like date by its heavier construction. This is true, not only of the frame, but of the top. In the instance before us and in a fine American trestle-board the top is thin. English tables have been found with pine tops.

A REMARKABLE Table owned by the Connecticut Historical Society. It is seven feet and a half long and thirty inches high. The wood is cherry except the upper frame rail in the back, which is pine, with a molded edge. The legs are 3½ inches square, also the front stretcher. The back stretcher is 2½ by 3½ inches.

There has never been a leaf behind. The feature of peculiar interest is the great wear shown on the back and stretchers and the freedom from wear in front. This is proof positive, since the parts are all original, that the table was used at the back and ends only. Now the back is the place where no wear would occur had this been a side table. We must believe the table was used in a public room, like a court room, or an official's office. The nature of the wear, besides the hight of the table preclude the supposition that it was used as a communion table. There is no wear on the rule joint of the leaf, showing the table was used standing regularly with the leaf raised. There is a fine molding on the stretchers, and the stretchers of the gates are molded on all four corners. The front stretcher is chamfered as clearly seen. The feet show much wear, and one is somewhat disintegrated.

The joint in the front rail is cut on a radius to permit turning the leg. The table is carefully made. It has in chalk on the back rail: "Chas. Hosmer, Hartford, Conn." This gentleman has been called the father of the historical society there. The legend is probably a shipping direction. We are no doubt indebted to him for this splendid specimen. His date was 1785–1871. The table date may be 1730–40.

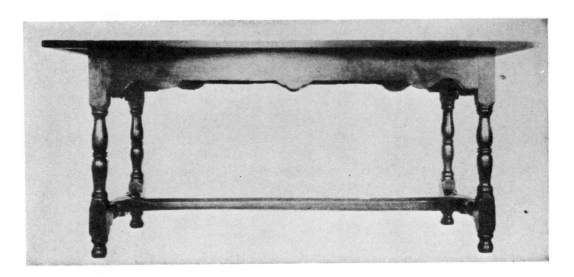

A MEDIAL-STRETCHER Table. Owner: William G. Erving. M. D., of Washington. The top and rails are pine, the legs maple; the stretcher ash. The frame is 24½ by 54¾ inches. The hight is 27¾ inches. The top is 32¾ by 64 inches. The brackets on the frame, next the legs, add strength as well as ornament; the central scroll being merely ornament. Brackets indicate a date, we should say, inside the 17th Century. They are important. Date: 1690-1710.

Below is a remarkable American Oak Table with carving on one side of the frame. It was found in Southern New Hampshire. The author can vouch for its authenticity. Its length is about seven feet. Picture furnished by Wanamaker, New York.

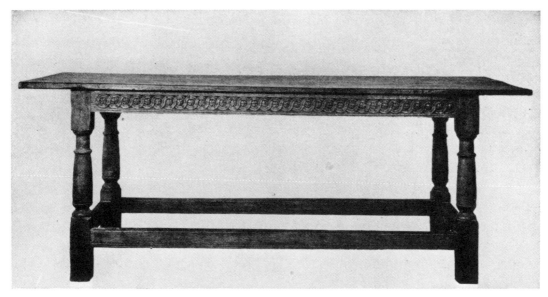

A ROOM of all cross-stretcher American pieces, a highboy, lowboy, chair table, desk, and two stools.

AROUND THE HEARTH

Since men have learned how to make a fire, the hearth, for every generation, until our own, has centered around the hearth. Here was the altar. Here, sitting behind the elders, ardent youths held hands in the silent wooing of the shadows. Here they were married. Here babes were born. Here the cradle stood, while the mother watched it at her labors. Here she presided, the mother of statesmen, poets and inventors. Here her sweet wisdom ruled, and her wheel and loom clothed the household. Here the aged sat, in the chimney corner. Here they passed at length into the unseen world.

From the hearth our fathers got warmth, light, food. Fire was the first object they recognized, after their mothers. It taught them their first lesson in self-restraint. Every day till senility claimed them they gazed into the blaze. Fire was the precious, first focus of civilization.

In the evenings the romantic sense was called out by the fire. The sagas of the ages were born and sung there. There leaped the ghosts; there loomed the giants; there played the fairies. Is it a wonder that all men love, with undying, intuitional affection, the hearth?

A BRACKET Refectory Table, with Drops. Owner: Mrs. John Marshall Holcombe. This remarkbly fine example was used in the Grant family, of East Windsor Hill, Connecticut, as a dining table, before 1700. Date: 1650-1670. It was possibly the property of the settler, Mathew Grant, who was a surveyor, and whose tripod was among the family treasures

The style of the turning is close to the earliest American work. The shadow mold on the frame is the same as that appearing on American oak chests. The brackets are boldly scrolled, and the drops add the last touch of style to complete the heavy turned table of this date.

The frame is oak. Size of top, 32¾ by 70 inches; frame, 26 by 58½ inches; hight, 31 inches.

It was a surprise to the author, on tallying his information on refectory tables to find them so few. A beautiful specimen is owned by Mr. H. W. Erving. One with carved frame was in the hands of the writer. The specimens here shown nearly complete the list of the other fine examples available.

AT the bottom of the page is a large kitchen table belonging to Mrs. F. Gordon Patterson of Boston. It has turnings identical with a small table known to be very early, and its brackets to stiffen the frame are a feature of merit. The slide is missing. The end leaf may mark a very early survival, suggesting the leaves of the table on page 345. Some other features would point to a later date. We therefore endeavor to be safe by placing it between 1690 and 1730. As we recollect it, the top is pine and the frame a close grained hard wood, very light in color.

We could scarcely expect to find in kitchen tables subjects of importance. But the facts prove otherwise. The great rooms in a house of the Pilgrim Century, were the parlor (dining room) and the hall (kitchen). The term hall for the room of entrance came later. In the Pilgrim time it was the porch or the entry, often very meager in proportions. The hall could be used as a dining room, though in homes of any pretention the parlor was used for that purpose. It was not till later that the parlor was shut up and set off as sacred to great occasions only.

The hight of tables is one indication of their use and age. As pointed out elsewhere a table much exceeding 30 inches high is likely to be, if large, a church communion table; or if small, a side table. But such small tables are scarcely found. If below 29 inches in hight, without the loss of any part of the feet, tables are for occasional use. Any large table of only 27 inches in hight, or even 28 inches, should be examined with care, for in all probability something is wrong. Feet are often so turned that the loss of one ball is overlooked by any one not expert.

A KNEADING-TROUGH Table with a drawer and cross stretchers; in the Metropolitan Museum. The drawer, the front of which is built on a slant, carries quaint carving. The cover removes, opening a hutch, which was most likely designed as a bread mixing trough. The huge wedges which hold in place the middle truss carry out the sturdy effect of the piece. The cross stretchers are slightly scrolled as are also the straddling legs; the material is pine.

One cannot resist the conclusion that a piece of this sort was a gift constructed by a young husband for his bride. The honest and not unsuccessful attempts at decoration are indicative of affection in the fingers of the artificer. Such pieces carrying decoration where it is not really required are always lovable because they mark a generous nature and speak of a kindly humanity. Date: 1670–1700.

A KITCHEN Table in Pine. The great thickness of the trestles and the still greater spread of their bases or shoes are points of attraction. The method of tenon and mortise is certainly crude enough, and possibly afforded the suggestion of the mission furniture. In reality it is only a make-shift arrangement to supply the lack of good joinery. This table had a slide, the groove for which may be seen immediately under the frame. The object of such slides, which were not uncommon, was partly the extension of the area of the table and partly an accommodation to a worker sitting by the table. The lower level afforded a convenience; as for instance, when the children shelled the peas. The great middle truss or stretcher also served as a shelf. While an English origin is claimed for this table, it has more the style of the Pennsylvania Dutch. Date: 1670–1720.

THIS curious table is owned by the Metropolitan Museum, but is not yet on exhibition. It contains a box or hutch below the top, which latter is made to slide, the cleats being in the grooved form. The panels are encroached on at the bottom by the base mold of the frame. It would have been far better style to raise the panels so as to give the same width of rail above and below. This is a puzzling but an original feature. Of course a good deal is missing from the legs. The massive character of the piece renders it very attractive indeed to the real lover of 17th Century furniture. The top is made with mitered end cleats, which form a part of the top, in addition to the grooved runner cleats below. The construction has more than one foreign suggestion, but the table is called American by an excellent judge of such matters. The only manner of gaining access to the hutch is of course by sliding the top. Date: The earlier part of the 17th Century.

No true refectory table has a leaf. They were used before the time of leaves, and a leaf, can only be sustained by a slide. We count tables with such slides as always later than the refectory period. If in the 17th Century and earlier a larger table was wanted it was added by placing tables end to end. The idea of a table as a board was deeply fixed, and but slowly eradicated. Once the leaf table came in it speedily put all refectory tables and trestle-boards out of fashion. Their use has never been revived. Hence their extreme rarity. There is a report that a six-leg American refectory table exists, but one never gets to see it, and meantime we claim the right to be doubtful.

A LARGE Walnut Library Table. It is owned by the author. Date: 1700. The top is 31 by 66 inches. The frame is 25 by 53 inches. The hight is 29¾ inches. There is a little central drawer, as appears, between two large drawers.

It is now common parlance to name tables of this type library tables, but no one knows for what use they were designed. The side overhang, about three inches, is too little to admit of sitting at the side either for eating or writing. The author uses this table for writing but is obliged to sit almost facing the end. The tops all being made removable, by four hand dowels, we arrive at an early date, as the effort was to procure a large table that could be carried about in sections, like the trestles and their boards. These tables therefore are a standing puzzle to all antiquarians. Whatever use suggested raises a very valid objection. And yet the tables were somewhat numerous. Pennsylvania is their usual "habitat."

They differ from the usual large "standing" table by having drawers, and by the method of attaching the top. They are also from thirty to forty years later in date, and are in walnut rather than maple or oak. They also average a smaller size. On the other hand they are distinguished from the tavern tables by being larger and having movable tops.

A "LIBRARY" Table, with Scalloped Skirt. These tables are rather rare with such skirts, but, with plain skirts, they are brought out of Pennsylvania in large numbers, twelve at a time being the spoils of one tour, noted at a dealer's.

As on the preceding page, the material is all walnut. The top is removable, and measures 32¾ by 48½ inches, by 28¾ inches in height. The frame is 28¾ by 36½ inches. It will be noted that the drawers in these tables are seldom paired, but one is longer than the other. If we named this a serving table, ignoring the higher sideboard table, we should possibly be making a guess as good as any, since a grounded opinion seems impossible. We should not hesitate at all in this decision, were not these tables found, occasionally, in such large sizes. Date: 1700–1720. Owner: the author.

It is humiliating that we human beings, with every facility for making records, should so often leave our successors in the dark concerning our works and ways. The pictorial art, using photography, will save the coming generation much trouble.

A LARGE Walnut Table, with scalloped skirt. It was once in the possession of the author; the present owner being unknown.

The turnings are much bolder than usual. The stretchers show much use—a mystery, as one cannot place a foot on a stretcher anywhere without hitting the knee on the frame! And on the sharp scallops, at that.

This table has a little drawer in one end. It is about five feet long. Date: 1700–10.

With this table we pass out of the class confined practically to the 17th Century. The gate-leg table was so much loved that it could not die, and though it began many years before the 17th Century went out it continued, a solitary example of style, long after its period. Among the many revivals of early furniture the "library" table and all 17th Century types except the gate-leg, are allowed to sleep, despite the occasional refectory type.

A PENNSYLVANIA "Library" Table. The frame is in maple; the drawer fronts as well as interiors and the top are in pine. Its sturdy type, its two drawers with the large knobs typical of the origin, and the plain end and medial stretchers, afford a piece of interesting character, wholly original and in natural color. The top is 34 by 68½ inches—a generous size. The overhang at the ends is 13½ inches! At the sides it is 4 inches. Had the possessors desired to use this as a refectory table they might easily have done so. It will amply seat eight persons. Owner: the author. Date: 1700–10.

The overhang of this table is so great that unless it were pinned down, disasters might occur. Hence, we suppose, the pins. Of course the entire table is a solid weight.

In the restoration of Greek temples the practice is to place a wholly new, and apparently new, pillar in place of a missing one. Such work can be seen on the Erectheum at Athens. How meretricious it would have been to scar and mar a new column to make it resemble the old!

We expect such bad work to be done on furniture by unscrupulous persons trying to pass it off as all original and sound. But collectors should be wiser.

SELECTIONS from the furnishings of the Hale Mansion, South Coventry, Connecticut. It was built 1776 by Deacon Richard Hale, father of Captain Nathan Hale, the "Martyr Spy" of the Revolutionary War, who was born in an earlier house which was demolished soon after the present house was erected and which stood but a few rods from it.

The maple gate-leg table is one of the most delicately beautiful specimens. Size: top, 41 by 52¼ inches; hight, 28 inches. Date: 1700–30.

The table on the right is a very rare specimen, called in Connecticut a Windsor table, from the town, not from the Windsor chair. It is of hickory, oak and maple. It was found in Hartford. Size: 28¼ by 21 1-8 inches; hight, 24 inches. Date, about 1700. The owner is Mr. George Dudley Seymour.

The room is beautifully paneled on the fire-place side. Much honor is due the owner for salvaging this fine old house.

A FOUR-GATE Table of Walnut. Owner: Mrs. Lewis Sheldon Welch, of New Haven. Date: 1690–1730.

The very existence of tables with four gates has not come to the attention of many collectors, except as they see illustrations of such tables, because so few exist. The writer knows of six, has heard a rumor of two more, and presumes that a dozen may soon be known. This work shows three; there is a fourth in the Metropolitan Museum, a fifth at the Albany Historical Society, a sixth in Hartford. Two of these have often been illustrated. These we show have hitherto appeared in no publication. The origin of the table here shown is presumably Connecticut.

Of course the drawer handle is not original. The existence of a good number of Virginia or English walnut tables in New England raises the question whether such tables were native here. From their style we conclude they were native and that they were made, as hinted elsewhere, from walnut brought in from the South, or sporadic trees here. They were in every known instance found near or on the tide-water.

A FOUR-GATE Table of Walnut, originally brought by the writer from Richmond, Virginia, and now in the possession of Mr. Chauncey C. Nash. It is somewhat small and low, for a four-gate table, and the turnings are in the fashion more often found in the South.

In giving these tables the name four-gate, the author feels the inaccuracy and possible confusion that would arise by a term often heard— double-gate. Those who use that term are thinking of one side of the table. But as a single-gate table means just what it purports to mean, a double-gate and a four-gate should mean what the words naturally signify. Date: 1690–1730.

Of course the purpose of four gates was to hold large leaves with stability. Four gates also add very much to the beauty of the table, giving a little forest of legs, and when the table is open the symmetry is not destroyed.

The top of the table above is mostly original. The plain stretcher we surmise is more often found in the South. The gate-leg table is now very rare there, as is all furniture of its date. This is partly owing to the war of 1861, and partly to the giving over to slaves the ancient furniture, which they did not preserve.

A WALNUT Four-Gate Table. Owner: The author. This table was found near York, Maine, in 1921. The top was about 66 inches in diameter, and very nearly round. Restorations are required in the top. There are two draws. The frame is very solid, and has nearly all the original feet, so that the effect, whether open or closed is very beautiful. The frame dimensions are 20 by 51 inches. The height is 29 inches. Date: 1690–1730.

The great gate-leg in Albany is six by six and a half feet, and the gates swing from the center, that being the only one known in this country with the center swing. It is without question the finest example now known.

The effect of one of these four-gate tables, when opened, in the center of a room, is startling in its impression of beauty and dignity. The revival of interest in the gate-leg table is well merited. Beautiful and useful in all forms, in its four-gate form it is supreme.

The Albany gate-leg has at present no drawer but there are indications that it once had one or two. It is peculiar in having a small half round attached to the edge of the center part, next the leaves, to guide the rule joint.

THE TABLE above really belongs in the class of stool tables. It is maple; 21 inches high. The legs spread in all directions. The frame, at stretchers, is 13½ by 16½ inches.

The table at the bottom of the page is a solid plain frame specimen, belonging to the author. Date: 1680–1700.

TWO Gate-leg Tables belonging to the Metropolitan Museum. They are quite similar in their turnings, varying in the size of the legs and frames.

These tables are of the type commonly known and in good style, having the stretchers turned.

It is a good point in construction that the leg should not swing out beyond the edge of the leaf. If the frame is designed in connection with the top the leg can be kept, in any part of its orbit, some inches away from the side of the leaf, and so avoid awkwardness of appearance, and still more important, prevent the collision of human with table legs. This feature is also assisted by a generous overhang at the ends. There is a considerable variation in this regard, ranging from four to eight inches; averaging about five inches, though more is better.

It is not possible in a small table leg to secure bold turnings. Hence the large legs are prized not only for their early, quaint, massive effect, but also because they afford room to allow the turner's chisel to cut deeply and shape fully a strong, rich design for the leg and stretches.

The nature of walnut in table tops is likely to cast some doubt on the collector's mind. In English Walnut there is an occasional bluish streak, running with the grain, perhaps every inch or two. This is quite obvious after one's eye has once been trained to look for it. Black walnut will bleach to a color like fresh English or Virginia Walnut. On the other hand these latter walnuts are often very much bleached on old table tops. They should be examined on the under side.

A GATE-LEG Table, with unusually fine turnings, owned by the Metropolitan Museum. One notices the long effect of the frame, in proportion to the width. This picture shows the slot in the frame above regularly made to receive the leg top, which is halved to fit in completely. These cuts are a distinct blemish in any open gate table, as seen at the bottom in this picture. The table looks best when closed.

The turnings in this case are bold, but they are so, always, at the expense of strength. If the leg is very large there is leeway for bold turnings.

Gate-leg tables usually have one drawer reaching about two-thirds the length of the table. If the table is very large there are two drawers. In the earliest types there is often a central slat under the drawer, on which it slides.

We do not remember to have seen grooved runs on gate tables, in more than a half dozen instances.

A SOMEWHAT stockily turned gate-leg table, in the possession of the writer. It has lost its feet but is otherwise original.

The turning is usually, as here, a doubled vase and ring. The leg, cut in two in the middle, would give two identical turnings. But on pages 364, 371, 376 and 382 we have single vases. There is little to choose between the styles, if each is of the best character, but the double vase is usually better done.

The table above is of medium size, is of maple, including the top and dates about 1690-1720. It has the tongue and grooved joint, where leaf and center join, resembling the modern matched board, only less pronounced. This sort of joint is counted the best, though some very fine specimens are found with the rule joint, generally called by modern cabinet makers, a table joint. From the point of appearance the rule joint is better, but later. We doubt if any gate-leg was made with a plain joint, that is with edges at the junction, square. The claim is often made of great age for such edges. The burden of proof is on the claimant.

Tables often have a thin block attached under the leaf, as a stop to prevent the leg going too far.

A LARGE Gate-leg Table with fine turnings. One should notice that in the finest style all legs, including the leg which acts as a hinge, should extend to the floor, as in this example, as contrasted with the table on the preceding page.

The relation of uniformity, so important in a gate-leg table, is thus mantained. It is only necessary to see two tables together, one with and one without this refinement, to feel the great superiority of the hinged leg with the addition at the bottom. It is matters like these that contribute to the charm of this most important style. The table below is a good maple specimen.

The table above is owned by Flayderman & Kaufmann, Boston.

A GATE-LEG Table, the property of Mr. J. H. Stiles, York, Pennsylvania. Date: 1700-1730. This piece is possibly unique in the use of an X stretcher. The solidity gained by such a method is apparent although the top of the table itself would seem to reinforce the rigidity of the frame and make such a stretcher superfluous. Nevertheless, the design is appealing and excites our interest.

Of course the top should be oval and not square. Possibly some gate-leg tables had rectangular tops originally, but no such table has come to the author's attention. The shape, we say, should be oval, but there are a few instances of circular tops. The oval is longer across the top than along the frame. That is, it is short the long way, and long the short way, so to say! The very marked oval, showing an extreme drop of the leaf is counted most desirable. But there are many things to be thought of, and confusion of judgment is easy. It is necessary to tell all the points over, one by one. Are the balls, or "pears" on the feet; are the stretchers turned; is the turning fine and bold; is the top original; what is its shape; is there a drawer; what is the wood; what is the leaf joint; the condition; the color, the size; and many other questions.

A GATE-LEG Table with large bold turnings and the flat gate. Ordinarily a flat gate is the mark of an English table, but in this instance, and some others in this volume, it is not so regarded. This table is walnut and has not turned stretchers; they would not be natural with a flat gate. The uniformity of the legs is lost in the flat gate style, nor has the flat gate advantages beyond ease of manufacture, and even that is slight. It does not require to be cut into, to secure complete closing.

One notices in some gate-leg tables in this book an end frame which is scrolled on the under side, sometimes with a cupid's bow curve, sometimes more simply. It is an added touch of style, but, unless the end has a wide overhang, is a further hindrance to the legs of the sitter.

A SPANISH-FOOT Gate-leg Table. Owner: the author. Date: 1690–1710. These tables are very rare. Perhaps a dozen are known. They are very fine in connection with Spanish-foot chairs. This specimen is maple. The top is 45½ by 47 inches. The hight is 27½ inches. The frame is 14 by 33 inches. There is a drawer. The feet project, as they should, well beyond the square of the leg. These feet are formed of attached pieces. Practice in this respect varied. Sometimes the foot was carved from the solid wood on the post. More often the "toes" were glued on. One should beware of being hoaxed by a new carving on a foot not designed as a Spanish foot. The failure to project beyond the line of the leg is a plain indication of the deception, unless the foot is added bodily, being doweled on, which may be learned by examination.

Such tables have, in the rough, lost some parts of the feet, unless they are carved from the solid.

A SMALL Gate-leg Table belonging to Mr. G. Winthrop Brown. It has a drawer, and the tongued and grooved leaf joint.

Little tables like this are very much desired, as they are not only beautiful, but adapt themselves readily as occasional tables.

The frame of a gate-leg sometimes, as in this case, is made to take the drawer directly under the top. In other cases there is a cross member, a half inch to an inch thick on the frame, above the drawer. This member seems to add strength, but the greater part of the best tables do not have it. We mention the matter because we have heard this cross member challenged, but we are certain it was original in several instances.

A DAINTY Little Gate-leg Table. Owner: the author. The turnings are especially fine. It is all in walnut. The drawer has an odd hook handle of wood. The turnings are striped with bands of red paint, which is old, but not, we suppose, original. The condition is excellent, and original. it has the tongue and grooved joint on the leaves.

Dimensions: Top, 24½ by 28¾ inches. Hight, 27½ inches. The leaves are 10 inches wide; and the top 8¾ inches wide. Such pieces are very rare, having all the original feet. The difference in condition of feet in tables of the same age arose from the fact that some of them were kept and moved about on sanded floors.

A "TUCK-AWAY" or Single Folding Gate-leg Table, in the former collection of the author. The top is pine and the frame, we believe, is maple. Both the stretchers being turned and the shoe being scrolled both on the bottom and on the top give greater importance to the piece. This table was found on Cape Cod. The top is in one piece, chamfered on the under side. Its size is 25 by 35 inches.

The attachment of the top to the frame is by butterfly hinges.

A TUCK-AWAY Gate-leg Table. Otherwise called a single- or folding-gate table. Owner: the author. It is usual for such tables, which have oval, one-piece tops to swing, so that the long way of the oval stands up and down. This table swings the other way. It came from an ancient family and bears a brass inscription with its genealogy, which we will not quote. It is maple. The stretchers are not turned as in the table opposite. The top is 20 by 26¼ inches; and the hight is 26¼ inches. Date: 1690-1720.

AN All-Pine Vase Trestle Gate-leg Table. Owner: Now unknown. It may be questioned whether the top, with no joint molding, is original, though old. The effort by a country cabinet maker to produce a trestle gate-leg is delightful in its quaintness. The shoes, or trestle-feet, are very thick. They have lost something of their contour by wear. They originally extended somewhat farther on the floor. The scrolled end and bottom brace, and the fluting of the end are the principal decorations. Date: 1680–1710.

A FOLDING Trestle-gate Table. Owner: the author. Wood: mahogany; this being the only mahogany piece of furniture shown in this book. We are, by announced design, carrying through the gate-leg tables to their decline. The style of this table, which came from the South, is early; it is perhaps an instance of the use of mahogany in 1720–30; The leaf has the rule joint. So also has the great table in Albany, already mentioned. That is in walnut. It is impossible to determine when the rule joint came in but it seems to have been well established by 1750.

When folded the thickness of the table is 6¼ inches. The top is 35 inches long and 42¾ wide—a very strong oval. It has a fine thumb-nail molding. The height is 24½ inches. The piece has good style with long overhang, and a large top in proportion to the base.

Mahogany examples are known in the first decade of the 18th Century.

A WALNUT Trestle-Gate-Leg Table. It is owned by the Metropolitan Museum. The center board is only 6½ inches wide and its length is 43 inches. The thickness is three quarters of an inch. The leaves are 10½ inches wide. The hight is 27½ inches. The shoe is 9 inches long and 2¼ inches square. The legs are 1⅝ inches square. The top of the stretcher is 5⅝ inches from the floor. The frame is 35¼ inches long. The examination the author made of the table was some time since, and he cannot say whether the top is original. The shape is against the presumption of originality; so also is the narrowness of the leaf, which should for the best style be clearly double what it is.

The table is extraordinary, being the longest folding gate we have seen. It has lost a half inch or more at the base. Date: 1670–1690. Tables in this style are very convenient, as they occupy little room when not in use.

A HEAVY Turned Trestle-Gate-Leg Table. Owner: the author. Date: 1660–90. Wood: cherry. It is a very early example of the use of cherry. It would seem hardly necessary to slot the base for the flat gate, but so we find it; an unusual form.

The shoes are pretty well worn down, on their uppers, as one may see. They were once scrolled with a double curve. They have probably lost a good inch or more. The hight is now 27¾ inches. The thickness, closed, is 15¼ inches; the leaves are 17⅛ inches wide each, and the length is 36 inches. Thus the oval is extreme. The top and the flat gates are ¾ of an inch thick. Tops on small tables, in hard wood, are very commonly of this thickness. The posts are stocky for so small a table, being 2⅝ inches, flush, square. Of course trestle tables can never have drawers.

A CORNER Gate-leg with a single gate, the property of Mr. George F.
Ives, of Danbury Connecticut. If this piece is not unique at least the
author has never heard of another example. The top, without a doubt
original, is in pine. We count the piece of sufficient importance to show
it both extended, and with the leaf dropped. It suggests a small three-
cornered table in the Metropolitan Museum in its treatment of the corner
posts which are, of course, triangular where they ordinarily would be square.
Corner tables seem always to possess a charm probably arising, if we are
to study the psychology of the matter from their evident adaptation to their
location, and to the sense of snugness, and the utilization of space. In
the same way any corner furniture is popular.

WHILE the stretchers of this piece are plain, we count it scarcely less important for that reason. The turned stretchers are more sought for and of course more decorative, but it is probable that the very earliest tables did not have them. The tavern table is a case in point. In gate-leg tables the failure to turn the stretcher is counted a greater objection than in other styles; but while this should be true it is not obvious, unless it is because we have come to think of the gate-leg table as a beautiful piece, and demand some ornateness in the turning and the carrying out of that idea of turning as far as possible. Date: 1670–1700. Size: top, 31 inches square. Hight, 27 inches.

Any one who has not forgotten his *pons asinorum* may work out the diagonal. Since picturing this table the author heard of another, only to discover it was English. One advantage of bringing such pieces to light is to challenge others to search. We have no doubt other examples will be reported.

ABOVE are Two Split Gate Tables. On the left is a very early example of a card table. The frame being triangular, is adapted for a corner, but the top on the other hand is almost an exact circle. The scheme of splitting the gate like a split spindle which shows as a complete leg when the table is closed, seems to have come in a little later than the gate-leg period and it is possible that the origin is not English. The top of this piece is soft pine, a flush inch in thickness. Date: 1680–1700.

At the right is a split gate leg with a gate on each side and with flat plain stretchers which, of course, are cut into in order to form the gate so that the stretcher is split, as one may say, as well as the post. This piece is in hard pine and is reputed to have come from Bilbao. The top is thin, about three-quarters of an inch, such as is often seen in small foreign tables. Nevertheless, we are not prepared to pass judgment upon the origin of this piece. It should be compared with the large split gate-leg opposite. Date: 1690–1700.

This style in tables seems not to have been popular, as there are very few found, and even today they are not at all eagerly sought by antiquarians. In this connection it is amusing to note that there seem to be waves of popularity, first of one sort of furniture, then of another, in the mind of collectors. The same has proved true in china; the blue china was much sought for a few years since, being now unpopular. Slight incidents not properly a logical basis for action, effect these waves of popularity. At the present moment decorated furniture, butterfly tables and Carver chairs would seem to be sought for with feverish intensity.

A LARGE Ball-turned Split Gate-Leg Table. It was in the author's former collection. Present owner unknown. It is attractive, as a fine example of its kind, but the kind has not appealed to all. Perhaps there is a suggestion of weakness in the splitting of the leg, but these tables seem strong.

One hesitates to say to what lengths the love of the gate-leg table may take some persons. There is an eagerness for their possession, as if specimens were few. Fashion demands them. In England there is a specimen with as many legs as a banyan tree has trunks. The leaves fall on all four sides. We may account for the rarity of massive examples from the fact that the very genius of the table demanded closing and moving. One large table, with four gates, of walnut, weighs 216 pounds!

A WALNUT Gate-leg Table. Owner: the author. The legs are in a fine state of preservation, and the top has fine large original butterfly hinges. The frame is 11 by 29 inches; the hight, 28 inches; the top, 40¼ (with the grain) by 39½ inches. An odd instance of a gate-leg table which is actually longer *lengthwise* than cross-wise! The turnings are excellent. The original drawer is lost. The table was found in Southern New Hampshire. It is a question what was the source of its red, that is, Virginia, walnut. We simply presume that in such cases the piece was long since brought from a point farther south, or that the cabinet makers on the coast brought up walnut by coastwise vessels at the time when it became fashionable. Not a few Virginia walnut pieces of furniture were made in New England.

A BEAUTIFUL and beautifully preserved slate top table, owned by Mr. Daniel Staniford of Boston, appears on page 387.

Its frame is of walnut. The top is inlaid with what appears to be apple wood, with a single marquetry design on one side. The stone is original, and whole, its size being 14½ by 29½ inches.

The table is in very fine condition. The stretchers are deeply and delightfully worn on three sides, the fourth side having been, probably, against a wall.

The grandfather of the owner taught school using this table for his desk.

Its top is 40 by 25 inches, the width of the border outside the slate is 5¼ inches. The frame is 25 by 19½ inches. The hight is 28 inches. The date is 1690-1710. On page 388 is shown again the table in the Antiquarian Society at Worcester.

On this page appears the dining room of Mr. Geo. F. Ives.

A BEAUTIFUL little butterfly table in curly maple. Owner: Mr. Geo. F. Ives. The top is the narrowest we have seen, being only six inches outside the frame, leaving no room for a draw. The wings are quaintly and unusually shaped. The top is 23½ by 33 inches. The frame at the base is 14 inches, showing a rapid spread. The wings of these tables are always thin—from a half inch to three quarters of an inch.

AN unique Table belonging to Mr. H. W. Erving. This piece combines some features of the butterfly with quaint brackets, which are not at all like the butterfly design. It suggests to us a little the style of the crane bracket. The turned stretcher and the short T of the turned post which sustains the main member of the brackets combine several elements of quaintness. The setting of the bracket under the frame in the gate-leg style, of course, made it necessary to cut away the remainder of the bracket except the outside strut which is framed into the horizontal member. Doubtless the maker had in mind a middle stretcher table and sought to adapt the butterfly design to it. The result was certainly one of great interest and rarity. The eye loves to follow the uniform idea of turning throughout such a piece, a style which indicates a sense of harmony in the mind of the maker, very satisfactory to our thought. This is one of a half dozen pieces in this book which have been published previously. The size is 33 by 37 inches.

Date: 1670–1700.

A VERY dainty small Butterfly Table, the property of the Estate of Mrs. Reinholt Faelten. It is only twenty-one and a quarter inches high. The turnings are highly meritorious. For some reason very small butterfly tables are more sought for than the average size. We may presume it is that defect in human nature which loves the unattainable. The top of this piece is in pine with the tongued and grooved joint. We would not undertake to say what parts of this table, and that on page 402 have been supplied. The molding on the edge of the frame is called by cabinet workers a stone molding, and is quite the usual thing on many old tables. The student will observe there is a considerable difference in the rake of the legs of butterfly tables. In this case the rake is rather extreme but no less attractive. Date about 1700.

A BUTTERFLY Table in the collection of Mr. B. A. Behrend of Brookline. This piece has all the marks of wear which are so delightful to the collector because they enhance the sense of humanness connected with old furniture. The wear of the stretchers is especially noticeable. The table is small and has an oval top. The object of slanting the legs of these tables is obvious. Greater stability was secured, and the slant afforded room for the bracket to swing back against the frame without awkwardness. When the leaf fell it reached the slanting leg which seemed to come out to receive it. The bracket is usually slanted inward somewhat, on the back. Date: 1700—20.

A BUTTERFLY Table, having a pine top with tongued and grooved joint, and a flush drawer. The brackets in this piece are somewhat clumsy and perhaps not original. In this connection an unsuspected refinement in furniture is revealed. Any failure of relation between one part and another instantly asserts itself even if it is no more than one eighth of an inch difference in a bracket. This piece, of course, has lost its feet, but the turned stretcher partly compensates. Date: 1700–10.

This may be as good an opportunity as any to refer to the method of fastening the joints of furniture. Frame work was, of course, always fastened with square pins preferably oak, driven in round holes and bored slightly staggering; that is, the hole on the tenon was a trifle toward the outside of the post. Thus the pin when driven tended to draw the joint together and originated the phrase, perhaps in the mouth of Edwin Simons of Hartford, "a draw-bore pin." The tops were also so bored as to assist the pins in offsetting one another, that is the pins were inserted at different angles so as to overcome the tendency to pull the top free.

A SMALL Trestle Table, with leaves and butterfly brackets. In the possession of Mr. Dwight Blaney. An unique piece. It combines two much sought for forms,—the trestle and the butterfly table. Of this the trestle style is more rare. It is compact, quaint, light and convenient

The other small trestle tables we know have either the one-piece top, or are in the gate leg style. The charm attaching to uniqueness was gained through the little one-man shops of early days. Date: 1690–1700.

A BUTTERFLY Table belonging to Mr. George Dudley Seymour. Curiously the drawer seems never to have had a handle.

The table came from the Captain Charles Churchill House, Newington, Connecticut. Built 1762–3. This specimen, made of cherry, may be later than the usual 1700, and date from Captain Churchill's marriage in 1747. It may, perhaps, have belonged to his forbears, but its fine condition and its being made of cherry favor a later date. The table is in absolutely original condition. It has its original feet and an interesting touch in the curious bosses at the lower ends of its leaf-supporting wings. The leaves are hung on large butterfly hinges. The turnery though simple is refined and well understood. Hight, 27½ inches; top, 40¾ by 45½ inches.

Mr. Seymour has a companion cherry butterfly table, also from the Churchill House in Newington, which table has a rectangular top.

A LARGE Square-leaved Butterfly Table, the property of the Rhode Island School of Design, from the former Nutting Collection. The top of this piece appears to be original, but in matters of this kind there is no absolute certainty, as the top may have been in place for a hundred years. It is indeed often possible by tearing a piece apart to ascertain certainly the originality of a top, but the author frankly believes there is no other way of knowing. This table has an interesting detail in the sockets for the extended cleats of an additional leaf placed at both ends, undoubtedly subsequent to the making of the piece. Thus a table of good size was obtained for a dining room. The oval style is regarded as a better style.

An interesting peculiarity of this piece is a circular hole in the bracket, enhancing the butterfly effect just as a large spot often appears in the butterfly's wing, although this opening was cut more likely to give lightness to the piece where strength was not required. Careful examination by more than one expert has established the originality of this aperture. Date: about 1700.

A BUTTERFLY Table, owned by Mr. H. W. Erving. The design, while simple, is good. The elongated pear feet which have escaped wear are a good example of their kind; the turnings are simple. Date: about 1725.

Below is an interesting variant of the butterfly table, in that the posts are vertical and the top very wide. This style necessitates a different

method of cutting the top of the bracket so that the edge of it shall fall into a slot in the frame.

Date: 1700–30.

Opposite is a small square cupboard with a cut corner panel, and ball feet; also a butterfly table, which are the property of the Rhode Island School of Design. The date of the cupboard is about 1690-1700. That of the table may be 1700–20.

A BUTTERFLY Table, with Plain Stretchers. The draw is not flush, but has the projecting edge with lip, helping us to a date a little after 1700. The present ownership of this table is unknown. Its legs are very much heavier than usual, and resemble more the legs of the standing tables of the 17th Century. The top has an edge which we like, though without reason. It is a rolling edge, without the thumb nail feature. The wood is maple, in the frame; pine in the top. The size is medium.

Butterfly tables are becoming very scarce in their good forms, or even in any form. They have appreciated enormously within five years. It is hardly possible to find a good example within the means of the average collector.

A BUTTERFLY Table, in the possession of the author. It has a drawer with knob, and is all original. It lacks, however, the balls on the feet.

The tongued and grooved joint found on this table and on most pieces before 1725, is counted desirable as a mark of date, yet some of the finest tables in existence have the rule joint. The material of this piece is maple throughout. The size is above the average.

Although Connecticut seems to be the home of the butterfly table, some are found in Eastern Massachusetts and some in Southern New Hampshire so that we must doubt the conclusion at which some persons have arrived that the pieces were all from Connecticut. It is probable that the earlier types had plain stretchers as here shown, whereas the turned stretcher came slightly later, but even this is a point about which it is dangerous to be dogmatic. The turned stretcher is counted more desirable, other things being equal, but size and general style may over-match the lack of turning.

A feature of these tables is that the drawer is slanted inward at the top to correspond with the frame, producing a quaint effect. The handles should always be small wooden knobs. The drawer is usually sustained by a bottom central runner and in a few instances there is a drawer in each end where the table is large. Date: about 1700.

A CURLY Maple Table with crane brackets belonging to the Estate of Mrs. Reinholt Faelten. This table has all the characteristics of the butterfly style, except for the bracket, which is framed together and is very light and thin. Nevertheless, brackets of this type are stronger than the ordinary brackets of a single board, which was very liable to split. The explanation of the rarity of the crane bracket undoubtedly lies in the greater difficulty of construction.

Curly maple came into use, in some instances, probably before the close of the Seventeenth Century. It became very popular for a time and then completely went out after about one generation. The principle of the decoration is against the use of curly maple in a turning, as a turned piece of wood is decorative in itself, and to use double decoration at the same point is confusing to the eye. As a consequence the curly grain should appear only in the plain parts of a piece as the top, the frame rails and the stretchers. Size: Top, 26½ by 35 inches, an ellipse. Hight, 25½ inches. Date: about 1700–20.

A SMALL Turned-bracket Table owned by Mr. Harry Long, from the author's former collection. It is in black paint crackled. The very simple turnings and the odd device by which the bracket member is halved into the frame, like a gate-leg table, are the special features. The device of the bracket, however, allies the piece to the gate-leg table in another way also, for the frame is made vertical, not with raked legs, as is necessary in the "butterfly" pattern. The table is not as stable as the "butterfly" and hence the leaves are made narrower. The top is a circle. Date: about 1700–20.

A CRANE-BRACKET Table. This piece closely resembles that on the preceding page in design. It, however, has great beauty in respect to its turnings, since the crane-bracket is turned to correspond with the rest of the piece, and there is a middle stretcher to stiffen the center, owing to the thrust of the bracket at that point. As there are few other pieces to assist our judgment on dates we must naturally allow a somewhat wide range, but we shall not be far amiss in naming 1690-1710. The original was not available for a photograph hence this sketch has been made in pen and ink. Of all leaf tables it has appealed to the writer more than any other. It has the general appearance of a gate-leg table in all respects except the bracket. This table and the preceding are often classed as butterfly tables, but erroneously so, as they have few features in common. The writer has ventured to add to furniture terms the name "crane-bracket" to apply to these pieces.

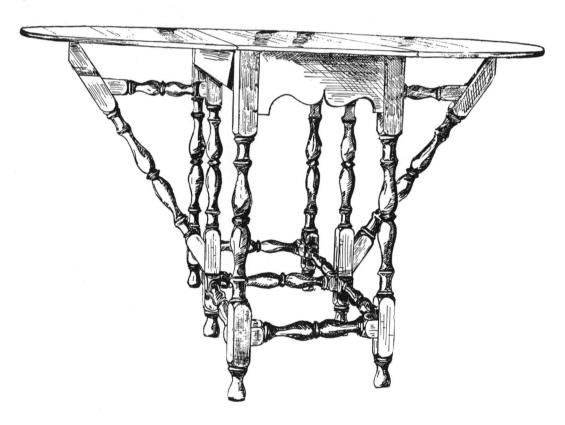

WE enter here upon a discussion of tavern, or tap-room tables. They were so called because of the habit, in early times, of bringing a table to a customer wherever he took his seat. They were therefore small and light, so far as a table for one or two to dine at, could be. But in our day any small table without leaves, and larger than a light stand, is called a tavern table, unless it was clearly made for some other special use, as a dressing table, for instance.

The table above is a fine example in maple of a medial stretcher. The turnings are rarely good. The frame is 17⅝ by 24⅝ inches; the top is 23¾ by 37½ inches, and 25 inches high.

Owner: the author. Date: 1700–10. The lateness of the date is marked by the drawer, which is not flush, as it would probably be, if earlier. The turnings also, one should note, resemble those on the desk, page 115, more particularly the stretcher.

THE Ball-turned Table with high stretcher and scrolled skirt, is of maple, with pine top. Owner: the author. Date: about 1680–90.

The top is 28½ by 37½ inches—a very wide top. In a table of this shape we presume the great width, in proportion to the length, was intended to make a roomy table for four persons.

One notes the absence of any low medial stretcher.

Compare with table on page 418.

Below is a small tavern table in maple, with a small leaf, probably original. Several such tables have been found. Owner: the author.

Such light turning make it certain frequent moving was intended. This table has wide end cleats, a part of the top, as usual. In many cases the cleat was very narrow as in the other table on this page.

The wide cleating was by mortise and tenon; the narrow was merely nailed on. The drawer is flush, but the lightness of the frame suggest 1700–30 as the date.

In the old inventories tavern or tap-room tables are seldom, if ever, mentioned. This arises from the fact that the name has lately been extended, as defined above. Such tables in private houses would be called, if defined specifically in inventories, merely small tables, or perhaps joined tables. That they were common in private dwellings as well as inns has been abundantly proved.

A TURNED Table with Brackets. Owner: Mrs. Insley Blair. Date 1670–80. A fine example with heavy turnings in the vase pattern. The thickness of the top, which has lost its cleats, in more than would be found on a light table. The bracket and the turned drops are marks of good style, and rare. Compare with table on page 411, but more especially with that on page 413, which is strikingly similar, except the top.

It is rightly questioned whether such a table was ever used in a tap room. No doubt this and similar examples, were made for private houses. Indeed their weight hardly classifies them as tavern tables, but they are placed here for want of a better place. Almost all heavily turned tables, in this style, or anywise resembling it, belong in the 17th Century, and not near its end.

A SMALL heavy Oak Table above belongs to Mr. H. W. Erving. Its turnings are the earliest. It resembles those of the chair, page 177. The size of the frame at the top is 14¾ by 8¾ inches and it stands 21 inches high with the feet missing. The date is 1640–60.

At the top of the next page is another very remarkable table. The ownership is private. The legs rake in both directions. It is all original and has a long overhang. The sturdiness and style of the turnings lead us to think it as early as 1660–70. No doubt tables with tops and this overhang were designed for two, one sitting at either end.

At the bottom of the next page is a lighter tavern table with stretchers on the outside. This piece while not important, has much that appeals in a practical way, because it is so light. It is in violent contrast to the other two tables which we thus purposely set off by a more usual example. Owner: now unknown. The turnings are a good example of what may be done with insufficient size of leg.

A HEAVY Oak Table, or Stand. There is here a suggestion in size and sturdiness of the table on page 408. The top is from another old table and is probably too short, it being now 25 by 18¼ inches. The hight is 22¾ inches. The frame at the top is 13⅞ by 8⅝. It is of oak with pine top. Owner: the author. Date: 1660–80. One would say this is rather too small for a tavern table; and a stand is probably a better name.

The number of American oak tables has not been tallied but all known perhaps do not exceed three or four score. By a rough approximation one may presume that about a half of the furniture, left in America, dating before 1700, may have come to light. If we say a somewhat larger ratio of the great pieces, like court cupboards, is known, and a much smaller ratio of the smaller pieces, we shall be nearer a fair estimate.

A WALNUT Heavy Turned Table. Owner: William G. Erving, M.D. The large cup turning, so striking, appears on one or two gate-leg tables we have seen. This table is too heavy for a tavern table; it most probably was used at the side of a dining room. Like most cabinet work of the period it shows a "stone" molding on the upper members of the frame. The legs are massive, and the drawer is on side runners. The top of the table is 29 by 41¾ inches. Its hight is 28 inches. The frame is 21 by 32 inches.

Date about 1680–1690. We think of the furniture of our fathers as heavy. Their passion for permanence was greater than ours. But our impressions of them are not accurate, judged by their remaining work, for the heavy work mostly survived, the lighter being lost.

A HEAVY Oak Tavern Table. Date: 1670–90. Owner unknown. The crude heavy brackets and the general character show the traditions of the middle of the 17th Century. The feet are missing.

The tools of the 17th Century were, with the exception of saw mills, hand tools. The abundant water power introduced the saw mill within a very short time after the settlement. Hewn timber is not even a suggestion of antiquity. Many structures of this generation were hewn, and are being hewn now. It was a question of nearness to a saw mill. The condition of roads was such that transportation of logs by oxen was prohibitory, beyond a mile or two. The turning lathe was the only machine except the saw mill and the lathe was often driven by the foot.

It is necessary to dissect old furniture to understand its structure. Its anatomy will be known and approved in this process. So many old pieces are ruinous, requiring to be re-glued, that we are able to trace the motives of contruction, always a fascinating study, to those who wish to be thorough. Thus at a very early date turned furniture was popular because it was the simplest good style combined with strength. The use of oak in the under body followed the tradition of English strength. The early cabinet makers had none of the fatuous confidence in glue which marks their successors. They knew pinned joints would remain good. Thus they pinned and glued, but if they omitted either precaution, it was the glue.

A HEAVY Bracket Table, with Drops. Date: 1670–90. We do not know about the top, whether it was originally in this form.

Owner: Mrs. G. C. Bryant, of Ansonia, Connecticut.

The tools used by the people of the Pilgrim Century were of wood so far as they could be, as metal was relatively higher in cost then than now. The most numerous tools were molding planes. A builder recently died near his hundredth year, in Portsmouth, who had two chests full of molding planes. A cabinet maker in these times has none, because his work is mostly fitting and assembling. The bit is said not to have been in use. Augers, chisels, saws, and the broad axe, formed the great part of the other tools. Sand paper was not in use. The plane marks can be seen on all early work. The finish was inferior; the substance was superior. The best of the work was out of sight. Now the best shows.

Tables like the above are increasingly rare. Perhaps a score are known. In the inventories such tables would be mentioned as framed, joined or standing, without sufficient description to separate them from other styles. The drops and brackets are never mentioned. But the love of style was very manifest, because it was very rare to omit some effort, in turning, at ornamentation.

TWO Tables of the tavern size and style. Their origin is Pennsylvania. They were in the former collection of the writer. They are of walnut. The scroll of the frame on the upper table is an interesting effort at decoration. The feet of this piece are partly missing.

The table below has on the drawer a crude scratch inlay, a scroll filled in with a white wood. Date: 1700–30.

The medial stretcher on these and other tables was an obvious device to give room for the feet under the table. Incidentally the invention added to the attractiveness of the table. The strength was hardly less, because two mortises at the same hight on the legs, necessary in outside stretchers, were avoided. The turnings of these tables, flattened on the bowl of the vase, are characteristic of Pennsylvania.

The love of ornament is much more strongly marked on the continent than in England. The Welsh seem to love ornament more than the English. But the furniture ornament of America, when not English, was Dutch.

The evidences of Dutch feeling in New York, Pennsylvania and New Jersey, in the carving of kitchen utensils and the decoration of cornices and table frames is very marked.

One wonders at the failure of Italy to impress America directly in the 17th Century in the matter of decorative art. What we had from Italy was first modified by passing through the Dutch and English developments. This is the stranger since an Italian discovered America.

A MAPLE Medial Stretcher Tavern Table. The turnings are odd,
but not specially meritorious. Altogether, however, the table has a charm,
partly because it is all original, unfinished and complete, lacking only a
little of the feet. Date: 1690–1700. The drawer has a lip, hence the late
date. Origin: New England.

Vast numbers of tavern tables have been destroyed. When, about a
generation since, the Wayside Inn tables were sold at auction, they were
knocked off four for a dollar. One man had a stack of them like a winter
wood pile, behind his barn. The American bar was the cause of the loss
of these, among other things. Tavern tables, of a kind, which are more
often mere domestic occasional tables, are among the commonest antiques.
But fine patterns are now scarce. Good specimens are still coming from
their hiding places, and as no two are alike, they afford much interest in
the way of comparison.

The slant leg specimens are most valued. The scrolling of the skirt,
the sturdiness of the turnings, the hight of the stretchers, are points of
importance.

A VERY well turned large tavern table, in the author's possession. It is maple with a pine top. The frame is 21 by 31 inches. The hight is 25¼ inches. The top is 27¾ by 40⅝. The brackets add to its importance. Date: 1680–1700. Below is another tavern table. Date: 1690–1700.

A TABLE in Birch, with High Stretchers. It is the property of Mr. B. A. Behrend. The date is 1660–70. Only the feet are restored. It was found in Milford, Massachusetts, in 1917. The top has a very long overhang, eleven inches or more, greater at one end than the other, proving it was attached without measuring. The balls have between them an incipient ring, and are very sturdy.

The mystery of the high stretcher has never been solved. It was much more in the way of a sitter than was a low stretcher. Yet we prize this style most of all. This is the earliest piece in birch that has come to the author's attention. Occasionally, on the hills, furniture birch was found in Southern New England. Most of the birch in lower New England grows in clusters like tufts of grass, of the gray variety, and is punky and worthless as a furniture wood.

Birch at its best requires a very cold climate. The yellow and black and "canoe" varieties supply a very fine hard wood, not a whit inferior to maple, and better than soft maple. When large, the color is fine. The birch used in the Pilgrim Century was not, for furniture at least, the great trees with dark wood, but the smaller sort. The yellow variety was dark enough without finish.

A HIGH Stretcher, Scrolled Frame Table. It was formerly in the Prouty collection, and is now owned by the author. It has been previously illustrated. We feel the public will not object to seeing a dozen old subjects among so very many newly shown. The scroll of this frame is markedly worthy. The drawer has grooved side runs. The turning is a refinement of the plain ball. Paired plain vases are inserted in the center of the long turnings. The molding carried around the frame is another refinement. The frame is 20½ by 23¼ inches. The top is 22 by 30½ inches; the hight 25¾ inches. Painted black over red, the wood is birch, or maple. The brackets on this table are constructed according to the usual plan. Their ends on the leg are tenoned into a mortise on the legs, but their other ends are merely nailed down to the frame rail.

A BALL Turned Table, with Open Brackets. This table which is owned by Mr. Clauncey C. Nash, is simpler than the preceding. It has the same general features. As an amusing instance of the rapid manner in which a discovery of such a table arouses interest, this table as soon as found changed hands five times in five days, the owners being in three states. It has since been sold twice, and is now apparently where it will remain for long. Date: 1670-90.

In this connection we have the answer to the question: What is the source of so many antiques? In the first instance some seeker finds an antique piece, and sells it to a dealer. Frequently that dealer passes it on to another dealer, who specializes in that particular subject. It then reaches a collector. Collectors are mostly elderly gentlemen. If their fortunes change they may part with their treasures. Their estates, at any rate, are very frequently dispersed and the process begins again. Thus one of the best articles known has been owned by nine different persons in four years. There are not many remarkably good pieces, but they get into the market many times in a changing world.

A HANDSOME Walnut High-Stretcher Table, belonging to Mr. B. A. Behrend. The top is also walnut. The table is one of the most attractive anywhere to be seen. It is small, as appears from its hight in proportion to its other dimensions. We place it very high in order of merit among tables of this kind. Date: 1680–90. Every line is good.

The explanation of the frequent absence of an owner's name lies in the fact that the author has for years, when he has seen a good example of very early furniture, procured a photograph of it. Since then many such examples have passed into various hands which we have not always been able to trace. We are more interested in the style and the period than in the personal equation.

It is unfortunately necessary in this work to crowd rare pieces into small space, and at times to give more than really necessary space. The advantage however of a description immediately adjoining the illustration is too important to abandon.

A HEAVY Turned Bracket Table. Owner: The Metropolitan Museum. A superb example, which should be compared with similar and possibly somewhat inferior previous tables. The frame is 23⅞ by 18¼ inches. The top is 36⅜ by 36¾, intended of course to be square. The leg is 2½ inches square. The hight is 26¼ inches. There is a four inch drawer. It is 12¼ inches to the top of the high stretcher, and 4½ inches to the top of the medial stretcher.

A table so large is an obviously small dining table, or what in modern times we should call a "center" table—a bad name! Date: 1650–70.

Another fine example of a somewhat lighter larger square table, appeared in New York a little time since and was eagerly carried away by a fortunate collector. Perhaps no table is more desirable. It vies with the trestle table, the largest gate-legs, and the most important refectory tables. It lacks no feature counted strong and important.

AN Oak Tavern Table. Date: 1670–90. An oak frame is quite rare and very early. Size of frame, 20½ by 30½ inches. Top, 26 by 40¼ inches. Hight, 26½ inches. The top is pine. The table is wholly original. It was not built with a drawer. Taste in the matter of tables like these has advanced very much in a brief period. Many good judges are much taken with pieces of entire simplicity, if they are in oak and all original, because they convey a strong feeling of unity with the typical life of the 17th Century. Owner: the author.

With this review, we turn our attention to occasional tables. They are always fascinating, because so individual. They assume a wide variety of forms. Before entering on those that could be used for any purpose we show a few dressing tables. These are among the difficult pieces to find.

A CHERRY Six-legged Lowboy, owned by Mr. Chauncey C. Nash. It was originally owned by Anna Rush, whose monument, erected by the women of Streatham, is in the cemetery.

This important little piece was found in Streatham, New Hampshire, where it had always been in the same family. It is all original, neither needing nor having had repairs. Dimensions: top, 34½ by 20½ inches. Hight, 30¼ inches. Frame, 29½ by 17½ inches.

The author does not remember to have seen another low-boy with six legs. Many high-boy bases are masquerading under the name of low-boys, but their larger size and obviously new tops show what they are. Date: 1700–20.

A CROSS-STRETCHER Dressing Table. This example has extra members in the turning of the legs—a pleasing variation. The small drops are missing. The wood as usual is walnut. The balls of the feet on this and most lowboys look very large. That was the style. There is a single arch molding about the drawers. Owner: Mr. Hollis French. Date: 1690–1700.

The derivations of styles of turning, are, like the sources of all things, obscure. The earliest turnings known on English furniture, on great tables, beds, court cupboards, and such pieces were crude, and not classical. The Gothic tradition was reponsible for some forms. Later, the vase shapes are more definitely established and modified to suit the rather attenuated forms of table legs. Italy and the classic ideals were the sources. The ball and ring is also a modification of the classical. So long as turners felt their real purpose of imitation all was well. A turning that cannot be explained is comparatively uninteresting.

A TRUMPET-TURNED Lowboy. Owner: Mr. G. Winthrop Brown. The name of trumpet given to the legs of this piece describes them with accuracy, especially as they are at the tops, without the cup, or inverted bowl turnings of the two lowboys that follow. The double arch mold dates this specimen a little later, about 1700-20. The X scroll stretcher is very simple. The feet here are smaller than any others we have seen. Like other examples, it has the thumb-nail molding. Like all, except the first shown, on page 423, it has the walnut veneer.

The legs of these pieces in walnut, are very often of other woods. Bass is a common wood, and very unsuitable, as it is weak, and this six-leg style is always weak in the legs. In fact, in the corresponding highboys, it is seldom that one or two legs are not broken. On the other hand the scrolled stretcher on a walnut piece, is generally walnut.

A WALNUT Cross-Stretcher Lowboy. With the single arch mold, the date would be 1690-1710. It lacks, as is often the case, the drops on the frame rail. A very large finial at the intersection of the stretchers does its best to make up the loss. Owner: the author.

The trumpet-leg is here capped with a cup, or bell. One notes the bail handles. Such were used, somewhat, at a period as early as this. The lowboy was bought not far from Boston. Eastern New England was very rich in such pieces, mostly lost.

One should measure lowboys and highboys carefully a few times, and thereafter will never be deceived. On reference to pages 72-86 it will be noted the highboys are, on the frame, higher, wider, and deeper from front to back. The lowboy here is 29⅜ inches high; the frame is 18½ by 31½ inches; and the top is 21⅞ by 33¾ inches. The cross stretchers where used, are clearly to afford the user greater convenience for the feet.

A WALNUT Cross-Stretcher Lowboy. Owner: Mr. W. of Boston. Date: 1690–1700. The huge middle drop is a striking feature. It is perhaps not necessary to point out that these drops represent the place where legs would otherwise have been, and show the process of development. In this case the early type would have had five, not six, legs. The stretchers here are more boldly and fully shaped than others we have seen. They are very handsome.

One may see that the drops, and the finial on the cross-stretchers are really only sections of legs tapered off.

There is usually present the thin bent lining under the edge of the frame rail, and forming by its slight projection, a bead. This piece also has only one drawer. For what it may have been designed one hardly knows, as the center drop prevents sitting at it as a dressing table.

A WALNUT Lowboy, with Outside Stretchers. This odd specimen resembles that on page 423 in the style of its stretchers, but unlike that, it has only four legs. The date, with single arch mold, is 1690–1710. The author owns it. The drops are not original, and not correct. They should be larger and bear more resemblance to a section of a leg. This lowboy catches the light in a way to exaggerate, but by that very means to exhibit clearly the condition of the veneer on most lowboys. It is hungry for oil and shows some tendency to chip off.

Though we lament the passing out of most forms of 17th Century furniture we do not feel the same way regarding the flat top highboy. In this we may not speak for any considerable body of collectors. But the impression of fragility which these pieces convey, and their veneer rather than the solid wood, that preceded them, are not as satisfying. Their greater elegance and finer finish probably appeal to a great number of persons.

A WALNUT Table, belonging to Mr. W. of Boston. This rare article shows ball turnings with variations of elongated balls and a ring at the center of the stretchers. The frame also is scrolled, in a half-way contour between ogee moldings and a serrated edge. The top is 13¾ by 23¾ inches, and the hight 25 inches. The molding on the frame rail adds to its importance. Though the feet are missing the bottom stretchers are well up above the floor. Photographed at very close quarters it looks large and high, as compared with the fact. Date: 1680-1700.

A BEAUTIFUL and dainty table owned by Mr. Geo. F. Ives. The turnings are very delicate. Enough of the balls of the feet remain to show their beauty. We have seldom seen so much legitimate wear on stretchers— a thing of much charm. The simple ogee scrolling of the frame, especially on the end, is very attractive. The turning is perfect of its kind. The date is 1690–1710.

The frame is 19 by 26 inches; and the top is 25 by 39 inches. The hight is now 26½ inches, which originally must have been about 27 inches.

It is articles like these that make collecting a joy.

As to the use of such tables, they were admirable for writing or reading, if one placed feet on the rung, and one did! Possibly also such a table might have answered in a tavern, for my lady to sip her—sweet cider, in the parlor.

A MAPLE Table, with a false drawer. The property of Mr. W. of Boston. The hight is 24½ inches; the top is 16 by 25 inches. The knob is original, but the table never had a drawer. With its scrolled frame and plain stretchers the little table boasts no one remarkable feature, but as a whole it is very attractive indeed, being quite perfect, and in the wood we best love. Date: 1690–1720.

An occasional table like this adds much in the way of charm. It seems easy to say that. But—find another! When we think of the multitude that have gone the way of the wood pile, and think of the glory that has departed, we wonder why we degenerated.

AN Oval Maple Table, owned by Mr. W. of Boston, measures 20¾ inches high, to which to get the original hight we must add a good bit.

The oval is 18¾ by 27¾ inches. Small tables are more often in this form than the tavern table. The table on the next page varies slightly from this— a good test of a quick eye for shape.

One may see on this table the usual cleat running across the frame to prevent the breaking off of the overhang. These cleats are let, full size, into the frame. They are very necessary as the tops are thin, generally of pine, and easily split off.

The heavy plain stretchers are early. Date: 1680–1710. It is very light and a joy for convenience.

AN Oval Maple Table belonging to Mr. W. of Boston, similar to but a little larger than that on the previous page, the scale being smaller. The hight, minus the feet, as it stands, is 21¾ inches. The top is 20 by 31 inches. Date: 1690–1720.

On the right is a little table which one might say was a joint stool, so far as size is concerned, but the rather slight turnings incline us to count it a table. It has slant legs, one way, like joint stools—and tables! It is 19 inches high; the rectangular top is 12 by 18 inches, just right for a joint stool. A pleasing doubt arises. Let us call it both, and we have, as the original owners had, two articles in one. The hight is not objectionable for a stool, as at one period chairs ruled higher than this. Of course one must add balls to the feet to get the first hight, and then we have a table! Date: 1690–1720.

We have in the three pieces shown on the two pages open before us a remarkable series, for their harmony, and the strong presumption is that they were made to go together, as now.

A LITTLE Square Stand of oak, with chamfered legs and square stretchers. It came from the Churchill family, Newington, Connecticut. The top and drawer are of pine, and the top has notched carving at the ends like that seen on many chests, bible-boxes and stand-feet. It is in the Wadsworth Atheneum, Hartford, and is owned by Mr. George Dudley Seymour. Date: 1670–1700.

We usually infer in the case of a table with chamfered rather than turned legs, that no lathe was available for the workman. The method of chamfering therefore was used, as on great beams in house construction. It is an attractive style, but required more labor than turning. Pieces to be turned were never sawed first, always they were split.

At the bottom of the page is a rare table, present ownership unknown, with the legs slanting in both directions, and a very well scrolled frame. The feet are well preserved. The few tables of this sort have for the most part plain stretchers and rectangular tops. The date is 1700–1730. The noggin on the left and the other articles were in general use at the date named.

These tables are marked by a wide overhang of the top. Lacking that, one suspects that something is wrong. Table tops are the continual bother of a collector.

A SMALL Octagon Table, in the author's collection. This piece was found in Plymouth. The piece is very perfect and has never been tampered with, or restored, nor does it require it. The top is pine. The paint is all original. The points of merit are the boldly scrolled skirt and the fine condition of the feet and the unusual shape of the top. There is much satisfaction in a piece of furniture which may be left wholly as found.

Size: Top, 27¾ inches; hight, 26¼ inches; frame, 21½ inches square. Date: 1680–1700.

A SKETCH, since a photograph was not available, of a very small table, with hinged top and a hutch under it. The rudimentary vase shape, the simple shoe, the touch of a scroll on the cleats, all suggest, with the heavy fine construction, an early country-made piece of no little charm. It is about two feet high. Date: 1670–90.

Below is what we will name an instep table from the odd shape of the arched shoe. The sides are apparently identical, top and bottom. It is a light, quaint little affair in pine. Owner: Mr. Chauncey C. Nash. Date: 1680–1700.

In the construction of both these little trestles the uprights are mortised into the shoes. The dating of such pieces is frankly

problematical, but in the 18th Century the shoe base of tables seems to have been abandoned almost wholly, even at the beginning.

Pine when knotty as we now find most of it, is difficult to work. But the clear pine available in the 17th Century was a delight. Furthermore where not subject to wear, it is far more durable than oak. Old side wall shingles of shaved pine never decay. In table tops however it literally wore out. In process of time our fathers learned how to use best the woods in their new country. For many purposes pine is the best wood in the world; far better than was available in England.

THE Porch of the Iron Works House, at Saugus. This room is formed by
a square projection in the center of the side of the house, about nine feet
wide, and the result is much to be commended in its effect. There is a
probability, however, that it was shut off from the stair and the doors,
which open on either hand, by a partition, on the house line, under the
main girt. There was no need of that partition, as neither the porch nor
the stair was heated. This house, no longer owned by the author, ought to
be, and may be, sometime redeemed as one of the finest examples of its
kind. The porch is a restoration, but the mortise holes in sill and on girt
were found, also the slant showing how the covering gable had been cut on
the roof boards.

Incidentally the porch exhibits a perfect setting for 17th Century furniture, and already some drawings have been made of the house, with the
purpose of copying it. We cannot too greatly regret that no early collection is yet housed in a sympathetic setting.

A SPLAY-LEGGED Drop-leaf Table, in the former Nutting Collection. This piece, although it has lost somewhat from the feet, is a stocky, quaint, very early specimen. It differs from the usual splay-leg table in this, that the legs spread both laterally and longitudinally. The scrolling of the wide skirt is another interesting feature. It extends around the ends as well as at the sides. The top is altogether original and the leaves are attached by hinges riveted through, an early and a very substantial method. The maple top has acquired the beautiful bleached effect so much sought for in the quaintest and earliest tables. While smaller tables are often made in this style they are extremely rare with leaves. It will be noted that the leaves are narrow so that, contrary to the rule, the top is longer following the grain than across it.

The overhang is very marked and it is possible to sit up to the table without any interference of the legs.

Tables having stocky legs are considered more desirable, in the Seventeenth Century styles, as a sturdy character is consonant with the period. The table was made without a drawer.

Size: 44 by 52 inches, the long dimension being with the grain. Date: 1670–1690

A THREE-LEGGED Table, with a one piece top, in the author's former collection. These tables are sometimes made with three drop leaves, and sometimes with solid one piece tops. This piece is all original. In most cases the feet have to be restored. The advantage of raking the leg was found in increased stability. Three-cornered tables are rare, especially in the Pilgrim century. All that the author has seen have plain stretchers. The tables vary from medium to small sizes, this piece being two and a half feet across, a very large size for the type.

Date: 1690–1710.

AN Oak Triangular Table owned by Mr. Chauncey C. Nash. It is 25 inches high and 28¾ inches across its round top. Date: 1690-1710.

Below is a triangular table, in the Metropolitan Museum, already published, which has three drop leaves operated by swinging the top on a swivel of wood, when all three leaves drop. Date: 1690-1710.

A drop leaf triangular table has been seen, the top of which did not turn. The leaves were held up

by slides, pulled out from the frame, just under the top.

Other things being equal, the slant leg three-cornered table is regarded better than the vertical leg.

The three-cornered table was so made for decorative reasons only, as the cabinet work was more difficult than in the usual form. Such tables have no drawers. The lower table here is very rare in having two ball turnings below the bottom rails, rather than the usual pear turning, corresponding with vase above.

A BEAUTIFUL and rare table belonging to Mr. Geo. F. Ives. Except for the loss of its feet it is in fine condition, and one of the most interesting pieces so far found, of the sort. The turnings are bold, with outside stretchers. The scrolls on the frame are different on the sides and the ends, but in both cases very good. Not once in a blue moon is such an article found. With so narrow a frame so deeply scrolled there could not be a drawer.

Such pieces were of course made for the "best rooms" and we suspect not a few, with drawers, were dressing tables. Sometimes they were convenient as sewing tables. And when a table goes by no other name "occasional" table will do. For use out of doors they were very convenient, for our fathers lived out of doors more than we do.

The date is around 1700. This turning was used for some little time before and for many years after that date.

A SMALL Stand, beautifully turned. The present owner is unknown. The top is not original, and may be three inches too small. There is a resemblance in the turning between this and that on the previous page, with the preference perhaps in favor of that table. A good feature of this table is the bracket effect on the frame secured by merely cutting away. This stand is exactly square, and the top is a circle. Date: 1690–1710.

Below is a triangular stand of small diameter, owned by Mr. B. A. Behrend. Comparing it with that on page 439 it is much smaller and lighter. A good Betty lamp, a very odd candle stick, to hang or carry, and a sand glass rest on it.

A feature of maple, of value to the turner, was its susceptibility to a smooth finish. As it comes from the tool, without polishing, it has a delightful smoothness as if rubbed. Oak on the other hand is rough. Birch and beech also turn smoothly, the latter being remarkable in that respect. Pine turnings were little used, as being weak. Hickory was smooth, but ash became rough. Yet ash was popular because it split in a smooth, straight line, and was thus quickly and with little effort prepared for the turner. As soon as saw-mills become numerous, we note the disappearance of ash from turnings, as maple was better.

TWO small stands owned by Mr. W. of Boston. The upper one of maple, is 23½ inches high, and has an oval top 17 by 23¾ inches in diameter. It is dainty in its turnings, in beautiful condition and has plain stretchers. Date: about 1700. The stand below is only 21 inches high, and the top is 14½ by 15 inches. It has a drawer. The all turned frame is very attractive. We are surprised at the smallness of the top, and at its being square. This is the smallest well-turned stand the author has seen, containing a drawer. Date: 1690–1710. These tables, with those on page 432 and 433 are a rare conjunction under one roof.

One readily infers that the scarcity of little stands like these arises from the fact that a simpler construction, with a single center shaft was usually adopted. In that style two pieces or at most three, took the place of the eight turned members appearing here. Stability and beauty are found in greater degree in the articles here. The use of the lower piece was perhaps as a work stand, with a candle. Candles were placed on lower levels than our lamps, in order to be very near one's work. Such pieces were also convenient at the bedside, or for temporary out-of-door use. Thus the "cobbler's" light was devised to bring it almost in contact with his work. To the introduction of better lights in the "kerosene period" we owe the destruction of stands.

AN Oval Stand, with legs slanting in all directions. It is of maple, and belongs to Mr. W. of Boston. The hight is 21⅜ inches; and the diameter of the top is 18¾ by 25¼ inches. Date: 1700 or thereabouts.

The all-slant leg stands have been called common. It is very seldom one is seen. We know of a dozen or so in different sizes. Of what size a piece must be to be counted a stand rather than a table is largely as one pleases, on the dividing line between 16 by 21 and 20 by 26 or something of that area. Below the smaller size one should not doubt that the piece was a stand, that is, made to sustain a candle or other small object rather than for general use.

The preference of the early cabinet-makers was for square rather than turned stretchers, because they secured greater solidity with the square stretcher. The turning of the stretcher was purely for ornamental reasons. One should not therefore look for something better than a square stretcher. It is found on the earliest and best furniture.

ON the right a stand, with a frame 12½ by 15½ inches; a top 21½ by 24 inches; and a hight of 23½ inches. Period of 1680-1700. The top is oval. It is all original. Owner: the author.

At the bottom is a small table with a band-box of wood. The name was acquired through the use of such boxes for starched bands before their use for bonnets and hats came in. The cover snaps on with a wooden spring. The table is prettily turned, and is all original. It is the prop-

erty of the author. The frame is 14¼ by 20¼ inches. The top is 18 by 27 inches; and the hight, 24 inches. Date: about 1700.

The literature of band boxes comes under a later period, but it may answer some question to say that the quaint paper on band boxes was put on them to match the rooms in which they were kept for guests. Thus, whenever the room was repapered the band-box had another layer added, and was thus kept fresh. A box like that here shown was for transportation with its handle, and so made of wood. The leather hat box was not so early.

The name trunk early appears in inventories. It is therefore not an Americanism, but an English survival.

A SCALLOPED Frame Table belonging to Mr. Geo. F. Ives. The top is 24 by 31 inches. It is 27 inches high. The idea of the wide frame rail, against the legs, is to secure great rigidity. The effect is good. The turnings are odd. Compare this table with that on page 444. The date is about 1690–1700.

The distinctiveness of local types of furniture arises from the difficulties attending transportation in the early days. There was much moving, owing to the unrest felt in a new country, and the desire to take up land in quarters beyond. But in such cases auctions were frequent. So that which was made in one district remained there unless it could go by stream.

Below is a stand with a large pewter pitcher. They are the property of Mr. B. A. Behrend. It is small in the frame, but like most small tables of the period has a long overhang. Date: About 1700.

Curiously the name stand does not appear in the early inventories. Table was made to do service for stand. We find standard very rarely, but its meaning is somewhat doubtful. We fail in the published inventories of this time to find even a wash-stand. And it is always a candlestick, never a candle stand.

A discussion as to what was used for a wash-stand cannot be dismissed by the flippancy, "they did not wash." Small tables were used.

A SMALL Stand which passed through the hands of Mr. Henry V. Weil of New York City. The feature of special attraction, of course, is the turned cross stretchers, combined with the raked leg. We ask ourselves in wonder why pieces of this sort which are so captivating were not oftener constructed. We must, with humility, conclude that our race is not marked by prevailing good taste. Let us at least seek in furniture for that which possesses some charm aside from the purely utilitarian aspect. It was very convenient to draw between the knees.

A SMALL High-stretcher Trestle Table, the property of the author. The top is pine and the rest maple. The features of special attraction are first the trestle form and second the high turned stretcher. This piece is altogether original and unrestored. It was found in Connecticut. The chamfered shoe appears as in the rare great trestle tables. The convenience of such tables is apparent, as they can be drawn very close to the sitter, and were available as tap room tables, light stands, or for any purpose where a light removable piece was desired. The use of a foot or shoe of this character seems to have gone out completely about 1700. A curious feature of construction is that the cleat is almost precisely of the same contour and size as that of the shoe so that we really have a double T, braced together and surmounted by a board.

Size: Top, one piece, 30 by 18½ inches. The shoes are 15½ inches long. The hight is 25¼ inches. Date: 1650–1680.

A SMALL Trestle Table owned by Mrs. Anna H. Howard of Whitman, Massachusetts. Comparing it with that on the previous page we see this has two turned trusses, while that has one, but that has a high truss. This has an oval top, that a rectangular top. They are great rarities. Date: 1660–1680.

A peculiarity here is that the shoes are wider than the posts. These tables belong with the trestles and boards, but date a little later.

THE Parlor in the John Alden house, Duxbury. The picture was made in 1921. It is understood that wherever paneling appears in a 17th Century house it represents an addition to the original finish. The paneling here may have been added around 1720–30. It is quite unusual for an arch to show on a colonial fireplace. This instance therefore is full of interest. The author remembers generalizing on one occasion, with the statement that the fireplaces of the early American house had a flat top. Here is the low arch! The spinning jenny at which Priscilla is always drawn by artists is shown here awaiting her. Also the candle stand, on the floor. It is of tin, at the base, a simple and good sort which is elsewhere shown in other shapes in this book.

The effect here of the five small panels above the large fireplace panel is very good. The corner cupboard was originally, of course, without a door above, and was oval at the top.

This house is owned by an association of the Alden family, and is thus, if it escapes fire, destined to become a shrine of the highest interest to Americans. In process of time, we may look for restorations to be made in the house, at least in the kitchen, though the paneling in some of the other rooms might well remain. No other spot except Plymouth Rock has so many fine associations connected with it.

THE subject of little stands, and candle stands proper, has never received much treatment, and we therefore have laid special stress on placing them before the reader in some profusion.

On the left is a little trestle stand belonging to Mr. Chauncey C. Nash. It much resembles the larger stands on pages 448 and 449. It will be noted that in the true trestle styles the shoe and the cleat above, whether or not attached to the table, are similar, so that the effect is that of a capital I with the horizontals much extended and chamfered nearly to a point. Date: 1660 or thereabout.

The other stand has a movable rod in a socket, with a wooden thumb nut to secure it. The minute feet, mere pins, are droll. Little adjustable stands are often called shoemaker's. It is quite impossible to date this piece accurately. We may say 1700–30. It passed through the hands of Mr. Henry V. Weil who furnished the photograph. In its turnings and general contour its like is hardly known.

TWO Candle Stands of which the left hand one is maple. Its heavy construction and general lines make it desirable. The cross-base is very good. It is maple. The hight is 26½ inches. The diameter of the top is 12 inches. Date: 1670–1700.

The right hand stand is of walnut. The hight is 25½ inches, and the round top is 12 inches. The foot is neatly molded. The post is set on the base quartering, and is fluted part way up, showing the influence of the architecture of 1720–60. The date may be 1710–30.

The feet of this piece have worn down somewhat, so that it may be said to be suffering from fallen arches; but the other pieces were created flat footed. They are both the property of the author.

The need of candle stands in the old days was imperative, as one reading required the feeble light directly beside his text. We remember seeing old people read, holding candles in their hands.

A PAINTED wall and stair in the hall of the Warner Mansion at Portsmouth. This picture is inserted here to suggest the relation between decorative furniture and painted walls. The construction began on the Warner House about 1712, it being perhaps the earliest example of a gambrel-roof in this country. The wall decoration is fairly well drawn, but without the slightest reference to perspective. It is carried from the base of the stair to the second story, spreading out in the well room above the landing to a wide extent. What we see here is a dog protecting a child from the attack of an eagle or vulture; behind is seen the mother of the child at a spinning jenny. The photograph appears indistinct, but the fact is that the painting itself is so injured by time that a better effect is perhaps not possible. Various figures of persons and animals appear on the landing.

The furniture of this house is to a considerable extent of the period of its erection, or only a little later.

The painted wall came in as a substitute for panel work, just as a little later wall paper served the same purpose. The panel was retained in the form of a dado only to a hight necessary to protect the plaster

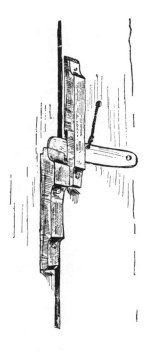

THE Latch-string is out. We are "at home." When we wish to be private we pull it in. The courteous understand.

The latch is all of wood, and will outlast an iron one. Let us go in and see some of the details of 17th Century work. The edge of the drawer shows the construction of the period 1640, with the great nails and the beginning of the groove on which the drawer runs.

The other drawer edge shows the early style of dovetail. The other end of the drawer was sometimes dovetailed and sometimes nailed. The bottom of the drawer was set in as a panel at a later period. Before 1700 it was usually entered in a groove of the drawer front, but on all other sides was nailed. In the vast majority of instances these interior construction pieces were of pine. Sometimes, very early, the sides of the drawer were oak.

The right hand example has an oak side and a pine bottom. It is from a court cupboard of 1650. The other example is from a chest of drawers of 1700.

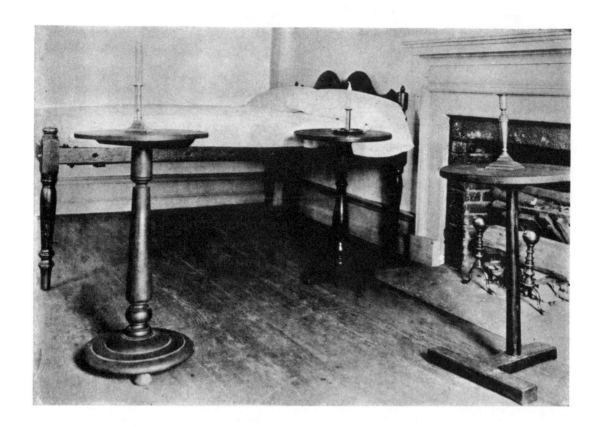

A CHAMBER in the Nathan Hale birthplace at Coventry, Connecticut. Mr. George Dudley Seymour has at much pains restored this fine old house. But the time he has expended on it is still more valuable. The picture shows an oak bed. The correctness of the restored feet, the owner states, may be debated. The date may be late 17th or early 18th Century.

There are in this picture three excellent candle stands, each a type of a class. That with a circular base has three ball feet. Hight 28 inches; diameter of top 16¼ inches. Date: about 1720–50.

The remote stand has a spider base, with arched oak cross members, supporting a maple shaft, mortised to receive a profiled cleat sustaining the round pine top. Hight, 27 inches; diameter, 16 inches. Date: 18th Century. On the right is a T-base stand, so made that the part supporting the shaft is between the feet of the sitter, who placed his feet on the other cross member. The post is maple. Hight, 25 inches; diameter of top, 17¼ inches. Several such stands are known; another is shown in this work.

OF all Candle Stands this one, which has only one or two known counter-parts, is thought most desirable. Its merit consists in the complete carrying out of the idea of a screw post, which is adapted also to the small wood hand screws under the candles, in order to lift them as they burn down. The writer who found the stand in old Concord, does not know the present owner. The round table screws up and down on the post, as well as the candle bar. The parts are all maple; the diameter of the little table being about 14 inches. The stand has never been painted, but is in the natural maple. The date is impossible to fix but is thought to reach back to the 17th Century. The table has a slight lip; the ends of the bar have small turned knobs.

The metal sockets on such early stands are usually of tin. The use of heavy brass is always suspicious, showing probable restorations from Russian candles. It is impossible to know whether tin candlesticks are early. While these adjustable stands were of course used by cobblers it is a mistake to restrict them to that origin. They are too good for that use, many being quite ornamental. They were reading or sewing lights. The best homes required something of the sort.

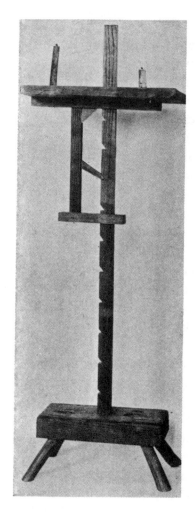

ON the left is a poor relation, owned by the author, of the stand described on the previous page. A considerable number have been found, and they are prized, having both bar and table. The right hand piece is a ratchet candle-stand, having a device to take the place of the screw in raising and lowering. It is owned by Mr. Geo. F. Ives. These pieces, and similar stands, were made all through the 18th Century. Some of them may go back farther than that. The crudeness of some of them indicates that they were mere work stands, for cobbling, or any close work requiring good light. A toggle arm bracket of wood attached to the wall was also used. It was made like the modern five-foot sectional rules.

ON the left is Mr. B. A. Behrend's stand surmounted by a Knicker-bocker or Pennsylvania carved spoon rack—a good decorative piece, with all the flavor of Dutch love for decorating simple things.

The stand on the right, Mr. G. Winthrop Brown's, is very fine in its style. The heavy shaft with its huge ball at the base and the well-turned legs are notably good. A well-decorated pipe box and a Betty lamp, on a standard, are on the top. This is a rare form of the lamp.

A QUAINT Stand has its cross-bar raised and lowered by inserting a peg in holes at intervals on the pole. The third light, on the top of the pole, was the one, probably, left burning when a member of the family was out late! The other two stands are very simple. On the left hand stand we see a wedge inserted in a hole of the bar beside the post, to keep the bar in place. Others similar are known. The other stand which has a square, rather than a turned, shaft, on good feet, holds up candles caught on its bar by the handles of the candle sticks themselves. Originally a better balance must have been devised, as the candles tip too much.

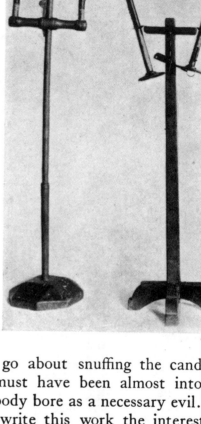

There are other endless varieties of little stands. It was necessary, on occasions of importance, to supply something like a hundred candles in a sizable house. One may imagine a corresponding variety of stands. One servant was deputed to go about snuffing the candles. In summer without screens the insects must have been almost intolerable. But nothing is said of what everybody bore as a necessary evil.

Since the author began to write this work the interest in candle stands has led to some remarkable achievements on the part of the unscruplulous. Some stands, on examination, prove to be made by inserting spinning wheel legs in an adapted bed post! The mortise holes should be looked for as they can be seen easily, though carefully filled. Again, stands are sometimes "improved" by new tops, new legs and new candle sticks until their original makers would remark, as a widow did of a portrait of her husband, painted from memory: "That's he; but how the old man has changed!"

Of course the question often arises what is allowable in restoration. But the question ought to be speedily settled in the case of unimportant pieces that are half gone. The author recently saw in a single shop, a half dozen all-new candle stands, all masquerading as old.

MR. HENRY V. WEIL furnishes the picture of the left hand stand, an amusing instance of solidity. The maker, like the maker of the one-hoss shay, determined to build one that *couldn't* be knocked over. It has an octagon top. The ends of the feet are notch carved on three sides. Date: 1680–1700.

The other stand, belonging to Mr. B. A. Behrend, is a notably sturdy specimen, with notch carved toes, chamfered square post, and large round top. There is sufficient weight to permit a top larger than usual. We incline to date this stand inside the 17th Century.

In the construction of these stands the tapered cleat at the top, on the better specimens, is connected with the post by mortise and tenon. The cross base is halved together. The top is nailed from below through the cleat. We have reason to believe that the stands of wood were much more numerous than the iron stands. The convenience of changing a candle-stick from a stand to a table was no small item.

THE Parlor at the Nathan Hale Birthplace, owned by Mr. George Dudley Seymour. In the foreground on the left is an original rocker. The rockers are of oak. The posts are shown turned with a taper proving they were designed to dowel into rockers. The profile of the fine arms does not show. The hight is 45 inches. The origin was Willimantic. Date: about 1700–20.

The pair of spindle-backed mushroom foot side chairs are maple with hickory spindles. The turnings are unusual and fine. From the Capt. Charles Churchill House, Newington. The chairs may be called transitional. Date: 1700–30.

The table in the center is an excellent example of a small 17th Century turned table with square stretchers.

This room has a narrow door in the paneling at the left of the fireplace, opening through a closet and a kind of secret passage to the so-called "Judgement Hall" or room at the rear. The passage is called the fat man's misery, but a recent very large President of the United States got through, though minus certain garments.

The table on the remote left, with scrolled edges, is a little late for this work, but was a worthy specimen of its time.

ON the left is a ratchet candle stand, date around 1700, and a Betty lamp, on a piece of Virginia pottery. They are owned by Mr. H. W. Erving. The feature noticeable about many candle stands, as here, is their huge bases, to avoid the danger of oversetting them. The Betty lamp shows plainly the spike and hook. The Betty lamp standard is of red clay with a coarse black glaze, and is from the old pottery formerly at Morgantown, W. Va. It is similar in texture to the folk pottery of New England and Pennsylvania and is of early 19th Century date.

The candle stand on the right belonged to Mr. Henry V. Weil. It is odd in having a mere shaft on top of which the candle was fixed. The simple stick leg device, which preceded the Windsor chair type, was used not a little in very early stools and other small pieces as long ago as the 17th Century. It seems to be dateless, continuing to be made in this form now.

A certain largeness of view must be maintained regarding dates, and regarding uniqueness. We wish to go on clear record here as giving dates only on the opinion of the best judges. "Sports" in furniture, born out of due time, are known. And a thing that is unique today may not be to-morrow.

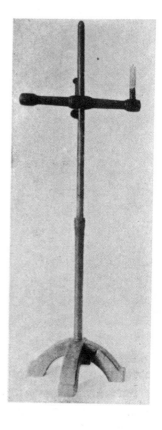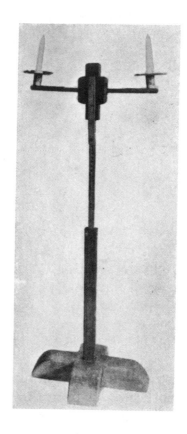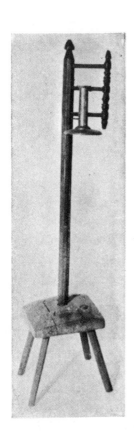

A WEDGE-BAR Candle Stand on the left belongs to Mr. Hollis French. The base is more strongly arched than usual. Date: about 1700–10. The middle stand belongs to Mr. B. A. Behrend. It is adjustable; the lower part of the post being hollow. The right hand stand, with the same owner, presents the oddity of three bars on any of which a candlestick can be hooked to change its elevation. These two pieces may date any time in the 18th Century.

There ought to be some systematic effort under responsible persons, to bring to light the remaining 17th Century furniture. At present intrusive and often uninformed persons press their way into residences remote from the great cities. The householder is suspicious and often has a right to be so.

If some of our reputable societies could father a scheme to make a careful census, by accredited agents, of all our older settlements, no doubt a hearty response would await inquiries now rebuffed. A photographic record could be made and a fair valuation given if desired to prevent subsequent exploiting by the unscrupulous.

A FINELY Turned Stand here shown, is the property of Mr. Geo. F. Ives. It properly has not a whirling table, as the screw is cut too high to serve for that purpose.

The turnings are very good. The feet have an extreme and humorous spread, so that they are nearly horizontal. Date: about 1680–1700.

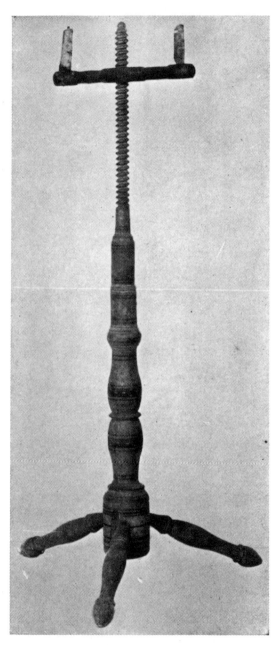

Among the societies which have interested themselves particularly in very early furniture, the Walpole Society, a small social organization of collectors, which has also published valuable literature, may be mentioned. The Society for the Preservation of New England Antiquities more particularly directs its attention to old houses. It is, however, gradually acquiring some early furniture by gift.

The Metropolitan Museum, through acquiring the Bolles Collection, stands at the head in the number of its important pieces. The Rhode Island School of Design is slowly acquiring such furniture to supplement its wonderful Pendleton collection of mahogany.

Collectors are humanly sensitive regarding their gatherings. One must therefore tread warily, especially in New England, among private collections, if one wishes to live there. There are, it is true, some collectors too proud to show pride. Their generous enthusiasm is hidden behind the New England reticence. We must take it for granted that rare judgment is not found among the boastful.

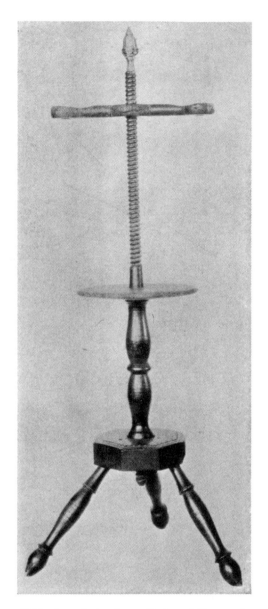

ON the right is a Pair of Rare Candlestands, which were evidently made to go together, as the turnings strongly resemble one another. The lower piece shows the desirable type of a heavy shaft into which turned legs are inset at an angle giving sufficiently broad base. These pieces are the property of George F. Ives, who is to be congratulated upon their possession since they are perhaps unique taken together.

On the left is a fine example of a wooden candlestand, the property of Mr. Ives. It is peculiar in that the small table is not fitted with a screw to rise and fall, but sets upon a shoulder formed by the turning. The finial of this piece is in brass. Date of all three stands: about 1690–1720.

FOUR Candle Stands belonging to Mr. B. A. Behrend. Similar types have already been shown, except the second stand, which with a large saucer shaped hub, exhibits some differences. The pieces date from 1690 to 1730.

The fine but small collection of 17th Century furniture in the Concord Antiquarian Society's rooms has already been referred to. The Essex Institute of Salem has a few important pieces, but their wonderful costumes are their chief asset. The Brooklyn Public Museum possesses a considerable collection.

The Worcester Antiquarian Society collects only that furniture which has an historical flavor. The Wadsworth Atheneum and its allied societies possess or have on loan many good pieces. The Deerfield Museum has a few very early specimens. Pilgrim Hall at Plymouth has a few priceless relics.

Unfortunately the local historical societies are often warped from their higher usefulness by the social feature which compels them to accept unworthy furniture. Gradually, it may be presumed, they will adopt rules by which nothing late can be accepted, and nothing of any date accepted without being passed on by experts. One such organization, outside of New England, has been sadly hoaxed.

A PAIR of Candle Stands both with unusually well shaped feet, but otherwise not claiming description other than that already given. Owner: the author. Date: about 1690–1710.

Private collectors in America have within the past twenty or thirty years gathered to themselves the most of the best 17th Century furniture. The private collector has the advantage of all necessary authority and enthusiasm on the spot where a particular article comes to public attention. Since each collector specializes on, or at least best loves, certain classes of objects, the result is that the important articles are gathered and classified. Thus, leaving out of account all mahogany furniture, there is more than one private collection more important than any public collection with the possible exception of the Metropolitan Museum.

Up to the present time no great museum has systematically sought Americana in furniture.

A CANDLE Stand of much attractiveness, and out of the ordinary is that on the right, which passed through the hands of Mr. Henry V. Weil. It is beautifully made.

It has its lower and its upper table. The upper table stands on a small sliding standard, which is held at any desired point by a wooden pin thrust through a hole in the standard. The lower, larger table has a good rim. The base and uprights are maple; the shelves or tops are pine. Date: 1700-1750.

Below are three simple stands, one with a perfectly square hardwood chamfered base. This sort was in most common use.

The wedge adjustment is not as crude as it looks. It was the quickest, most secure device of all.

The burning of tallow candles was at first too expensive. The bayberry furnished a wax much used, and now revived

by lovers of the quaint. The pine knot was the commonest original light. The influence of artificial light on social habits might become an interesting study.

No doubt the pilgrim habit of rising with the sun was induced by an early and successful effort at daylight saving. "Early to bed" made one wealthy. "Burning the candle at both ends" passed into a proverb. One who passed through the tedious process of making candles, as the author did when a boy, was not likely to waste them. A thrifty habit was supposed to be shown by careful use of candles. The classic story is that of a dying man who on seeing two candles burning, uttered as his last word, and with a deeper pathos than he intended, "One candle is enough to die by."

AN Octagon Hub Candle Stand, with sturdy turned legs. In this specimen the candles were stuck directly into the holes in the candle bar, without tin sockets, and were held in place by a good fit only. It belongs to the author, and dates about 1700.

The principal occupation of the early home, aside from food preparation, was the manufacture of the household textiles, none of which were bought. Wearing apparel, aside from buckskin and fur, was exclusively made of wool or flax. The housewife was complete mistress of the art of taking raw wool or flax and carrying each through every process until the product of the flock or the field appeared in the completed garment. The flax process consisted in ripening, beating and hatcheling. The wool process was carding. Then each, carried so far, must be spun and woven or knitted. This process occupied in many cases more than half of the waking hours of a house-wife.

On the right is a tape loom.

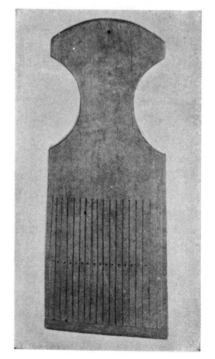

The art of weaving as practiced by our fore-mothers was carried on sometimes in a special room, as a full-sized loom occupied a large space. The parts of the loom were very heavy, traditionally, to prevent vibration. Hence the Biblical phrase, "a weaver's beam" as a simile for great size and strength. The bleaching was done as now in Ireland, by exposing the finished linen to the sun and rain on the grass. The dyes had nothing to do with the manufacture of munitions. Indigo might be imported but butternut was a standard for men's wear, and various vegetable dyes locally concocted answered for all other shades.

[470]

THE distaff on spinning jennies varies from the staff here to a less elaborate sort as seen in the piece below. This is prettily turned and very daintily made. This spinning jenny has the well wrought wheel, the spokes of which are neatly turned. Such wheels, of course, are made in segments and are turned with beads, and in some cases are very decorative, especially when made in parti-colors. Owned by the author.

Below is a rare form of a spinning jenny, with double treadles. It is owned by the author. There is one in the Stanton House, Clinton, Connecticut, and Mr. H. W. Erving of Hartford, also has one. The construction almost suggests the shape of the chair frame. The double treadle, of course, added greatly to the convenience of the operator, especially if she were not thoroughly skilled. A feature of this piece is that the hand screw at the left near the top of the post, when loosened, permits the head to be swung upward and inward so as to be out of the way. Incidentally also, when the head is lowered again it can be set at any degree of tautness, a great convenience, as the pulley was inclined to stretch.

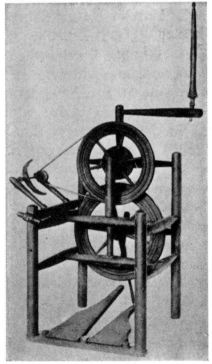

THE LADY spinning above was caught in the act, not posed for the occasion. She is using the ordinary spinning wheel which accomplished in wool for household uses the purposes of the spinning jenny for flax. The wool wheel was used up to a later period than the flax wheel. The spindle was attached in leather; a turned stick called a "wheel pin" was used to avoid the blistering of the fingers in turning the wheel. The lady above stands in a recessed porch. She was eighty-four at the time this picture was made and had always spun for herself everything needed for the mittens and socks of the family.

The hand-spun yarn was usually rather coarse and soft and made warm material when knitted. For weaving it was necessary for good work to spin a finer yarn. The attics of the country still hold many thousands of wheels like that above. They are in no respect desirable in modern homes, except to fill a vacant space, which certainly they are amply qualified to do as they are large and awkward. A sharp contrast is suggested between the time when all such work was done by hand and the present period when it is estimated that one firm of cotton spinners is making as much yarn as every woman in the United States could spin if she devoted all her time to the work.

A DOUBLE Spinning Jenny is a rarity. The one here shown is arranged to spin two threads at once. It must have required a spinner of wonderful skill to keep it going. Fingering four part music on the piano would be easy in comparison. The double wheel was the foreshadowing of the machinery that was to follow, so that one spinner could attend an entire battery of jennies. Date: 18th Century. Owner: Mr. L. C. Flynt, of Monson.

The wheel below is a bobbin wheel. On it was wound the yarn to prepare it for the loom. The bobbins were placed within the shuttle. It was a long and intricate process. A card for combing the wool lies on the frame.

The various contrivances for making butter and cheese are too simple to require illustration further. Hulling of corn by wood lye; braying of corn in a great mortar, before the day of mills; the manufacture of hominy, called now in the South grits; the sanding of floors; were a part of the duties with which a housewife could amuse her leisure hour. If any time remained there were candles to dip, scouring to do, braiding of mats, boiling of rush lights. Every one was supposed to be busy when not asleep.

The men in stormy days had clapboards to split, shingles to shave, ax and scythe and fork and shovel handles to hew. The littlest girls were knitting with grandmother. The young boys made birch brooms with grandfather, and always, when all else failed, children were told to think of their sins. This method prevented them from thinking up new ones.

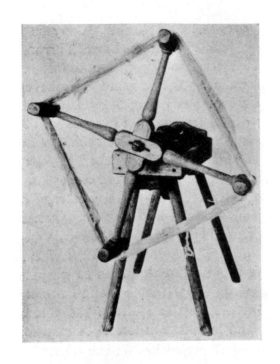

ON the previous page are four forms of reels for taking the yarn off the spindle where it was spun. They all have some device for checking the lengths into skeins.

The lower left one with rare bent legs belongs to Mr. B. A. Behrend; the others to the author.

Above is the process of weaving rag rugs, such as that on the floor. Weaving is still done by hand in the South, and Northern people have encouraged a fad for "homespun." It wears well but has little other merit.

ABOVE is an embroidery frame of much interest. It is owned by Mr.
W. of Boston, and the construction is a nice piece of work. It has the trestle
foot, or shoe. The frame swivels on the posts, and
is held in the proper angle for work by two hand
screws. The work was kept taut by turning the
wooden nuts on the side bars, thus making the frame
adjustable to any length. The worker stood before
the frame. All parts are turned. We are unable to
fix anything like a definite date. We regard it as an
18th Century piece.

The other smaller frame was adjustable in hight
as well as in slant to the convenience of one sitting.
There is a universal joint of wood, the female member of which is split and adjusted rigidly by a hand
screw. The hoop is wound with cloth and a second
hoop is clamped over it, avoiding any need of
basting.

[476]

A SPINET with Spanish feet. Made by Thomas Hitchcock. Date: about 1690. It is said the frames, and the pine music drawers were made in this country. Hence, the piece is introduced here. The strings are plucked by quill plectrums. The feet are a specially good adaptation to a light leg, and are a good example of how the thing could be done. Attention is called to the matter, since there are so many awkward Spanish feet. These instruments have but one brass wire to each note. The piano had not been invented. One should notice that the figures after a maker's name on the early instruments are not a date, as so many suppose, but the number of the instrument. This piece was in the Hazen Garrison house, Haverhill, and we think is now in the Brooklyn Public Museum. The shape is quite like that of a baby grand piano. The wood is walnut, with inlays in front.

The tops of these instruments were so thin that in most cases warping cannot be prevented in a modern house, where the air is too dry for the good of any furniture. A method of cutting very fine parallel lines, with a saw, on the under side of a warped top is advised. The cuts stop short of cutting through to the opposite surface. The board may then be flattened easily, and kept in place by working into the narrowed saw cuts a composition of sawdust and glue, or very thin pieces of wood.

A HARPSICHORD, that is, a harp-shaped instrument of music. It is a larger and more elaborate, and a better instrument than the spinet. It was the immediate precursor of the piano. Some of these instruments were very large—even exceeding in this respect the modern piano.

There were spinets and harpsichords both square and upright in shape, but the style here is the finest. There was usually more than one string to a key, sometimes as many as four. There were sometimes two keyboards, for soft and loud effects respectively. These instruments were regularly used in all dramatic music. The instrument shown is in the Benning Wentworth Mansion, Newcastle, New Hampshire, near Portsmouth. These instruments are of the 17th and 18th Centuries.

As to fine musical instruments as well as clocks, the 17th Century was too early to develop such articles to any extent in America. We find American cases, or parts of cases. The works were probably all imported. The wood is quite generally walnut indicating a date between 1670 and 1730.

In most households a pitch pipe or a tuning fork was all the instrument that could produce musical vibrations, except the fair throats of the pilgrim daughters. The words were lined out in church, and comical tales are told of audiences mistaking some interjected remark of the leader for words of the hymn, whereupon they proceeded to sing with fervor "My throat is very sore, I scarce can speak any more." Happily people can do what they must. Jonathan Edwards preached a sermon to prove it was a sin not to sing. Were he living now, in an apartment, he would know better.

A SPINET formerly belonging to the niece of David Brainerd, missionary to the Indians. It is owned by the author. He procured it in Haddam, Connecticut, from the family in which it had always been handed down. The name is Jacobus Kirckman, (*Londini fecit*).

The base is maple whereas the case is handsome walnut inlaid in front.

The method of adapting the frame to the instrument was curious. At the top of the frame were little iron spurs, pointing upward. Wherever the case is set down these spurs sink into the wood and prevent movement. But the placing of the frame must be about right to get the instrument to cover it perfectly. These spurs are an argument that the instruments and the frame were not constructed at the same place and time. Thus the case can be lifted off bodily, without tools. The brass hardware on these instruments is of very fine pattern and workmanship.

There was no special change in most musical instruments used at an early period in America, to warrant their introduction here. Of course even the spinet was rare. Small musical instruments prevailed, such as the harp, violin and pipes.

A ROOM arranged with highboy, lowboy, early Queen Anne looking glass, 17th Century high stretcher table and three Carver chairs. The fireplace is of the style closed in summer with variously painted fireboard. The minute pewter cup on the table was probably for medicine—it is too small even for the strongest strong waters. The warming pan is of the early variety, having the iron, rather than the wood handle. A foot stove such as was carried to church, and used in sleighs on cold rides, appears. The material burned was charcoal. The arms are somewhat earlier than the revolution and are preserved mainly because this room shows the gun room of the town of Framingham in the revolution.

Powder horns were often carved as in the one showing here. Good horns were translucent so as to reveal by holding against the light the amount of powder in reserve. The fireplace is twenty years late for our period.

After a careful inquiry the author is unable to find any authority to inform us when braided and drawn-in rugs were first made. The Indians understood braiding, but so also did the colonists. We shall probably never know how early braid was worked into rugs.

A ROOM in the Ipswich Historical Society's house, otherwise the Saltonstall house. It is in some respects the most interesting early American house, but not to go beyond our province, we show the great fireplace as a suggestion of the manner in which utensils and furniture were grouped about it. Mantels are often a later addition.

The tin oven also is after our period probably. The oven is in the wall in the rear of the fireplace, and never by the side of it.

The churn, in winter was drawn near, or placed far from the fireplace, according as the temperature of the cream required "to make the butter come." A swift, or yarn reel, attached to the table on the extreme right is the only one of the sort we illustrate. It was later than those that stood on the floor.

A broom made of one piece of birch shows. A large stick was stripped down in shreds and tied down, the remaining stick forming the handle. It was very serviceable.

A ROOM giving a 17th Century arrangement of a Hadley two-drawer chest, a "tuckaway," or folding gate-leg table, a Carver baby high chair, a Flemish-legged highboy, a 17th Century pine desk, a scrolled-foot side chair, a joint stool, a wainscot chair and a leather back chair, all original. Also a Spanish foot gate-leg table. The shutters are a little late for the setting, but only a score of years. Such other articles as appear may explain themselves.

The requirements in furnishing an entire room with ample intervals, if the space is about 16 feet square, are ten to a dozen pieces. More are here gathered at one side for a picture's sake, than would be wholly appropriate in use. The attraction of early furniture consists mostly in its grouping. The museum method is necessary perhaps for study, but charm is gained by a room setting.

Paint may have been used on walls, as we know it was in a decorative way, on furniture in the 17th Century; but the presumption, in America, is against it.

[482]

THE Chest picture above was received too late to supply data. It is a very interesting variant of the Hadley chest found early in this volume. The introduction of the sunflower or aster ornament, so generally found in the Connecticut sunflower chests, allies this specimen more closely with Connecticut. The other Hadley chests, obviously, were free from that influence. The photograph was furnished by Mr. Geo. Dudley Seymour.

To fit 17th Century furniture a room may have a wall covered with pine sheathed panel work. Every other board is thin, like a panel. No attention is paid to the widths of the boards. A long bevel forms a tongue to fit a groove. Thus the thin board has a tongue on both sides. There is no true panel with four sides, a thing which came later, of course for wall work. The ceiling may be composed of open work of small floor joist framed into larger timbers, while the floor above forms the cover. To deaden sound material may be placed between the floors. Or plaster, never smooth, may be applied between the joists.

THE three finials above are from Brewster and Carver chairs. Of those below the larger are from Carver and Pilgrim chairs, and the others from chairs dating later, about 1700. The plates are both half size—the only pictures made to scale in this volume.

THE Attic of the Webb-Welles house at Wethersfield, Connecticut. The attic is the most beloved spot a collector knows. It is one of "The loved spots that our infancy knew."

Into it went for two hundred years the discarded because "old fashioned" furniture. Many a New England house has today great treasures in its attic; which are unsuspected by the occupant of the house. And it is high time to add another sentence to that. Many an attic has worthless furniture which its possessor values at a fortune. The house-holders are gradually awakening to know that old furniture is good, but their knowledge is at present, and ever must be, confused. So they may sometimes count the worthless priceless, and the priceless worthless.

If articles are highly valued why are they kept in attics, where the excellent collector cannot come? Or if he comes, he arrives after much negotiation. If all the hidden things were revealed today where would be the sport of collecting for the coming generation? Yet we deprecate the sardonic grin, or the complacent aspect, of the collector who has "arrived", when he endeavors to comfort the collector who has not arrived, with the saying that there are just as good fish in the sea as ever were caught—the sea, in this mixed metaphor, being an unknown attic.

A ROOM with a low Oak Bed, which our first fathers used. Two chests also appear. We are presuming that the collections of a family for a century are here drawn upon, with some articles which were newly purchased about 1720.

The literature of the settlers would not, aside from the Bible, make enlivening reading now. Although many of the books of the period are of much historical value, and of present interest because of their quaintness.

In musical instruments they were especially poor. Music had charms for them, but those charms were regarded as inspired from below, as so much doubtless was in their English experience.

Hunting was an important occupation rather than a sport, because they needed the spoils of the chase. Fishing was, after agriculture, the first industry in importance. They became too weary for much athletic recreation. There was before them the big job of conquering a continent.

AN old "hall" setting. The hall in this sense is the main room in the house. What was later enlarged to our hall was then merely a porch or entry.

At the fireplace the flip iron was heated and thrust into the potation for the evening. The cheese could be toasted on the slender long fork shown on page 549. The chairs were made comfortable with cushions unless the seat was rush, which required no cushion. Children occupied stools. There was no effort to keep any room, except the great room, that is, the "hall," warm enough to sit in. The great chimney itself warmed somewhat the rooms above, and the floor even in a good house was not so tight but that heat could rise through the narrow cracks.

The winter evenings were spent in basket making, spinning, weaving and knitting. The musket was kept where it would not rust and the powder would be dry.

The width of the floor boards was such that they shrunk in winter and swelled in summer about a quarter of an inch. In this crack the sand of the floor sifted. The first homes being by the sea fine white sand was available.

The windows being very small required little drapery.

[487]

COLLECTORS' DON'TS

1. DON'T collect restored furniture. Get it "in the rough."
2. Don't collect furniture with new paint, which covers a multitude of sins.
3. Don't seek for bargains. Low prices on choice articles, at a dealer's, prove something is wrong.
4. Don't aim at rarity alone. An object must have intrinsic interest.
5. Don't hesitate when you are sure. The best things are lost by a day, or an hour.
6. Don't trust your own judgment in all things, because you are experienced in certain classes of things.
7. Don't forget Franklin and buy what is cheap, unless you need it.
8. Don't leave behind what you have purchased. People change their minds. Possession is nine points of the law.
9. Don't fail to keep sweet because you meet people who will not part with their treasures. Others have rights.
10. Don't restore more than is necessary. New furbished 17th Century furniture loses it charm. Mahogany is different.
11. Don't forget that an inheritor is often the poorest judge of the age and merit of his property. Traditions should not be bought.
12. Don't give attention to historical furniture. Don't "buy stories." They are good backgrounds, for good things only.
13. Don't fail to study both books and the furniture itself. Half the pleasure is in knowing.
14. Don't mix styles very much. The beauty of an old room consists in approximate harmony.
15. Don't make a house a museum. It is not as interesting as just enough.
16. Don't regard the discovery of specimens like rare pieces you already have, as a disaster. We ought to be glad for every good thing that comes to light.
17. Don't fail to let the knowledge of beauty and quaintness in your possession become public knowledge. We owe it to our generation to diffuse good taste. Patriotism calls for an adorned country.
18. Don't despair of getting what you want, if you seek long enough. Hunting is better than fishing.
19. Don't neglect to become an authority on some one thing at least, if it is only a tinder-box.

A ROOM with furniture of the year 1700, some of it a little earlier, some a little later. On the wall is a cocked hat box, three-cornered. It has a rest, within, for the hat. A flax wheel and a yarn reel are shown, with a leather back and a late Carver chair. A middle stretcher tavern table, candle stand and other articles, like the "ancestor" on the wall may tell their own story.

THE OBLIGATION TO MATERIALS

We have no right to misuse wood. We did not make it. We found it, like air, water and grass. The only possible manner of acquiring any rights over it is by putting the stamp of character upon it. The theologians tell us of sins, as if we were under obligation to a spiritual world alone. But sheer wickedness in the use of materials ought to cause even a materialist to shudder. Wood is one of the best things we have. Whether Grinling Gibbons puts his tool to it or we make a milking stool of it, men will measure us by the manner of our handling it.

Only people with a sense of reverence for materials can make good citizens. A man must use wood well, or he will mistreat his neighbors.

INTERIOR DECORATIONS OF THE 17TH CENTURY

FLOORS: Kitchens or Halls; Sand or Rushes; corn husk mats.

PARLORS, DINING ROOMS AND CHAMBERS: Drawn-in, otherwise called hooked rugs, made on a burlap base; braided rugs; knitted rugs.

CEILINGS: Open beams and floor joist with the rough boards above. The beams chamfered. Sometimes the entire ceiling was whitewashed. A second scheme was to plaster between the joist, with rough plaster. There is not yet any evidence found that ceilings were paneled in the 17th century. But inasmuch as panels were used shortly after the century went out, simple large panels, preferably unpainted, may be used.

WALLS: The most effective early style was in sheathed paneling. Every second board was a panel with a very long tongue. Every second board was grooved on both sides for panels. The boards ran to the beam, girt or cornice, and to the floor, or sill. The tongued boards sometimes were furnished with beads or quarter round molds to meet the panels. The style may be seen still in many old houses.

There was no half-way panel. The work ran from floor to ceiling. In this style the corner posts and the beams were left uncovered, being smoothed by the plane. The boards were pine, the timbers oak.

Plaster was used sometimes in the 17th Century, especially on the exposed walls. On the walls abutting on other rooms a finish all in wood was common. The sheathed panel work may sometimes have been painted. Preferably it was left natural, with no finish whatever, either oil or stain.

The doors were cleated, of the same construction as the wall sheathing, precisely.

BEDS: The material of the canopy was cotton, linen, wool or silk. It varied with the means and taste of the owner. Plain or plain colored linen covered by netting was used. Copperplate came later. So also did hand stamped calico.

WINDOWS: These were small and all the light was needed. Shades were not used. A single material to push away at the sides was the style. The same material as used on the beds was proper.

UPHOLSTERY: Cushions were made of leather, linen or silk. Cupboard tops were covered with rich cloths and cushions were placed on such covers, on which again were placed the finer pieces of plate, pewter or china. All wooden seats were probably provided with cushions, except simple stools. Couches (day beds) had cushions made in the same style as the chairs.

TABLE AND BED LINEN: It *was* linen, in great variety and richness.

ON the next page following are a remarkable pair of quill-work sconces. Owner: Mr. Francis Hill Bigelow of Cambridge, who has kindly furnished the author with some data regarding them.

The size of each is 21 by 9 inches. The frames are in all respects similar in style and materials to looking glass frames of the period. The obvious reason is that the looking glasses themselves were often used with sconces. The designer of these sconces went farther and filled his frames with decorative materials, designed to catch the light in front. The frames are of walnut.

The vase design, with the rosettes and border are of paper, gilded on the edge. The flowers, principally carnations and tulips, are made of wax, which is perhaps mixed with mica. Each petal is edged with silver wire. The colors are red, blue, purple and white, of varying shades. The whole sparkles from the light of the candle below.

They were made by Ruth Read, daughter of the Hon. John Read, a lawyer of distinction in Boston between 1722 and 1749.

In "Gold and Silver of Windsor Castle," 1911 (p. xxxi), Mr. E. Alfred Jones refers to this pair of simple scrolled candle brackets as being typical of such in use in England during the reign of Queen Anne. None of the English specimens seem to have survived the melting-pot. Similar brackets may be observed in Hogarth's engravings, "The Laughing Audience" and "The Analysis of Beauty." This pair of brackets was made by Knight Leverett of Boston (1703-53), and is engraved "RR 1720."

We distinguish here between the sconce brackets, which hold the candles, and the sconces, which are the portion against the wall—the framed section.

The pieces are supposedly unique. Their effect is excellent.

In not a few instances glasses probably had sconce brackets which have been lost, the sockets even being removed, so that there is scarcely a trace of their former location. The effect of looking glasses with candles was not overlooked by the designers of the period. The fashion of using such candles was continued into Chippendale's time and even later, only in the later time the candles were placed at one side rather than in front of the glass. We may suppose that the fashion of cutting the surface of the glass in ornamental forms was a persistence of the decorative idea such as appears in the pair of sconces before us.

A PAIR of Sconces in quill-work. The property of Mr. Francis Hill
Bigelow of Cambridge. They are veneered, apparently in walnut; three-
quarters of an inch wide, and are now painted black. More fully described
on preceding page.

A DECORATED looking glass, the property of Mr. Mark M. Henderson of Norwalk, Connecticut. The frame is small, and is decorated by painted scrolls which do not show in the picture.

It is said to have belonged to Peregrine White, though what the evidence is we do not know. He lived into the 18th Century, and was a substantial citizen, whose dwelling remains to this day. Many articles came down to us from him, and are in the Pilgrim Hall, Plymouth. It is natural since he was the only original member of the Pilgrim Fathers who lived into the 18th Century that we should know and have his relics. John Alden, who is said to have been the youngest signer of the famous compact, was a young man when Peregrine was born on the Mayflower in Provincetown harbor. Though Alden outlived all the other signers he died a score of years or so before Peregrine White.

A FRAMED Petit Point Needlework Picture of the 17th Century owned by Mr. H. W. Erving. This picture with its rich coloring, quaint drawing and perspective is characteristic of the period, and is particularly interesting by reason of the fidelity of the costumes displayed. It is introduced in this work, however, on account of the frame, which is of pine, well moulded and with a wide gold lining. In order to show the cloud effect the top is made with a double arch, and should be compared with the sconce on page 491.

A LOOKING GLASS, formerly provided with sconce brackets.

The glass itself is original. The author owns the piece. The frame is pine.

The places where sconce-brackets were affixed at the bottom are clearly designed for such a purpose, being practically the same in the contour of the frame as other glasses provided with brackets. Date: 1710-30.

The frame has been gilded and blacked. It is left as found, "in the rough," some parts of the gilding having scaled off.

The possession of a large glass, in the period we are treating, was counted a luxury. Little glasses crudely framed in pine, and painted, or in leather are found.

A LOOKING GLASS dating about 1700. It is all original, but there was a decorative scrolled top which has been lost. It is owned by the author. The frame outside is 27⅜ by 31¼ inches. The wood is walnut veneer. The glass is 18¼ by 22 inches. The bevel is discernible.

Whether the bevel originated in a desire to reflect light as from another face of glass after the manner in which precious stones are cut, we do not know. The bevel adds to the beauty of the glass.

The early bevel was very flat and soft. The edges blended more gently with the main surface than in the modern bevel. It is sometimes impossible to see the bevel on an old glass at some angles. The surmise that the bevel was cut to fit the glass more easily and securely in the frame is untenable. It will be seen as we proceed that the earliest looking glasses were nearly square, because the glass, expensive in any form, was least so in this form. Later came the two glasses, the one over the other, as a measure of economy.

The very earliest frames mentioned in America have stump embroidery but the only one known has been illustrated, and was not American, anyway.

Whether any glass as early as 1700 is American cannot now be known. The glass itself was imported. We believe that some frames as early as 1700 were made here. The glass industry was, in the heavy plate form at least, too specialized for a new and a poor country.

Cheap frames, or frames to be decorated, were often in pine. Fine wood frames were usually walnut, which also indicates their period.

THE GLASS itself on the next page is 13¾ by 16¼ inches. It has a three inch convex satin wood frame, with walnut outside edge. It is inlaid with thuya and tulip wood. The top has three inset panels of corresponding design. Originally the inlay covered the entire top. The veneer between the panels is now missing. A very rare glass. Date: 1710–20.

The word "mirror" in the quotation, "now we see in a mirror, darkly," means of course a metal mirror. Polished metal did not give the excellent reflection of glass, especially when, as shortly was the case, it became tarnished. Hence it was said "we see *darkly*." The significance of the word "looking-glass" is felt at once when we remember it was contrasted with the earlier mirrors which were not glass. The beauty and elaborateness of looking-glass frames arose largely from the expensiveness of the glass which must be honored by appropriate richness in frame.

Good mirrors, belonging to the Pilgrim Century, are more difficult to obtain than any other class of objects. They were unusual even in their period. Breakage has done for the most of them. Lack of appreciation of their merits is responsible for the loss of most of the remainder.

The loss by fire of 17th, and even 18th, Century articles is immense. An instance comes to our minds where a collector was burned out, but persevered and made a second collection, which was also burned!

Some of the finest work in the country is still in very precarious surroundings.

The influence of commerce on the diffusion of furnishings for homes is almost a history of civilization. The early Americans were a maritime people. Sea captains were not only on the lookout in foreign lands for cargoes to sell in America, but they were in the habit of bringing back to their wives objects of interest from all parts of the world. Thus the early china came from China, as well as from English importations. Early mirrors particularly were brought home because there were no such things to be had in America. We have instanced such a mirror being brought from Venice. It was from such articles that the American cabinet workers derived their styles. They often made in pine what had come here as walnut. But they did not hesitate to attempt more precise and elegant reproductions. We know that sometimes mirror glasses were imported without their frames.

A FRAME belonging to Mr. Francis Hill Bigelow. Further particulars are given on page 498. The reader is reminded that these looking-glasses are not shown in any scale.

THE looking glass frame above has its perfect original glass, but the silvering has been cleaned off and the coat of arms inserted. The frame is beautifully decorated with marquetry of the period of 1700. This glass was sold from the Wayside Inn, Sudbury, at the auction of its contents some fifty years since. It had been painted, so that when sold its character, as a walnut and inlaid frame, was not suspected. The cresting is missing, but the condition of the frame otherwise is quite perfect.

It is the property of Mr. Hill, the post master of South Sudbury, who inherited the glass from his father, the purchaser at the auction. The arms are those of the family who for many generations conducted the inn.

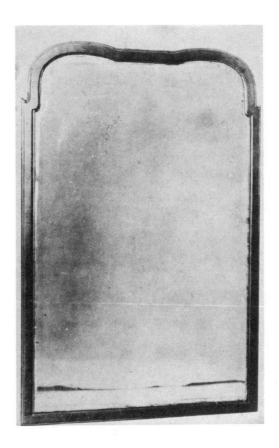

A LOOKING GLASS owned by Mr. Francis Hill Bigelow. The glass measurement is 21 by 32¾ inches. The frame, on its flat surface, is 1¼ inches wide. It is of walnut, with boxwood edges, inside and outside.

This is a large glass for so small a frame, and indicates what so many glasses did not that its principal office was use. Date: 1730–50.

When, as was sometimes the case, the only glass in the mirror was cut in some design, we infer of course that the chief purpose was decoration. In the case where, as in later examples, a sconce bracket was attached near the center of the frame the motive was the same as in light-houses, to increase the light as much as possible. When light was scanty, as in those days, reflection became important for any sort of satisfactory illumination. This purpose of course lay behind the numerous mirrors found in a single rich French room. This connection between mirrors and artificial lighting is often forgotten by us who enjoy such full and easy means of illumination.

In the invention of looking glasses the method of coating their backs with quick-silver was as important as the skill required in producing the glass. Since the ancients used mirrors rather than looking glasses, obviously no practical method of silvering mirrors was known in classical times.

A LOOKING GLASS belonging to Mr. Francis Hill Bigelow. The glass is 11⅞ by 17⅛ inches. It has a two-inch walnut frame with convex molding. The style of top is frequently seen in English mirrors, but with a crown and other royal emblems in the fret work. The presence of such emblems does not in itself prove that a frame having them is English. It only establishes a stronger presumption to that effect. During the reign of William and Mary and Queen Anne the loyalty of the colonists was such that royal emblems occurred here. Yet the mere fact that one lived in America showed that a seed of democracy was working.

These fretted frames appeared as late as Chippendale's time but with smaller margins, and the fret work extending on the sides. Date: 1710–30.

The backs of American frames are as a rule of pine, the edges of the backing being beveled. A thickened piece of wood near the top, with an opening for a hanging cord, was common. The top as shown here was stiffened by long splints run down on the main frame and often set dovetail fashion into it.

THIS Looking glass is also owned by Mr. Francis Hill Bigelow. The glass is 16 by 19¾ inches; the frame is 4 inches wide in addition. It is of walnut convex, inlaid with satin and tulip woods. This mirror evidently had a top which has been lost. Many, however, were complete as seen here. The inlay here was doubtless imitated in the glass shown on page 494, attributed to Peregrine White. Only in that glass the imitation was a painted decoration, to take the place of inlay. The date is 1700–20.

One should notice the marked resemblance between some mirrors of this period and the period of 1850. We have the same width of frame, but so far as we know, the late mirrors are always of concave contour on the frame. The earlier were generally convex as here. The latter mirrors were also of course in mahogany. But a complete novice might be deceived.

The late mirrors never had a scrolled or fretted top, and the glass in them was not beveled, nor often plate.

The convex mirrors, when seen sidewise, remind one, by their quick outward sweep of frame, of the blocked fronts of some early chests, from which very likely they took their style.

THE Glass here shown measures 15½ by 18¼ inches. The frame adds much more, the molding being 4¼ inches wide. This fine specimen is owned by Mr. Francis Hill Bigelow. It is in applewood veneer, showing end grain. In cases where we have covered the glass to avoid confusing reflections it may be understood as a rule that the glass is beveled.

On this frame the scroll is simple but effective. The shape so common, in the middle of the century, of the "broken arch," seen also on door heads, seems not to be found in the early years of the century. The date is 1700–20.

Looking glasses like the above are more rare than the long glasses, in two parts, which bear the name Queen Anne. If we are to use an English name to mark the period, William and Mary is proper for the style before us.

The old glass in these frames is highly valued by collectors, whatever its condition. This is true partly because it seems impossible to obtain commercial plate cut on the old bevel. Many old glasses have been resilvered, but the result is not fully satisfactory. It seems quite impossible to silver an old glass and secure a perfect adherence everywhere of the amalgam. Formerly mercury was used in an alloy with tin. Pure silver is sometimes used now.

The direct rays of the sun will soon ruin the silvering on a mirror. It is for this reason that old mirrors appear as they do. The suspicion arises whether new plate is not sometimes submitted to direct sunlight to give an old effect.

THE Looking Glasses here are both the property of Mr. Francis Hill Bigelow. That on the left has a glass measuring 21 by 33½ inches. The width of the side molding is 1½ on the flat part. The edges outside and inside are gilt. The frame is in burl walnut.

At either side below the glass are marks showing where plates, with sockets for candle brackets, were attached. Date: 1720–40.

On the right, the glass measures 11¼ by 16½ inches. There is a two-inch convex walnut frame. Date: 1700–20.

The question sometimes arises whether the tops of these frames were made flat and acquired convexity by warping, or whether they were made convex.

As wood does not shrink or swell endwise, the tops as they swell from dampness must either warp or split. A thin board too, which is veneered on one side only, is sure to warp in time.

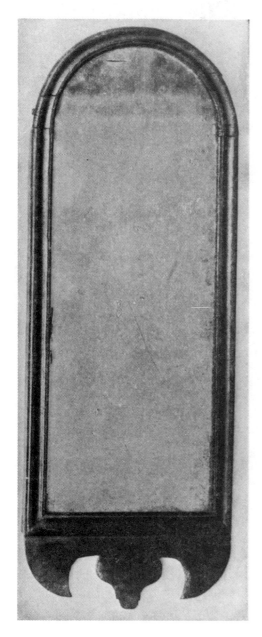

THIS picture shows what is probably a sconce glass, since there are two holes at the bottom of the frame showing that a plate with a socket held a candle bracket.

The glass is 7½ by 20¼ inches.

The frame is one inch wide, on the sides; the wood is maple, stained.

The scroll below bears a remarkable resemblance to that seen on the frame rails of tables of the period, or a little earlier.

Date: 1700–30.

The plain semi-circular top is unusual. Very narrow glasses of this character often came in pairs, and it may be that this specimen once had its mate.

It is owned by Mr. Francis Hill Bigelow. One should compare the molded frame of this glass with the similar molding running around the back of walnut chairs of the same period. It was a great favorite with the cabinet makers of that day who were capable of getting into ruts like those of the present. "We refer," as Dr. Hawes, of Hartford used to say, "to those to whom we allude!"

The back of any early looking glass, if it has not been tampered with, shows a mellow even pine surface which cannot be mistaken for modern work. One is never likely to be misled, who has once examined a looking glass back. This undisturbed condition is a merit much regarded by collectors.

A WALNUT Frame, with a glass 13½ by 21½ inches. The frame is only one inch wide. It carries a band of gilt inside and out. Owner: Mr. Francis Hill Bigelow.

The date of this piece is later than we should, perhaps, include in this book.

This glass shows the characteristic feature of the Queen Anne period—the shape of the scroll. At the very beginning of the scroll, where, on the side, it sweeps inward a trifle, is a motive found on great numbers of the looking-glasses of this time, 1730–50.

It will have been observed that the relatively wide glasses are made in one piece, whereas the narrow glasses are more than likely to be in two parts. The object of

making the frames narrow was probably to make possible the use of small plates. The cutting of the scrolls on some of the simpler glasses was a work in which the makers of that day seemed to delight. This simple frame, for instance, has a glass full of curves and angles, the cutting of which, as a commercial matter, seemed to cause no hesitancy in the mind of the merchant.

WE have included in this volume, for reasons already given, most of the hardware in use up to the 19th Century. But in the pilgrim century the householder himself made, or had made, most of these things. The first vessels were made by John Alden. Large and small vessels for liquids were nearly all made of staves with hoops. Thus dippers, noggins, pipkins, firkins, runlets, barrels and hogsheads, each one a little larger than the preceding, served as containers for liquid and dry commodities. The pewter was at first imported, also the iron up to 1640, when a beginning was made here.

The trenchers, trays, troughs and bowls were of wood, turned, burnt out, or fashioned by hand. Vessels of bark, and of splint were common. Basket making began early. Any knowledge our fathers lacked in this art they learned from the Indians. But then as now the bartering for baskets with the Indians was common.

The settlers hewed the handles for all their tools, whether for carpentry or the farm. A broadax man could hew a log half as fast as a primitive up and down mill could saw it. A forge must have been set up at once. Though they imported iron and steel tools, they kept them sharp with the forge or grindstone. They bent their own ox-bows and rake-bows.

The furniture was turned where possible. Crude beds in crude houses were made to answer. One has only to know how quickly woodsmen will erect log houses to understand why the houses of the first generation had such low values in the inventories. Probably not a particle of iron entered into the first houses. Even in England oak pegs still exist driven in slate or shingle. Floors at first were ignored. Hard clay answered; then halved logs, flat side up, called puncheons. Doors were hung with wooden pins and closed with wooden latches. The windows were holes closed by solid shutters, or a little later filled up with paper or wee panes of iridescent glass, with lead divisions. The windows were the most difficult thing to make; some of them were probably imported.

As to brick houses, one often hears, as if it were a necessary or remarkable thing, that "the bricks were brought from England." Brick kilns existed in America as early as brick houses. Bricks were brought from England indeed, but as ballast: the heavy lading of ships was on the return voyage. The settlers were in need of fine manufactured articles, rather than weighty freights.

No doubt the vast majority of the pieces of very early furniture were thrown away as soon as better specimens were available. There are only a few thousand pieces of American 17th Century furniture, and only a few hundred very fine important pieces.

A LOOKING GLASS, with a stained maple frame. The glass measures 11¼ by 17 inches. The narrow part of the frame is 1⅛ inches wide, and convex. The sheer simplicity of the design is rather pleasing. The odd button ornament and the somewhat wandering uncertain lines of the scroll are interesting gropings after beauty.

The date is about 1700–10.

It is often alleged, even in this book, that maple in furniture means American work. In a looking glass frame that allegation can probably be supported successfully. And of course where we see maple, the burden of proof is on the person who calls the article English. Nevertheless, maple was used in furniture in England, especially in turnings, to a considerable extent. What study

we have been able to give to the subject, however, inclines us to tne opinion that the 17th Century tradition was so strongly in favor of oak that maple would surprise one, in an English piece. Thus Flemish and other turned chairs in maple are generally conceded to be American.

As a general proposition the nearer we approach the date of the first settlers in America, the variation between English and American types becomes less. For the first score or two of years the settler, not having tested the woods unusual in furniture in England, would keep closer to the original types. Thus oak frames in dwellings, not a whit better than pine, continued through the century, with exceptions.

ON the next page on the left is a looking-glass, measuring inside, 13⅞ by 33⅞ inches. The flat walnut frame is 1¾ inches wide. Owner: Mr. Francis Hill Bigelow.

The glass in the top is beautifully engraved in a floral design, with birds, and conventional scrolls. Date: about 1710.

A glass as large as this forms an important part of house decoration. Whether the glass cutting on mirrors is to be counted as pure art, or art out of place and therefore untrue to itself is a matter to be decided. One feels that the introduction of looking glasses of a pretentious character, being an innovation, was accompanied by cut decoration partly as a *tour de force*, to show what the manufacturer could do.

THE left hand glass is mentioned on the preceding page.

The right hand looking glass is very large, 15¾ by 43¼ inches. The cut glass top is a simple design. The frame is 2⅛ inches wide, in burl walnut, and with the convex molding.

It is also the property of Mr. Francis Hill Bigelow. The date is about 1710. The scrolled lines have a decisive simplicity that is quite satisfactory.

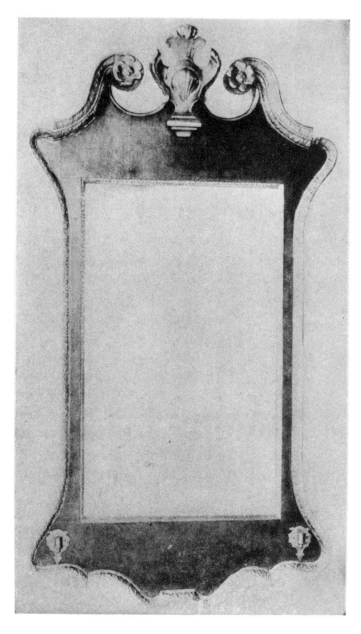

A SCONCE Glass of burl walnut. Owner: Mr. Francis Hill Bigelow. The date though well on in the 18th Century, perhaps 1730–60, will not exclude it, as we wish to make a somewhat complete showing of glasses with sconce brackets attached underneath, as in the earlier period. The size of this glass is 17½ by 29½ inches. The frame is gilt inside and out. It bears "engraved" brass plates with sockets for candle brackets.

This piece may have come from south of New York. It shows the cartouche decoration in the center top, which we look for at a late period. Yet walnut was not much used for mirrors after 1750.

If we set the walnut period as ending at that date we shall, it is true, include some examples of a decidedly late type, since there was no hard and fast rule. The plain rectangular glass, the only one we show, is decidedly late. The setting of the plates for sconces at one side is another mark of change from the earlier period.

A LOOKING GLASS the outside measurement of which is 18½ by 48½ inches. The frame is walnut. The decoration at the top, which shows somewhat indistinctly, is a very good inlaid design in tulip wood.

The great hight of the mirror makes it more important. The glass is not original. It had of course two glasses. Owner: the author. Date: 1710–20. The frame is walnut; the width being 1¾ inches; in the convex pattern.

The adaptability of walnut to the purpose of furniture making was recognized in the south of Europe at a period so remote that all record of the matter is lost. In the veneer it was used sometimes too thick. In the modern method we may hope it will hold its form better. With the mutations of two hundred years and more it has done well, but the tendency to curl is noticed in most heavy veneers. We take it for granted that the running of the veneer across the grain of the pine foundation was designed as a better decorative effect, as the grain of the wood is not very marked, and advantage was taken of every feature possible. It is very remarkable that the early cabinet makers were able to make a veneer that lasted as their work did.

The pine backing of so many early looking glasses is proof that pine was found almost necessary in England as the basis of the best veneer.

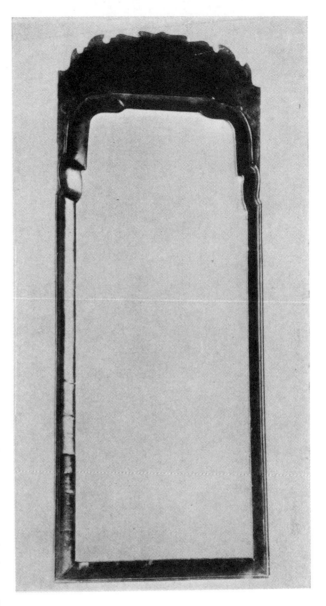

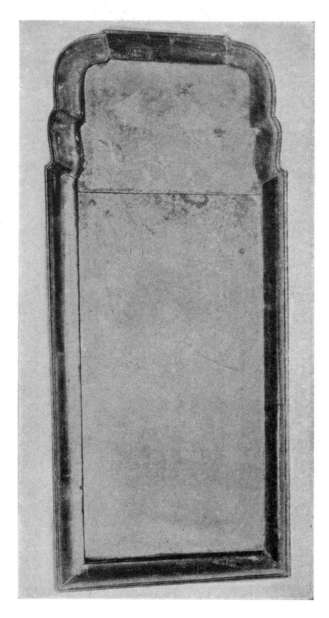

A WALNUT two-part looking glass. It is original in all parts. It was found in Eastern Massachusetts.

The full hight is 37 inches. The cutting on the upper glass represents that bird, sometimes called a phoenix or a pheasant, but which is not always recognizable by any of Audubon's illustrations! It was at least a bird; and a touch of mystery is rather an advantage.

This frame is somewhat heavy, as in the earliest styles of the two-part looking glasses.

The date is about 1710. Owner: the author.

In these glasses, the upper one lapped over the lower, and the rabbet on which the glasses rested was cut deeper in the upper section. The object of lapping the glasses was to give a continuous glass surface. Old mirrors, becoming a little shaky, are very liable to let the upper glass slip down. Hence many were broken.

The wood of this frame is somewhat bleached, showing how light walnut may gain a quite charming color. In this connection it is worth considering that new English walnut is by no means so much lighter than our northern black walnut as to make the distinction always easy. Unbleached black walnut, however, is very dark, and unless it were exposed to brilliant light for a long period it would not bleach, naturally, to a great extent.

A MOST interesting looking glass, belonging to Mr. Chauncey C. Nash. It has in the upper section, instead of glass, a wooden panel, on which is represented a ship in full sail. The colors are now very quiet but entirely distinct. All parts are original. The date is about 1710.

We see in this glass an interesting prototype of the immensely popular 18th and early 19th Century mirrors, bearing painted representations of ships, and everything conceivable on the upper glass, the painting being done on the under side. Here, on a wood panel, was possibly the inspiration of some of the later work.

The use of wood as a ground for pictures is extremely early. Though at first thought it seems not to be a suitable substance, yet the mutations of years have proved that it has some great advantages. The work done on it is more permanent than that on glass or canvas. Though the surface may scale the subject is never utterly destroyed.

Of course the painting on glass was an easy substitute for cutting, and being brighter it appealed to the declining taste on which it rode to popularity. The tops of long glasses were too high to be useful, hence they were made ornamental. We may presume that, in case a clear glass was used in the upper section, the intention was to have the glass low enough to secure the benefit of its entire length.

AN exquisite specimen of a great mirror of about 1740 which closes, perhaps, too late, our period. The property of the author. The hight is 69 inches.

The gradual shading off of mirrors in this style from the early Queen Anne to the Georgian, without a radical change, is a case of persistence of a beautiful type. One must get the date from details rather than the general contour. The earlier mirrors had two glasses, and the bird or other design was cut in the upper glass.

In this mirror the carving immediately about the glass is incised in the wood of the frame. The other carvings are applied.

A MIRROR of which the bill is still preserved in the Griswold family where it still is in Connecticut. It was bought in Venice, in 1737, and so absolutely fixes the date at which this beautiful style attained its finest proportions.

From the crest of the bird to the bottom of the mirror the measurement is 78 inches! It is the finest example of its type with which we are acquainted. All parts are original. While such mirrors were made in England and presumably here, the source of the pattern is made clear by this piece. As it has been here ever since it was made, we venture to include it.

Of course the material is walnut. Before the coming to light of the date of this mirror it would probably have been placed later. The elegant and the rich in all sorts of furnishings may be looked for anytime after 1700. The public taste was probably as good in furniture at that period, as it ever was. The time of poverty had passed. Painting flourished. Exquisite work was produced in nearly all the arts. America, removed from the seats of culture, bought well.

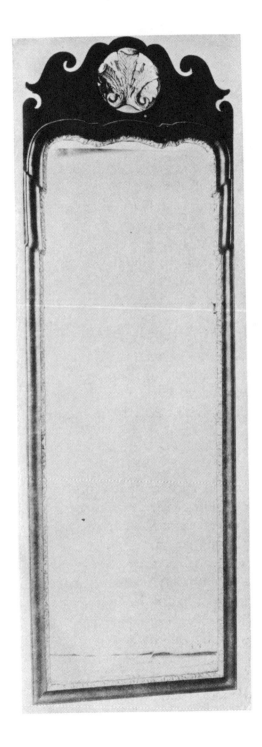
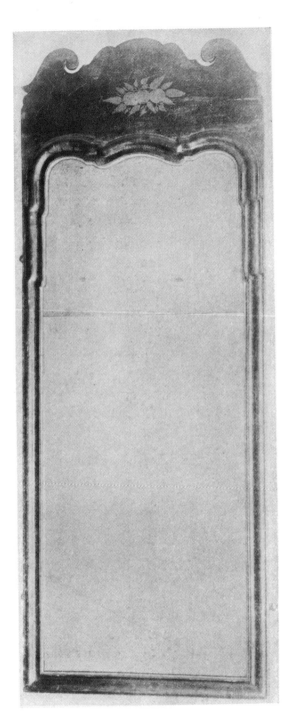

ON page 518 is a fine early example of a Queen Anne mirror, of date 1720–40. It is above five feet high. Owner: the author. It is all original except the feather ornament.

On page 519 are two looking glasses belonging to Mr. Francis Hill Bigelow. Their date is about 1720–40. That on the left is in walnut, the frame being 1⅞ inches wide, gilt inside, and with a gilt shell. The glass is 14¾ by 48¾.

The other example belonging to the same owner has a molded pine frame, 1⅞ inches in size. The glass is 16 by 40 inches.

The frame is grained in imitation of rosewood. It is gilt inside. The stencilling in gilt was probably added in the 19th Century.

The mirror on page 516 is 69 inches in hight, and is original except the bird. The wood is mahogany. All carved parts are gilded. It is owned by the author.

Such mirrors must have required at least ten-foot ceilings. In an ordinary colonial house the bottom comes very near the floor.

Date: 1735–50.

With this we close our treatment of mirrors, which really should have a volume by themselves. But the designs confined to the Pilgrim Century are limited and it seems better to show them here, with a few exhibiting the flowering of taste into the richer, larger designs toward the middle of the 18th Century.

Mirrors in very small forms were used in the 16th and possibly in the 17th century as decorations on the person. They were attached to the trimming of gowns to catch the light. The effect must have been striking. Allusion to such use is made by Shakespeare and others.

Little mirrors for shaving, too plain to require illustration, are yet very quaint. The use of oak for mirror frames is found in England in Queen Elizabeth's time. The frames were well carved. Examples are shown in *Benn*, "Style in Furniture."

It is not to be supposed that the Plymouth pilgrims had looking glasses to any extent, for many years after landing.

The Puritans, however, owned many. More than twenty are named in Essex County inventories before 1664 and more than thirty in the next ten years. As this was the era before walnut we much wish to know what the glasses were like.

A LARGE home room furnished as of the date 1700 or thereabout. The court cupboard answered for a sideboard.

The various appurtenances of the fireplace, like the warming pan, with iron handle, the earlier sort, the weighted jack for turning the roast; Pilgrim chairs; chests; and general household gear, are set forth.

The atmosphere of continuous occupation by the same family, the great charm of an old home, is highly important in forming a mellow habit of mind. We need an historical perspective and unless we gain it we are like nomads in the desert.

Dignity becomes the home of men. They have fought their battle through unknown ages. They have mastered so many sources of power and beauty, and arrived at so much knowledge that they deserve to honor themselves with something better than riches. That something is to surround themselves with the rich past in order to make the present richer. Hitherto in America we have lost what is behind us as rapidly as we have gained what is before us. The real wealth of life is to keep the best of the past, because manhood means more than ruining one age to build another.

IN the 17th Century, at least in the part of it when oak was still king of woods, we had not in America arrived at any such pitch of diversity in civilization as to make clocks. We must content ourselves with at least one type of English clock, the bird cage, otherwise called the sheep's head, from the shape of the wood bracket on which it was placed. This clock was built with the bob pendulum, in use in the earlier years of the 17th Century. It was adapted to the long pendulum, which came into use more or less in the last decade of the century. These clocks had but one hand, the spaces being marked so that one could tell the time within five or ten minutes.

The works were brass and the fret work in various patterns is the means by which the age is determined. This clock belongs to the author, dates about 1640, and has been shown in several previous volumes. It has been in America a great many years. It was the invention of the long pendulum, keeping better time, that induced the making of tall clock cases to protect the weights from meddling. They were too tempting for a child to resist. The first clock cases made in America were probably of pine, and very simple. Some cases remain which are of uncertain date, bordering the time of the incoming 18th Century. They are very crude, being merely for protection to the clockworks. The idea of decorating these cases, however, was too appealing. Eventually, a family had a decorated clock case, though the entire house might contain nothing else as good.

AN interesting and odd Clock, probably of Knicker-bocker origin. The face is carved; the entire front about the face being of one piece with it. There is a music box above. On the hour a tune is played on the zither which is strung on the back, below the face, protected by open scroll work carving. There are a multiplicity of weights and as each has two cords we have a whole battery of lines running down the front. We have no accurate means of dating this clock. It belongs to the author; was brought many years ago from New York to Providence and is in good running order. The color is a dull orange, some sort of paint having been used to give an appearance of mellowness. It is all original. It requires to be hung high on the wall, to give room enough for the long range of the weights.

Some European musical clocks are very ancient indeed.

The watch, invented at Nüremberg about 1500, was a Pilgrim possession. A wooden wall holder for a watch is not infrequently found. It was made with a circular opening through which the face of the watch showed. Sun dials were common. Crude marks on a window ledge sometimes served instead. They were accurate twice a year, and by a little calculation were made to answer for the entire year.

A "DUTCH" Clock.

Owner: Mr. L. C. Flynt, Monson, Massachusetts. This clock may serve to represent a large family under this name. They are exceedingly quaint. The pendulum is short. They date late in the 17th and early in the 18th Century.

The rather elaborate example here shows all the usual features—the pewter ornaments in great number, the turned wooden feet, the mermaid, and the hood or roof which is sometimes omitted.

We make no attempt at showing later clocks; nor can we find any 17th Century clocks of American make. Leads which we have followed disclosed, later on, European clocks.

That is to say our American tall clock in a 17th Century setting is an anachronism. That some American clock cases exist, made before 1720, one cannot successfully dispute.

Their works, however, are presumably not native. A simple Dutch clock, called a "wag-on-the wall" was the most popular style of early clocks.

A KITCHEN of the latter part of the 17th Century. Makes clear the method of treating the fireplace when the bricks were not left exposed. Here the drawing in of the bricks above the chimney tree permitted a wood finish. As we are soon to take up the matter of hardware we now call attention to the fireplace furniture. In this case there is no crane, but a pole above the line of the chimney tree.

The cooking was done in two ovens opening diagonally in the rear of the fireplace. It is supposed that the designation of this house for a garrison is responsible for the two rather than one oven. On opening the cupboard doors one may see the bee hive shape of the ovens.

One should not look for the side oven with its separate flue and fire box, until about the time of the Revolution. The crane also gradually came into more general use, as it "saved the face" of the fair housewife. Hence the hanging of the crane (which could be shipped in or out at pleasure) signified not only the setting up of a new family, but a gallant act on the part of the husband to save his wife from broiling herself with the dinner over the fire, as was necessary with the lug pole. The scene is in the Hazen Garrison House, Haverhill.

[525]

THREE little wall contrivances. The wider one could have been used for candles on a pipe box. Such little wall pieces are very good adjuncts in the furnishing of a house with antique objects. Sometimes baskets are designed to hang against the wall, like pockets. Little spice boxes, boxes to hold the scouring brick, boxes for candles and for pipes and tobacco, and many other purposes, were used.

Where an early house lacked pictures, as most did, conveniences of the above sort assisted in the furnishing as well as the decoration. There was usually small closet room in 17th Century houses. The kitchens lacking our kitchenettes, were arranged something like a ship's galley, with the utensils arrayed about the walls. Tin sconces, brooms, the implements of the chase, also contributed to the numerous list, until the walls of a thrifty householder's kitchen looked like an assemblage of the movable family property. It is often impossible to know the special use of an ancient article. We must presume that all little wall pieces were made for a particular purpose. When one does not know he naturally takes refuge in the term spice box. But candle boxes of wood were also common.

The loss of numerous articles, and their names also from our common life, makes it more difficult to understand many passages in early literature. We lose the local tang. The next dictionary maker should carefully go through a museum of utensils.

The small wall pieces, when simple, were usually of pine. When more elaborate they often appear in walnut.

PIPE boxes, a hanging box and an hour glass, owned by Mr. Arthur W. Wellington. The pipe box was a very decorative piece. It was invariably made to hang upon the wall and usually in two vertical divisions.

Others are shown in this work.

The little hanging box is initialled and dated. It is too early for matches and its use is not known, but it would have been convenient for many purposes.

The hour glass is made in two parts. While such pieces usually go by the name hour glass, a sand glass is the proper term. They were more often regulated for one, three or fifteen minutes than for an hour, and are found very convenient today.

Below are five different devices for striking fire, all the property of Mr. H. W. Erving. The first on the left is the usual tinder box, with the place for the candle. It contains a piece of flint, a piece of steel and a piece of tow. The next two pieces are to be carried in the pocket and are very daintily chased. The next is a combination knife and pick and sparker. The wheel sparker at the right was used by striking metal against the revolving wheel and thus dashing a spark into the tow.

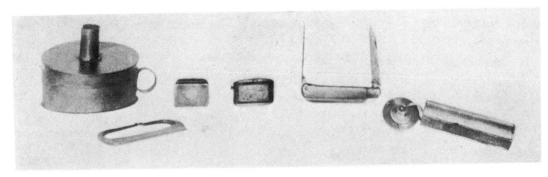

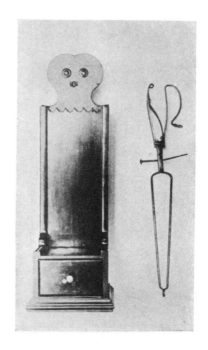

ON the right is an unusual pipe box belonging to Mr. H. W. Erving. There is a long, deep vertical partition in the back, into which were stuck the church warden pipes whose long, slender stems demanded a specially safe place. At the bottom is the tobacco drawer.

On the right of this box is a good example of pipe tongs. One cleaned out the pipe with the nail-like piece, which also served as a guide for the prongs. The tongs were to seize a coal for lighting the pipe. The flat thumb piece, at the end of the goose neck, was for pressing the tobacco into the bowl. Fine pipe tongs are among the rarest articles found.

The pipe box on the left belongs to the Metropolitan Museum. These boxes date from the earliest settlement to a time near the close of the 18th Century. They are often of pine, but later maple, cherry and mahogany appeared. No two are alike. Good ones are rather rare and are now eagerly sought. The drawer always has a small handle, generally of wood. There are sometimes two pockets for pipes. The kitchen was at once, in small houses, the den, the nursery, the living room, the library and the dining room.

A List of Odd Names of Early Utensils

Alchemy. A mixed metal like brass, for spoons, etc.

Beaker. A large drinking vessel with a wide mouth.

Chafing-dish. A vessel to hold coals for heating food.

Cob irons. Small andirons.

Cotterel or cottrel. A small iron window-bolt.

Cowl or cowle. A cowl-shaped covering for a chimney to avoid smoke.

Creeper. A low patten worn by women.

Dial case. For a sun- or possibly a clock-dial.

Fire dogs. Small andirons. Cob irons.

Fire pan. A vessel to carry fire.

Hatchel—hetchel, hackle, heckle. Iron teeth for cleaning flax.

Hake. A hook, especially a pot-hook.

Hanger. A short sword; also a pot-hook.

Keeler. A small shallow tub.

Latten ware. Made of mixed copper and zinc. Like brass.

Noggin. A mug of wood.

Peel. A long, flat shovel of wood or iron, for handling food in ovens.

Pipkin. A small wooden tub, with a prolonged stave for handle.

Porringer. A small, handled basin of pewter, iron or silver, for porridge, etc.

Posnet. A small vessel like a porringer, or more fanciful.

Pottle. A two-quart measure, for liquors, etc.

Runlet. A small barrel of 18 gallons.

Skillet. A small metal vessel with long handle and legs.

Slice. Same as peel (above).

Tankard. A drinking vessel, larger than a cup, and generally covered.

Tap. A wooden faucet.

Trammel. An adjustable pot-hook, with holes or saw-teeth.

Trencher. A plate, usually of wood.

Voider. A tray or basket for clearing a table.

Warming pan. Usually of brass, with cover and handle. Used with coals for moving about in a bed to make it tolerably warm.

We have, in the above list, omitted all modern well-known names. There were many utensils whose names are contained in no dictionary, and whose very use is now unknown. The inventories take it for granted that the names will be understood. Invention proceeded so rapidly that an old world was lost.

TURNINGS. That on the left shows the turned portion of the leg of the gate-leg in the Albany Historical Society, which has four gates. The size of the corner posts is two and seven-eighths inches. The inner, or gate legs, are smaller. The ancient turnings were strong and bold rather than delicate. This arose from the crudeness of the lathes of the period. Yet in some instances the approach to delicacy was very close, and a great achievement considering the handicap. Very small articles could not be turned. The age favored solidity.

The earliest traditions of furniture turning followed the Gothic. The prototypes of all the fine examples of wood turning may be found in the pillars, windows or screens of cathedrals.

Flat turnings for comfort in chair construction were not rare, in the arms and the back.

Turning came to be a fashion, almost a fad.

Hence half turnings, otherwise called drops, or split spindles, and bosses were applied on stair posts, cupboards, chests, chests of drawers, and various other articles. In fact, wherever there was a space where applied turnings could be used, they were used, at the end of the 17th Century. It was common to turn finials on stair posts, and probably bed posts except where the construction demanded that the body of the post should be square. The happiest effects, and unfortunately the rarest, were in the turnings of standards for candle stands. The so-called square turnings on stair posts were taken bodily from cathedral finials.

It is curious that the applied turnings did not come into vogue on looking glasses till a hundred and twenty years later. It appears that, before our time, discursive minds wandered back to early styles and revived such as seemed worthy.

A BURL Bowl, probably of maple. Owner: the author. The extraordinary character of the piece, owing to its size, the diameter being 23 inches, also its having ears carved upon it, and the great beauty of the wood, renders it highly important. It is presumed that the Indians found here by our ancestors, carved bowls like this, and that our ancestors imitated them. It is known, however, that they are made abroad also. The object of using the burl which is a growth—resulting from a wound on the trunk of a tree, rather than a root or a knot, was to secure a material which would not split. The grain is wholly distinct from that found in the crotch of a tree; it is snarled in every direction. Of course much beauty also attaches to the finished piece, owing to the grain, and a copy of it would make a beautiful wall paper design. The date may be any early period.

Below is a similar small bowl and a scoop of the same material, from the author's collection.

A SERIES of Utensils. The great mortar is rough shaped and is almost all a man can lift. In such mortars the corn was pounded if a mill was not available. Ordinary mortars, turned and unturned, are on the right and left. The shovel is large, and all of wood. The bowl beneath it is of burl. The handled vessel was used for dipping water. It is called a dipper. The knife, blade outward, in a haft, is a *froe*. It was placed on the end of a straight-grained small log of oak or ash with the point of the knife at the center. A blow with a great mallet, followed by successive changes in position of the *froe* as a pie is cut in wedges, resulted in making clapboards, thin at one edge.

All the early clapboards were made in this manner, and the writer has a nice bunch of oak clapboards made to test the matter. After the splitting one or both surfaces could be smoothed by a draw knife. As soon as our ancestors learned that they could shave pine shingles more rapidly than they could make clapboards, they did so. The shingles were more durable. On the rear of the John Alden side wall they are probably original. The long shingle is quainter. It could be used only where the best straight-grained pine was found. We frequently see long shingles on modern houses but unless they are shaved they will not be durable. The sawed shingle is cut always somewhat, and often very much, across the grain.

A PAGE of burl bowls, accompanied by quaint wooden spoons or ladles. The property of Mr. Albert C. Bates, of Hartford. The little instruments between the bowls, above, are Indian tools, consisting of minute parallel knives, for stripping up wood for basket work. The Indians made bowls and the settlers learned from them. It is often impossible to say whether an object is of Indian make or not. The bowl below has a decorated edge.

THE room is the old kitchen in the Cooper-Austin House, the oldest house in Cambridge, and in the ownership of the Society for the Preservation of New England Antiquities. It shows a vast fire place. The Society's seven houses are, sad to say, at present rather bare of early furniture. In time that lack may be remedied.

There seem inseparable difficulties at the present time to the gathering of proper furniture of the pilgrim period in a proper house. There is furniture, and there are houses, and there are persons interested in one or the other. To our thought a museum is not a satisfactory place for the exhibition of such furniture. It should appear in its natural home. The home thereby becomes attractive and the furniture no longer looks queer and out of place. Not until we abandon the thought of catering to persons who must be pleased, as the saying goes, shall we get down to the scientific assembling in a charming unity of the furniture in the house, neither to be accepted unless each is thoroughly right. Otherwise we shall learn little, and the objects so desirable will not be attained.

ON the right is the Parlor, no longer thus furnished, of the Iron Works house, Saugus. The fireplace opens nearly ten feet, and the room being a parlor, the fireplace was plastered inside and the inside corners were rounded. The great chimney trees of such houses were of oak, sometimes more than twenty inches through vertically. Where, as here, the hearth was of brick tile we can understand that a chair moved back and forth upon it for a hundred years would wear down to the rungs.

The other picture shows a spinning attic in the Wentworth-Gardner house. Herbs were hung about the sides of attics. This attic over the main hall afforded fine facilities for carrying on the spinning, though the heat of summer and the cold of winter were not escaped.

The walls of this room are paneled sheathing. The furniture is somewhat late for our purposes.

Below are a set of fine lanterns, the property of Mr. Rudolph Pauly.

THE means of locomotion in the early part of the pilgrim century were limited to boats and to "shanks' mare." The pretty fiction of Longfellow, in placing Priscilla on a led bull, was not intended, we imagine, to be taken for a gloss on pilgrim customs. Bulls were worked in the yoke, but were hardly available for riding. The boats did not help much inland from the New England coast, except on the Charles and the Connecticut. Edward Winslow went on foot when he visited the Narragansetts. Snow shoes, with "gaiters" attached, an ancient pair, are above. A shovel in quartered oak, though worn, still does good work. The churn was handed down in the Alden family. The barrel, probably worked out from a hollow tree, would have been scorned by John Alden, who was a cooper by trade. For a description of the quaint subject on the left we refer to the next page.

[536]

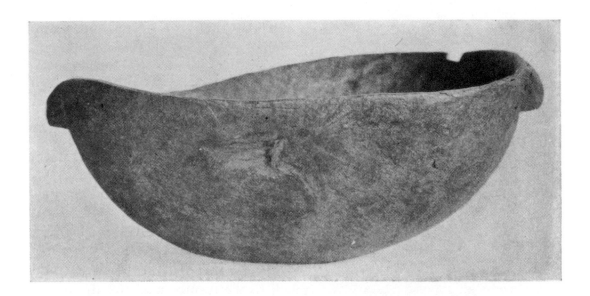

THIS great Burl Bowl is somewhat like a hat in shape. It has ears worked upon it from the solid wood. It belongs to Mr. Albert C. Bates. The object of cutting a bowl from a burl was to escape the danger of splitting.

Burl is the result of loss of orderly impulse in the tree, so that the grain is like a tangle.

At the bottom of the preceding page is a smoke jack, such as was used to turn the spit. The scrolling of the face plate is quite elaborate. The handle shows how it was wound up. The chain belt is not shown. The object of the wheel at the top was to give it a spin after winding, for the weight was carefully graduated so as merely to keep the spit moving very slowly. See another sort on page 548. We have here a worm gear, so much heralded in automobiles now. It is one of the oldest human inventions. There was a clock work jack invented and patented by Simon Willard, the famous clockmaker, but at a very much later date, for a vertical tin or copper oven. The spiders had very long handles, to keep one away from the blaze. The Dutch oven was a cast iron pot with a cast cover. It was placed on the coals; coals were also heaped on top of it, so that the bread could be cooked evenly. Hence the phrase, "between two fires." At the very first, some fireplaces had no brick ovens. Everything was cooked in or on the fire.

Boiling was a much more usual method of cooking than now. As in Europe our fathers cast into a great pot whatever edible things they found, to flavor the contents or to add to its strength. It was all in "one boiling."

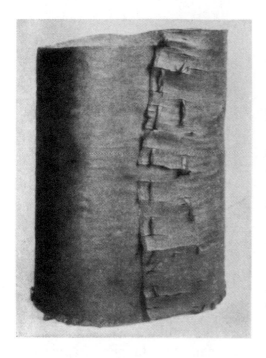

ON the left is a barrel of red-elm bark, belonging to Mr. Albert C. Bates. It is said the Indians used such articles. The wood of hollowed out barrels which has been called hornbeam, is beech or birch. They were once not uncommon.

Below are four pairs of bellows. One pair is flat, without decoration. One pair has a turned ornament. A third pair has stencilled ornaments. The fourth pair has a convex face and is well decorated with stencil work. This is the best sort. Bellows were a necessity with open fires. They add much to the furniture of the fireplace, especially since they are useful now.

Great kettles of iron or brass were a necessity in every family. It required, unless there was a crane, two strong persons with a pole to remove the great kettle from the fire. Those were "the days of real sport."

The carrying of fire from house to house arose merely from improvidence in keeping dry tinder. More use for the fire carriers was found in taking coals from room to room, for fires in the various fireplaces.

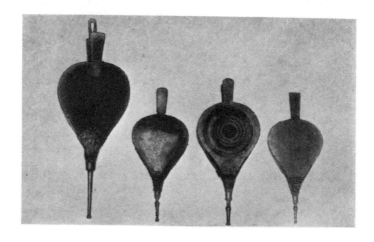

THE ordinary wall sconce in use for generations beginning soon after the country was settled is shown above in three styles of painted tin. It had the advantage of safety, convenience of moving, and cheapness. Sometimes these sconces were decorated with stencil or other painting.

The iron vessel is a cast Betty lamp. They are less common than the tin or hammered iron. The saucer base was designed to catch the drip. A hinged cover had a small opening at the lip end, where the wick protruded.

The little wooden wall box with door and drawer is a fine example of the undefinable home made articles that gave charm and individuality. The little row of decorative knobs was whittled out.

Below is a series of articles, which require no explanation.

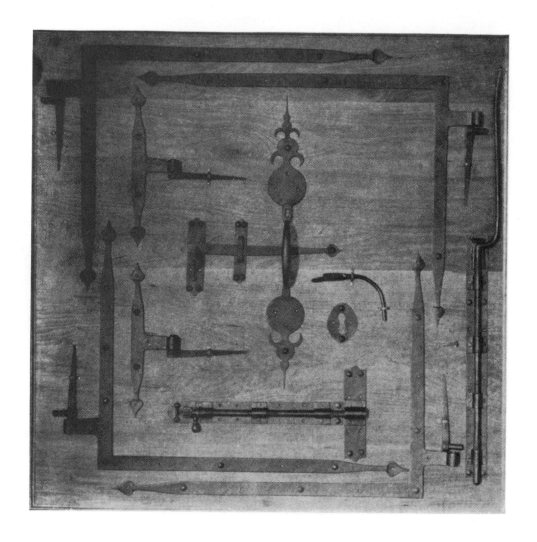

HARDWARE preserved from St. Stephen's Church, East Haddam, Connecticut.

Mr. Morgan B. Brainard, of Hartford, interested himself to see that this hardware was preserved, before the church perished. He has now mounted as above all the hardware on the doors of the church. While the period is not very early, there was less change in hardware than in furniture, from the 17th to the 18th Century. The Episcopal Society which erected the church was organized in 1791. The edifice was finally completed in 1795, and consecrated by Bishop Seabury.

The long push bar and the hinges are especially good. A handle like this we show elsewhere. We see here the transition from the plain guard and striker, driven directly into a door, to the same pieces mounted on a plate and attached by nails or screws. By this date screws were generally used in domestic architecture.

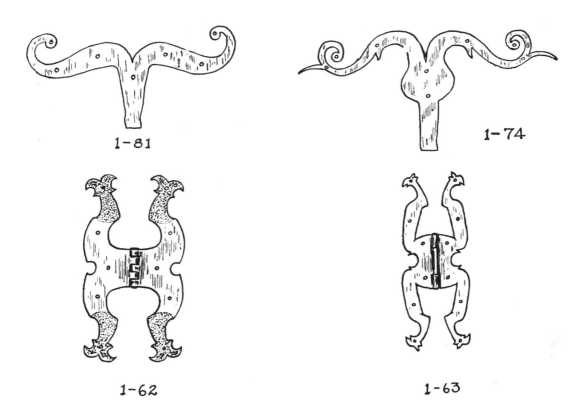

1-81

1-74

1-62

1-63

THE Hinge 81 is a ram's horn. It is a simplified form of 74, which in turn is greatly simplified from the scrolled Renaissance hinges so often found in Europe but not known in our Colonial hardware.

62 and 63 are two forms of the cock's comb hinge. On the left the example is hackled on the neck. The other form is slighter and more angular, but more generally found.

The cock's comb hinge was often made of cast brass. Its more usual application was on small cupboard doors. But at least one house which the author has visited had this hinge on all the room doors. It varies in length from three to eight inches. It is never found except on good woodwork, as it was considered a refinement and somewhat of a luxury.

None of these hinges were common. The upper examples were used with gudgeons, which were never ground but merely hammered.

The fastening was by hand wrought nails. It was custom to use a bit of leather, through which the nail was driven to secure a binding fit. This system is found in the best houses, as is also the clenching of the nails on the opposite side.

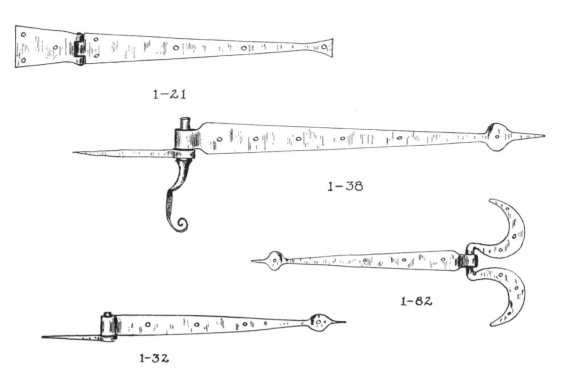

1—21

1—38

1—82

1—32

THE Hinge 21 is made with an offset on the short end of about an inch, or whatever the thickness of the material was to which attachment was made. It is called a chest hinge, though the usual chest hinge on American work was a pin hinge, like the cotter pin, two loops of tapered wire or larger iron hooked together.

The regular chest hinge above is occasionally found on cupboards, or wherever it was desired to lift the door as well as to open it. The European varieties of these hinges are sometimes richly wrought with intricate scrolled patterns. In 32 we have a very ancient example used still in the same form. The gudgeon is ragged, that is hacked to form small barbs, so that, once driven into the wood it cannot easily be removed. The more elaborate gudgeon, 38, is furnished with a scrolled end, in blacksmith's parlance a pigtail. It is not exclusively ornamental, as a nail was driven into the flat to brace the hinge.

The buck horn hinge, 82, was used on dwelling house doors. The scroll end afforded nail holes which did not follow one line and saved splitting the wood.

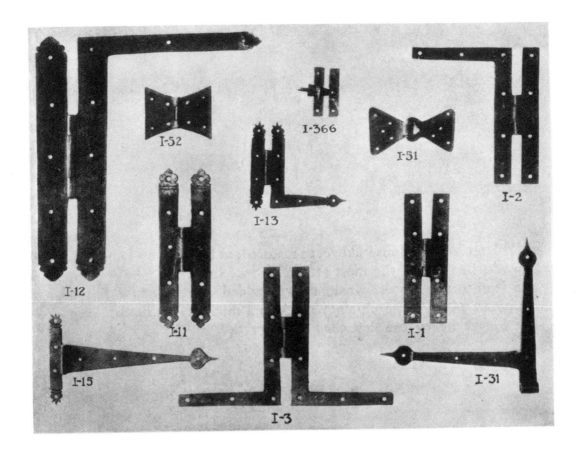

A PAGE of Hinges, of which the rarest form is 3. (In these notations I signifies iron and will not be noticed further.) The name is HLL. The purpose of the L was to strengthen the hold in the wood. The commoner form is the HL, number 2. At the top of a door it was placed as we see it. At the bottom the mate to it was reversed. In 12 we have the modified form with small decorative work at the ends, over dignified by the word scroll. In 31 we have a hammered form in which the branches not only taper but grow thinner toward the arrow end. This form also was attached by the pin, or gudgeon, and is earlier than the ordinary H and HL hinges, made of sheet metal. The plain H hinge, number 1, is the commonest of all forms; somewhat ornamented it becomes number 11. Number 13 is a hammered HL hinge with star and arrow ends. It was used on small work. The butterfly hinge 52 was used after 1700; the cruder form, without a pin, 51, was in use before 1700. Number 366 is a little latch for a small door made like an H hinge.

THE Iron Works House above, as restored, at Saugus, no longer used for that work, has one of the most attractive roof lines.

The lean-to was not original but was added about 1750. The ell followed about 1800. The chimney stack is a model of its kind.

The hinges below are described on page 548.

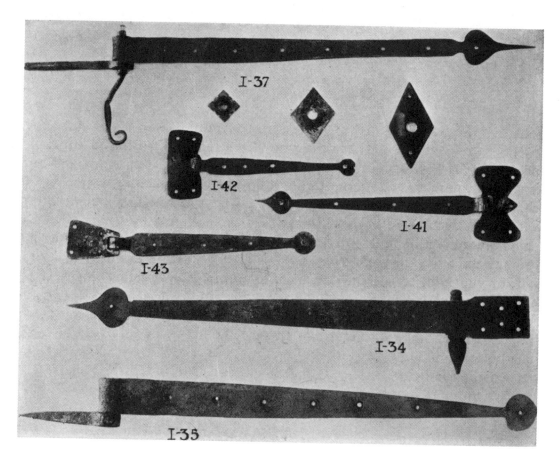

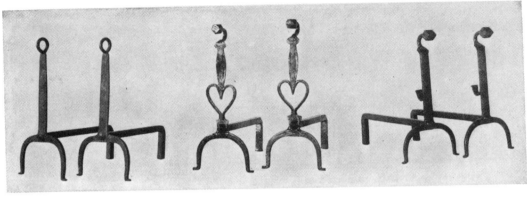

404   406   401

IN this Page of Andirons, 404 is the simple form, with a ring top. The heart pair, 406, is very rare. The crook neck octagon ball, 401, is a popular style. The hook on the inside of the standard is for the spit rod rest. The goose necks, 403, are quaint and were much used. The straight ball pair were heavy and high. The flat ball, with crook neck, 409, differs from those immediately above them in having plain rather than octagon balls. These patterns vary from 12 to 20 inches in hight. Unless otherwise noted the hardware in this section of the book is photographed by the author from original examples once in his possession. There is one exception.

All this work was hand wrought. Cast iron was very early used, but its forms are so manifold we can notice only a few.

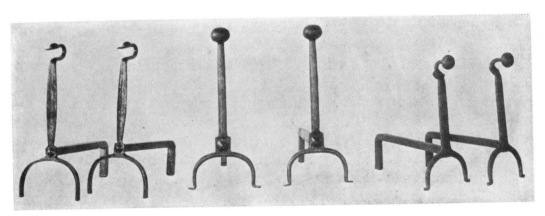

403   409

THE first pair of andirons differs from the last shown in that these balls are not flattened. The heavy flat scrolls, 402, were seldom found. They too much obscured a view of the fire. The pig tail scroll, 400, has a flattened section on top, where a small porringer might be placed.

The andirons below all belong to Mr. Geo. F. Ives. The cast pair of Hessians face away from each other—an error in photographing. The right hand pair of Washington andirons are rare. The Hessians have been so much copied that the original, like these, are the choicer, as imitation enhances the value of the original. The middle pair, with brass tips and flat feet, are extremely rare as the brass is made in a square molded section.

THERE is shown above the wonderful old fire room and fireplace in the Iron Works House. It is about ten feet across. In the same side of the same chimney in the lean-to is another fireplace, so that the chimney on the ground floor has dimensions of about 11 by 18 feet and the question of the fireplace furniture becomes an important one.

The clock-work jack, shown in position above, turned the rod below which rested on the large andiron. This method antedated many years the tin oven, which was a declension from the earlier, stronger style.

The small andirons in the rear, holding up the back logs, were called fire dogs. They were for use while the larger andirons were for ornament or to hold the spit. The meat of Queen Victoria was cooked on an arrangement like this during all her life.

The bunches of red ears of corn are hung here to season. On the right, on the wall, is a candle box of tin.

The pole hung from the ceiling was for hanging articles after ironing, a kind of suspended clothes horse.

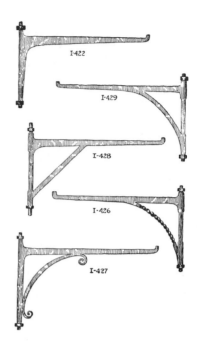

ON Page 544 is shown, in 37, a hinge with a screw gudgeon which passed entirely through the door post and was fastened on the opposite side, in the next room, with a diamond shaped washer and an ornamental nut. In 41 we have a 17th Century hinge named the strap and butterfly, a crude form of which is 42. This was used on good houses. A modification is the wedge and strap, 43. An offset hinge with ground joint is 34. The plain thumb end of 35 is commoner but not so good as the arrow end, 41.

On this page, on the left, is shown a smoke jack, which the author took out of a chimney in the Wentworth-Gardner house, photographed, and returned to its place. It was revolved, in the flue, by the draught. The bigger the fire the faster it turned, The long shaft, with worm gear at one end, at the other end stuck through the chimney breast, six or seven feet above the floor, and was connected by a pulley and chain belt with the spit rod below. A remarkable affair, dating 1760.

The cranes are various types, spiraled, braced, scrolled and plain. They should extend about two thirds of the way across the fireplace. The crane hangers are eyes with a shank which is built into the brick work. The upper end of the bearing was made long so that the crane could be unshipped.

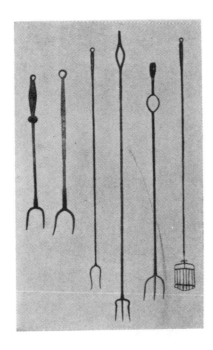 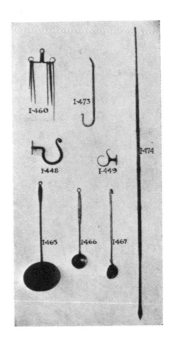

THE two Forks on the left are called tormentors. Some ask why. Evidently they are not familiar with the preaching of the past generations. The forks were used to take the meat out of the pot.

The slender little forks, third and fourth in line, were for toasting. The basket work affair last in line, was used for broiling an egg or chop. It had a swivel so as to reverse and cook on both sides. In the group on the right of the page, 460 is a skewer holder and its half-dozen skewers. An iron hook for sustaining the hole for drying articles in front of the fireplace is 473. The attachment called a jamb hook, 448 and 449, was fastened, on either side of the fireplace, to steady the shovel and tongs. The long rod, 474, rested on the hooks of the andirons, carried a little hollowed rim wheel at the end for the clock work jack, and revolved the meat attached by the skewers.

The other articles are hammered ladles and a perforated brass skimmer.

We do not seem to find cast ladles. The hammer marks on early iron are often eagerly looked for. But in the finest work those marks were often carefully avoided, so that they prove nothing except that the piece is hand wrought. They do not testify to age. Of late the market has been flooded with a great quantity of crude, spurious iron work.

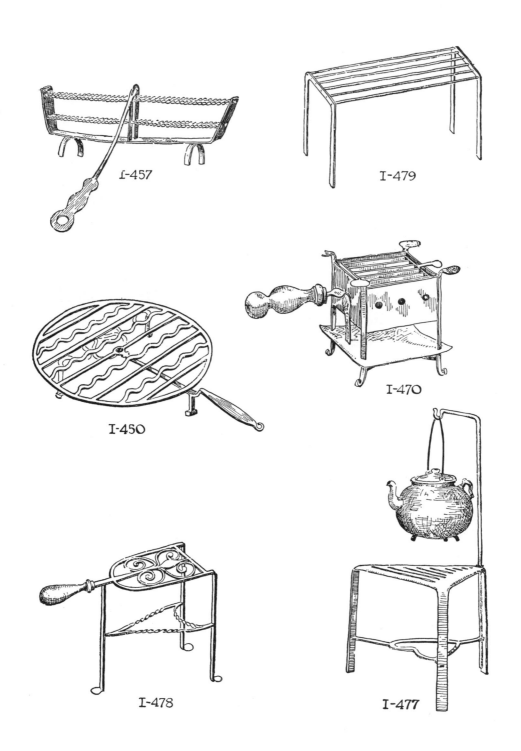

I-457

I-479

I-450

I-470

I-478

I-477

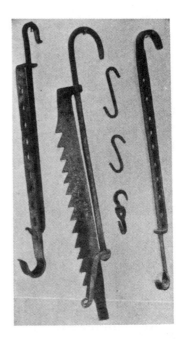

ON the preceding page, number 457 is a good early toaster. The handle is hammered in a quaint design, and the bars of the toaster are spiraled. A plain grill, or rest for a vessel over the fire is 479. A whirling spiral grill is 450. This and all articles on the page except the kettle, are hammered. A charcoal broiler or cooker is 470. The top is hinged for renewing the charcoal. A trivet, spiraled in its bracing, and scrolled in its table, is 478. It has a handle of wood. A trivet with a heart-shaped brace is 477. There is a detachable crane. A little fire on the trivet in summer; but in winter the entire trivet placed over the blaze.

On this page are various pieces of iron belonging to the author. The long, narrow trough is for boiling the rushes in waste fat. An excellent pair of early pipe tongs is on the right. The right hand group on this page shows the notched and the saw tooth trammels and pot hooks. The word trammel has an origin now forgotten. It confined, or held at the desired elevation the pot over the fire. The saw tooth trammels are rare. Some beautiful examples from the South have scroll work—"etching"—on the haft.

The trammel was a daily necessity. The pot was adjusted to bring it into direct contact with the blaze. The hight varied according to the size of the blazing logs. With a lug pole the same method, together with chains, was used.

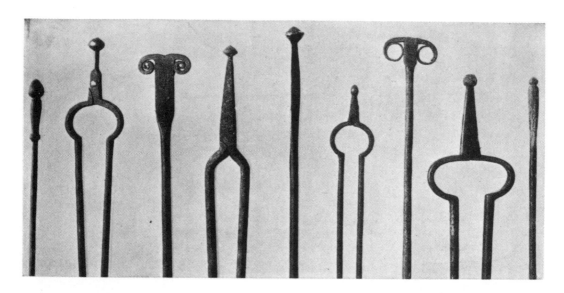

A SERIES of shovel and tong handles. None of these tops are brass; all are hammered. The third and the seventh are scroll shovel handles. The shovel itself was not used for ashes—a great shovel was brought in for that purpose—but for putting in and taking out food at the oven. This shovel was also called the slice, or the peel, because it peeled as it were the food from the oven bottom. It was sometimes made of wood.

The fourth and the eighth forms are tongs, the latter being best, with strong outward scrolls.

The round headed handles, some of shovels, others of tongs are good in their way.

The brass fireplace utensils came in much later, though in a few rich homes they might possibly, and rarely, be found.

The most used utensil at the fireplace was the tongs. The falling pieces of log required readjustment and powerful tools were necessary. Pokers were not in use. They go with a coal fire, or at least with grates.

A broom of birch stood by the fireplace to keep in their place the scattering ashes. The bellows, a long spider, kettles, pots, Dutch ovens (cast iron baking dishes), made up part of the furniture.

The ashes produced by the hard wood fire were all carefully saved for making soap. Also the lye made from them was used for hulling corn. In the backs of the fireplaces, well up, were niches for holding tinder, and the tinder box, or anything small that must be kept dry.

In the large chimneys recesses were provided, upstairs, for hanging ham and bacon to cure.

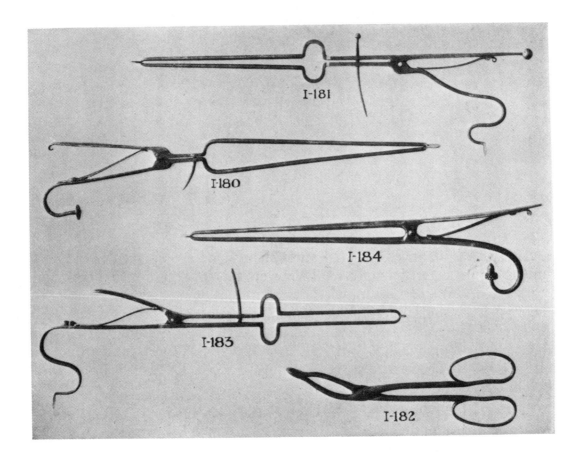

SEVERAL daintily wrought examples of pipe tongs have came down to us. At the top is the pair captured at the siege of Fort William Henry, by a scion of the Williams family in South Easton. They are engraved to that effect, with the date 1754. A pair owned by the author, 180, is not nearly so good. The little thumb piece for pressing the tobacco into the bowl was perforated to prevent putting out the fire.

The pair with an acorn end is hardly equal to the next pair 183, perhaps the finest example found. In addition to what one can see, there is on the hinge a series of little notch "carvings," and a flattened or halved acorn terminates the base of the spring. More properly it is a tear drop.

The bottom pair is a poor relation of the others. It merely supplies clumsy figures for the tongs, and resembles a pair of pincers. The delicacy of much of this work, very light and paper thin, is the highest achievement in American colonial hardware.

ABOVE are an array of candle sticks, lamps and a heart waffle iron. Also unique three-fingered snuffers. Below on this page are two fine candle stands of Mr. W., of Boston, with Betty lamp, snuffers and pipe tongs. On page 555 is a wonderful table candle stand, the most interesting we have seen. A series of lanterns at the bottom of that page shows examples of differing dates. The fourth is of wood. The fifth is a ship lantern. The third and last are late. The second was in use about 1800. The first is for carrying before one, or for use as a sconce.

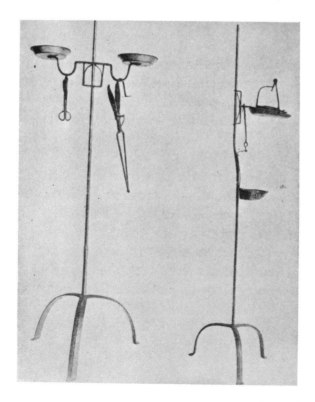

The date on such work is impossible to fix with any degree of accuracy but it is safe to say that they are at least pre-Revolutionary.

The variety of designs for holding candles, or oil, for lighting, is only surpassed by the multiplied modern fashions. But there is a quite notable scarcity of artistic forms. The elaborate European styles are scarcely represented in early American work. All efforts to trace the origin of the tall standards for candles have proved vain. We know they were in use in England. Spanish examples are numerous, but have been excluded here, except in one case.

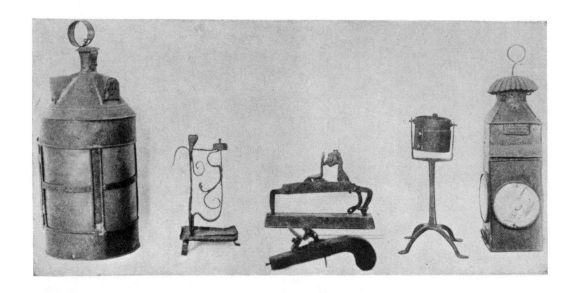

ALL the articles on this and the next page belong to Mr. Geo. F. Ives. The first above is a horn lantern. The next a quaintly scrolled candle stick. Then a pistol sparker and a gun lock sparker. A petticoat lamp follows, and a bull's eye. Below is a good chandelier with a crystal center. This, while not original, was provided for in the construction.

ABOVE is first a curious ladle or flagon. Next a reflector lamp, then a triple wall sconce with reflector. Next a swiveled pewter lamp made to hang or carry, and last a tinder-box combined as usual with a candle stick.

Below we have on the left a fine pair of reflecting sconces.

The other pair on the right may be unique. If not they are extremely rare. Their simple three branches are effective and seem to be the production, here, in iron, of the richer sconces produced abroad in silver.

Beautiful plates serving as backs for sconces in Sheffield ware appeared later. The best thing in use in our period seems to have been such reflecting sconces as those on the left. They were in their finest forms, composed of small segments of silvered glass. Their effect is very beautiful.

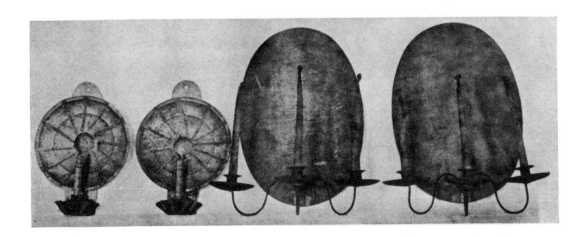

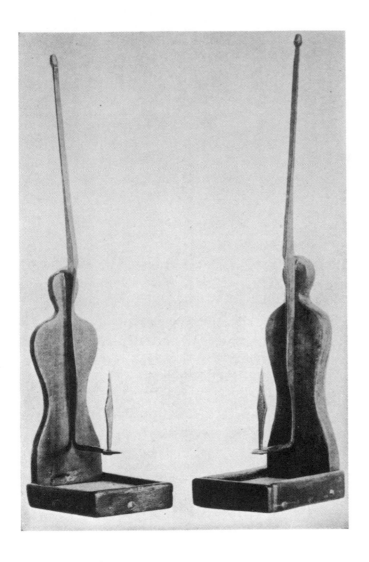
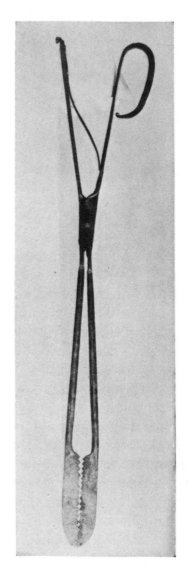

A PAIR of Sconces belonging to the E. B. Leete Co., of Guilford, Connecticut. The tips of the iron candleholders are of brass. The use of a spike, so common in Spanish work, for affixing the candle, is rare on American pieces. These sconces have been for generations in Connecticut, and their simplicity suggests that their origin is colonial.

There is an iron hook, the beginning of which is discernible, which goes over the back of the wooden support, resting in a slight slot. Thus the iron portion may be removed and hooked elsewhere. The pieces are designed as they stand, to rest upon a table. They are presumably unique and very attractive in their quaintness.

Hight, 17½ inches; hight of wooden base, 9 inches. On the right is a very large pair of tongs, with teeth, for filling a warming pan.

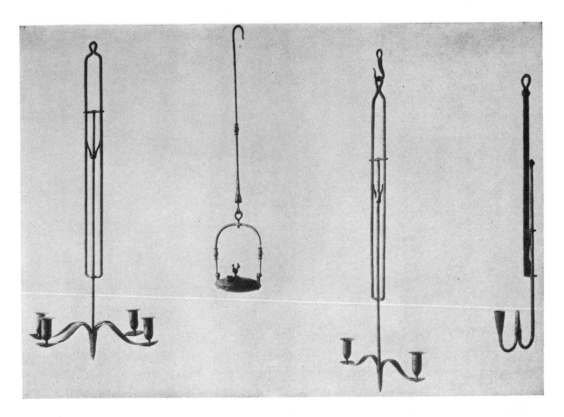

THE hanging sconces here shown may not in all cases be of American make, but they were all found here, except the first. The second is a nice piece of lamp work, of two saucer-shaped pieces of iron brazed together. The rooster, stopper and the turned ornaments are of brass. These hanging lamps were used at looms, as well as for other purposes. The third example is made with a sliding joint and spring to shove up and down. The last is a trammel form candle stick and rush light.

Below is a quaint little affair, a candle holder to be thrust into a wooden support or to be hooked to a mantel or a "high backt" chair. It was found in Connecticut, and is owned by Mr. Malcolm Norton.

A MOST attractive form of chandelier or "branch", as such pieces were called. The central portion is a wood turning eleven inches high by six inches in diameter. To it are nailed the sheet iron strips which form the branches. They are rolled over on their edges for finish and strength.

The staple and the S-hook at the top are for attachment to a hook in the ceiling or a chain adjusted to the hight of a room. It belongs to Mr. Geo. F. Ives, as do the lighting fixtures at the bottom of the next page

On the top of that page is a twelve candle chandelier the design of which the author had sketched from an ancient example. This piece is all in metal. The dates of these chandeliers are entirely conjectural, beyond the statement that they belong in the 17th and 18th Centuries, and there is no reason why some should not have been made until the time of the common use of the whale oil lamp.

The low ceilings in 17th Century houses where furniture of that period, left to us, was originally used, did not admit of central "branches" like the above, except in rare instances. The individual candle branches are about 11 inches each, horizontally. The hub is of pine. Similar pieces are now being eagerly sought. But there is little hope of discovering more than a very few. The author has lately seen one with two circles of branches, on different levels.

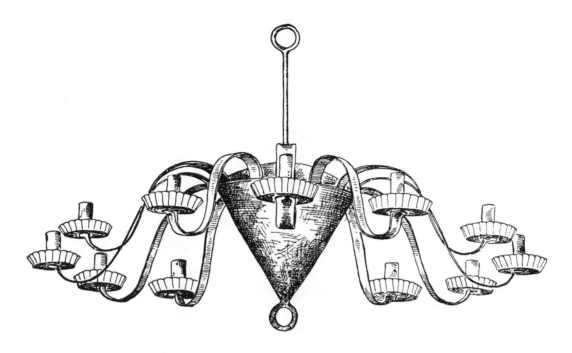

THE piece above was just described. Below are, on the ends, two very rare examples of Betty lamp stands, with the lamps. The Betty lamp was designed to hang, but obviously that was sometimes inconvenient. The second and fifth pieces are candle sticks, the fifth with square base being very odd. The fine wall sconce with minute facets for reflectors is a very rare example in this good state of repair. The fourth piece is a hanging candle, the fish hook shape of which does not clearly show.

A SECOND good example of a wood and iron chandelier owned by Mr. Geo. F. Ives.

The use of oil in the Betty lamp, which copied the classical form, was very early, but coincident with the use of candles. Metal or glass lamps with a wick and whale oil as a filler were of a later date. This brief survey covers most of the antique methods of lighting in this country until the introduction of kerosene. All lamps designed to burn it are too late to be called antique. The ordinary lights for general room illumination were as they should have been, at the sides. A chandelier was ordinarily objectionable owing to the low ceilings. Wall sconces of various degrees of elaboration were common. Ordinarily speaking no effort, except in ball rooms, was made at general illumination. The light was small and movable to be placed where most needed, hence the stick lamp, the hook lamp and the candle stick; some of these being attached to the back and others even to the front posts of a chair.

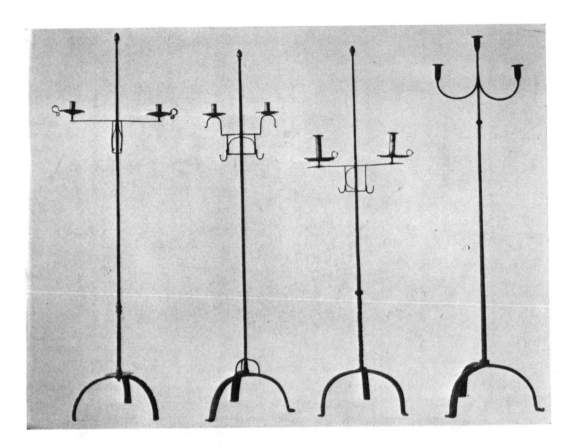

A SERIES of tall iron candle stands photographed from various examples. All except the last, which has more of a Spanish suggestion, were in the author's possession. These three have bars which adjust at any hight desired, a spring or two securing them. The second one came from the South, and is good and peculiar, perhaps unique, in having little arched braces to stiffen the high standard. In most cases the standard is four and a half to five and a half feet high. There is a cast and turned brass tip on the top of the standard. The candle sticks are sometimes iron, generally brass, and the latter are often cast. These candle stands tapered toward the top and are rather delicate in the old patterns.

The brass tip is always small. The more elaborate the specimen the more likely it is to be an imitation. The little frame containing the springs is called a cage. The light, when pushed down, was for reading. When elevated, it served to illuminate a room. We have never seen one of these early American standards with four lights. But there has been found a wooden stand with short T arms at the end of the bar, as if to take two candles at each end.

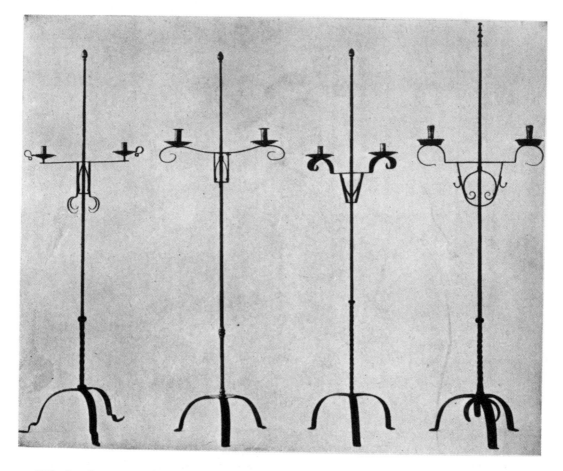

IN the first stand we have a scrolled foot. In the second the candle bar is scrolled, from a narrow section. There is a brass disc as part of the decoration, just above the tripod. In the third example, the candle bar is composed of a very wide scroll. In the fourth example, the bracket is more artistic than usual. At the base simple scrolls between each leg are added for decoration. This piece belongs to the city of New York, and is in the old City Hall.

Tall iron stands are now very difficult to obtain. When found they are generally in a dilapidated condition. It may well be that some of these old stands are not native. Most of them have a bar for two candles, but perhaps a dozen are known with a single bracket, for one candle. A few are found with wooden blocks for bases. These are usually simple and are not relatively good.

The classical stand was for burning oil in a lamp like a gravy boat, or Betty lamp, of elegant workmanship, in bronze.

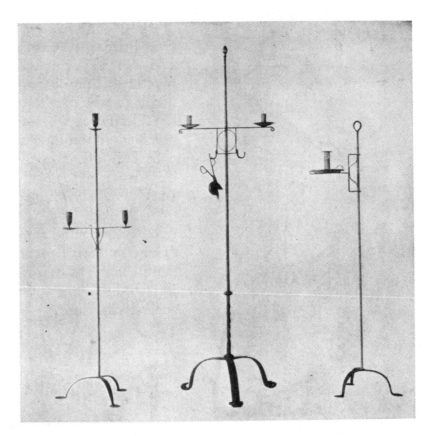

OF the stands above those at the sides are short and slight. One carries three candles. That on the right has a three pronged rest for an ordinary candlestick which is not attached to the stand. The middle specimen shows a hanging pair of snuffers and feet with curled up toes.

The matter of lighting was so important as to give the name chandler (candler) to merchants in many kinds of trade. We have only to consider what the oil and electric development is today to understand how large was the matter of candles in the old days. The wealth of New England came largely through the whaling fleets, which brought in oil to take the place of candles, or spermaceti for the best candles. The preparation of rushes for lighting was by peeling, except for a small shred on one side, and dipping in hot tallow. Rush lights are shown farther on.

A history of artificial lighting might disclose some odd chapters in human experience, from the pine knot to the 300,000 candle power light now being installed, to cast a beam eighty miles out to sea.

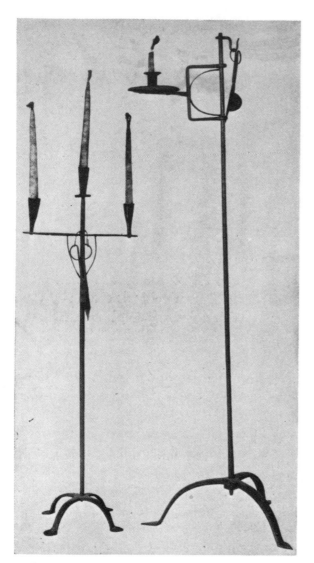

TWO interesting stands owned by Mr. Geo. F. Ives. That having three lights has practically no bases as drip basins for the candles. It must have been used where this defect was ignored, on an earth floor.

Several other good lanterns belonging to Mr. Rudolph Pauly, are shown at the bottom of page 535. One has a wooden frame and small wooden finials, and is of great interest. Horn lanterns were not subject to breakage and were in general early use.

A lantern such as that shown is now called, by the perversity of a fad, a "Paul Revere lantern." Of course it would have been impossible to see the light from such a candle, in a church belfry. These lanterns are simply tin perforated by nail holes. They were in early use and have continued up to the last generation in many country neighborhoods. They are now made in quantities. A few days is sufficient to coat them so effectively with rust that they look older than necessary. They are sometimes made in very large sizes

WALL Sconces that could not be moved were on that account objectional. Our fathers were accustomed to carrying lights in the hand, in doors and out.

The double sconce above is a very rare form whose origin is not known. The snuffers are hand wrought. Steel snuffers are of small account. They are always more fanciful.

The attractive, extremely rare, double table candle stand with shades has a brass post and handle at the top. The rest is iron. An important specimen. Below the lanterns are not very early forms. They were used on shipboard or in public halls, on walls.

Almost every man seems to have made his lantern to his taste. The forms are numberless. Few are very ancient. The materials were either wood, iron, tin, brass, horn. They should not be adapted to electric light. To do so is thoroughly incongruous.

[567]

ON the left is a rare swinging bracket torch holder. The ornaments are quaintly good. The date may be 18th Century. Small plates are nailed to the wall to sustain it, moving through a half circle.

The small single wall sconce on the same plate dates from the 18th Century.

The use of torch holders seems to be confined, of necessity, to light out of doors. Such holders were filled with any resinous wood. They marked the approaches to stately dwellings.

The table candle stands on the right vary little from the high stands already shown except in hight. The feet of the one on the right are more delicately made with hammered enlargements. It has nicely shaped little scrolls on the springs.

On the left at the bottom is a pole torch, the pole of course being missing; and a flip iron—a thing much sought after now—of course as a curio.

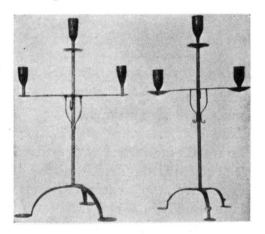

We suspect certain blacksmith's tools have been made to do duty as flip irons or toddy sticks. We are sure that the gophering iron, thrust into a hollow holder, is often called a flip iron. It was used in England, and perhaps here, to heat the gophering iron on which ruffles or flounces were smoothed. After the fashion of the gophering iron had passed out its original purpose was forgotten, but obviously no toddy iron could need a sheath, as it would be cold when taken from the toddy.

A loggerhead, served the same purpose, and, if too much toddy were taken, the imbibers sometimes used the loggerheads on one another's skulls.

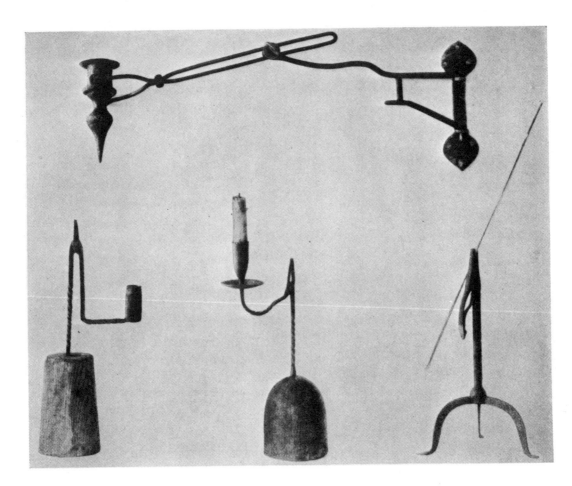

THE Bracket Candle Sconce, on a swivel, above, is one of the oddest affairs ever found. By means of a thumb nut and a toggle joint the candle holder may be changed in hight and extension. The little holder itself is on a swivel weighted below to keep it steady. Such a contrivance would have supplied a good reading light. Below are three forms of rush light holders. The writer was asked recently whether any holder for rush lights is American. Our fathers used rush lights not a little. So simple a thing could hardly have been imported in every case. These specimens were found in America, but there is nothing to prove they were not brought here. The left hand holder has a side prong for a candle, to use for guests. Meantime the weight of it kept the nippers closed on the rush, as shown on the right example, which has a spring for that purpose, and iron legs. The middle piece has a nicely turned base.

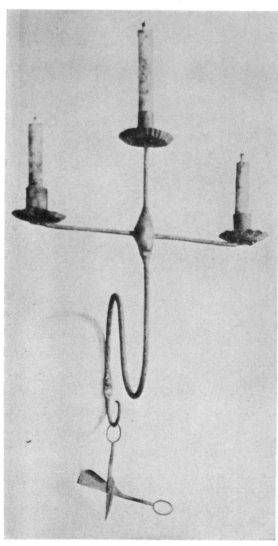

A REMARKABLY good set of three sconces, each with the lights, is owned by Mr. Geo. T. Ives. They have the true colonial feeling, much simplicity, but very good taste. The curl with which the pieces terminate is made useful as well as ornamental.

So far as known these specimens are unique. No doubt the less artistic reflecting sconces were found better for lighting. Hence the rarity of such examples as these.

Below is a much reduced picture of the corner fireplace in York jail, now converted into the local historical museum. The feature of great interest is the raised hearth, English-wise, which wastes heat; and the corner treatment in general, which is delightful.

In the fireplace, the error is

often made, when preparing it for a setting of early hardware, of doing the work too daintily. No glazed trim or pressed brick should be used, no colored mortar, and no arch allowed.

The hearth should be of old, or at least rough, red brick tile, about 7½ inches square. The rest of the work should be in common brick, old if possible, laid in common white mortar. The larger the fireplace the better.

[570]

THE Brass Box Lock was used on fine houses from about 1725 to 1795. When the author was rummaging among the unknown treasures of the Metropolitan Museum, he found a second specimen like this. They are the best examples that have come to light. The ordinary brass box lock was cast with perfectly plain square edges. The molded edge is one feature of beauty and rarity. Most old locks are screwed on from the face. This, in common with the better sort has a back plate screwed to the door. To this plate, the lock is attached by hooked studs and slots. One screw placed in the edge at the closed end, holds it securely. The striker is attached in the same way.

These locks, at least in the early period, were never made rights and lefts. The lock was simply turned over to accommodate itself to a door opening the other way. There was no outside keyhole, this being an inside door lock. Thus the polished plate was clean except for the drop handle. A bolt was shot by pushing the little stud shown on the bottom edge. Knobs are much later. Below is a drawing of the pine tree shilling, our first coin. The die was made by Joseph Jencks, ironmaster.

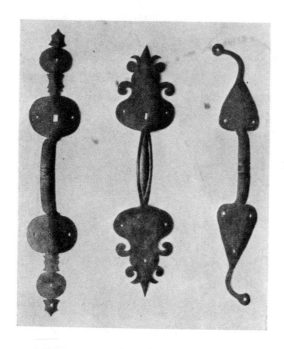 

OF the Latches the left hand one, in iron, is now on the back door of the hall in the Webb house, Wetherfield. It is above nineteen inches long. The second example is in brass. The third was taken from an old church door—we hope not without leave. Its length is sixteen and a half inches. The latches on the other plate are outside door patterns. The left hand one has fine hatcheling on the small triangles. One should notice the ornaments across the centers of the handles. The right hand example is called the triangle latch. The middle one ends with spear or arrow points and has extra little quirks at the bases of the circles.

No such rich hardware as is common abroad showed itself in America—at least none remains. And we do not regret it. These simpler designs are sufficiently attractive and mark the decorative sense of the colonists better than the mere importation of something on which they had not put out their skill.

The bars of these outside latches, which date in some cases earlier than 1700, were large, running to fifteen inches. Dependence was placed on a large wooden bar across the door within instead of locks.

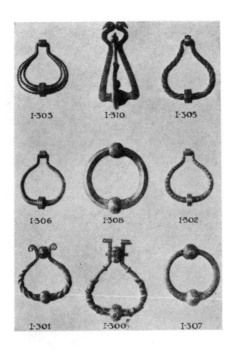 

OF the numerous knockers here shown, all in iron because the brass knocker is later, 302 was found on a door of a 17th Century house near Haverhill. It is like 306, except that it has stamped on it a series of decorative rings.

305 is a rope twist found in Newfoundland, as was also 300. The origins of the others have been lost sight of. 310 is a kind of cock's comb knocker. 301 is a simplification of 300. 308 and 307 are merely rings with balls. 303 is composed of several twisted strands gathered into a ring.

Some of these knockers were also latches. On swinging the knocker a latch bar was lifted by means of a post running through the door. This devise was doubtless the origin of the drop handle on brass box locks.

The three great latch handles in the right plate run from 22½ to 27 inches in length. Their shapes are quite suggestive of the finials on a Brewster chair. Of course, they are a reminiscence of the Gothic.

Such latches were used for the most part in America on church doors, or state buildings. They are among the rarest articles of American hardware, and what is worse, there is little chance of more of them being found. They are so prominent as to make their whereabouts known. One recently came to light with notch carving on the thumb piece. But it was not in this heroic size.

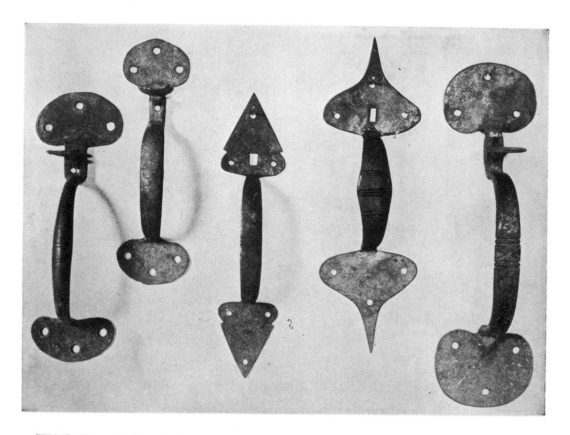

THE Fourth Latch in the line above is found on many good houses. It is the best design of the five. The handle portion is shaped more than in the others. This one was on the back door of the Wentworth-Gardner house. It was used as an inside and outside latch, in differing sizes.

The third latch is scrolled to secure a slight departure from the triangle, but the type is not so good. The other three latches differ mostly in the ornamental bars across the handle. They are common design, rather lacking in style. The large specimen was on an outside door.

Iron latches of this period are never attached with screws but always by clinch nails, which hold far more securely than any wood screw ever devised. The length of the thumb piece was accommodated to the thickness of the door and there were no adjustments to get loose. The hammering was so done as to leave the iron thinner and narrower near the plates, which themselves were thinned at the edges, like early brass cabinet handles.

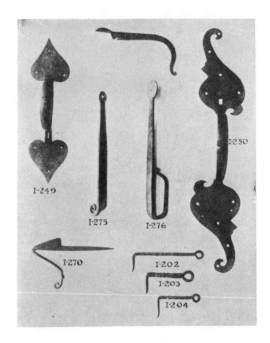 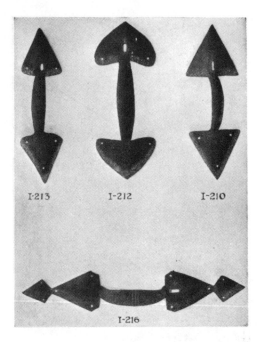

LATCH 249 has the Heart shaped Plate. The large well scrolled latch, 250, was on a church. The striker, 270, shows a scrolled support into which a nail was driven. The shaft was also ragged. At the top is shown a shaped thumb piece. There are also two examples of latch bars, 275 and 276, which have scrolls to lift them by, independent of the thumb piece. Below are examples, 202, 203 and 204, of various hooks, used with staples.

On the right hand side of the page, 212 is a quaint "round triangle" design. The other examples need no explanation.

Large latches were not used indoors. The latch with a turned handle and back plate was a 19th Century device, and was attached by screws, with its striker, and we therefore omit it.

The box locks with a patent mark, very numerous, are omitted for the same reason. There was a good design of a Pennsylvania latch with long twisted levers having flat enlargements at their ends, like half knobs. They are on the third story rooms of a Newburyport house.

Early hardware was, in the first designs, not made of plate iron, but was invariably thinned at the edges or ends, where less strength was required.

Owing to the quality of the iron used it was more free from rust, at least in the remaining examples, than our present iron.

A SERIES of Shutter Fasteners. The modern blind was first used in the last decade of the 18th Century, in one large old coast town. The spring fastener on the right was the latest and poorest type. It continually got out of order. The others are earlier, operate by gravity and cannot go wrong. The crude S fasteners should be compared with the somewhat later design, 390 on the next page. The types at the left are later than the S type, since they are attached by plates.

The shutter was solid or had a small opening, a star, a clover leaf, a moon or something of the kind to prevent total darkness within.

I-281

I-283

I-280

Below on the left are three types of spring latches of iron with small brass knobs. They were in use in Portsmouth in 1760, and earlier. Another name is the wishbone latch, from the shape of the spring. The one in the center is shaped with some attempt at artistic design. The attachment of the strikers by nails is a change from the earlier simpler method of a driven in striker.

A door having one of these latches and with HL hinges, all done in black, presented an effective display, especially if a square bolt were added above, and a little removed from, the latch. These latches were the last stage of progress towards the mortised spring latch with knob. These are much less likely to get out of order The passion for hiding construction was a mark of declining taste.

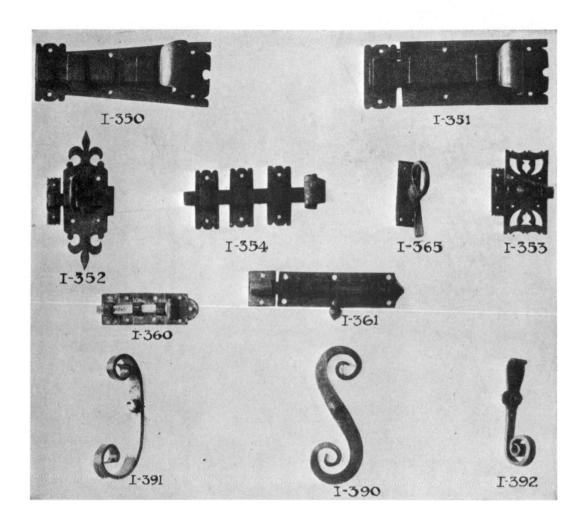

I-350   I-351   I-352   I-354   I-365   I-353   I-360   I-361   I-391   I-390   I-392

THE Scrolled Bolts were in use, the large ones on large outside doors in Portsmouth.

352 and 353 are cupboard catches of rather dainty and very rare design.

360 and 361 are the common slide bolts, though 360 with a square section is the older.

391 is a C shutter fastener; 392 is a J fastener, and 390, already mentioned, an S fastener. The last, in huge form, was also used as a chimney or brick wall tie, to prevent spreading. It is seen on colonial houses of the late period shortly after the revolution.

365 is the swing catch used in securing lattice casements—a very early device, reaching back to the first settlement.

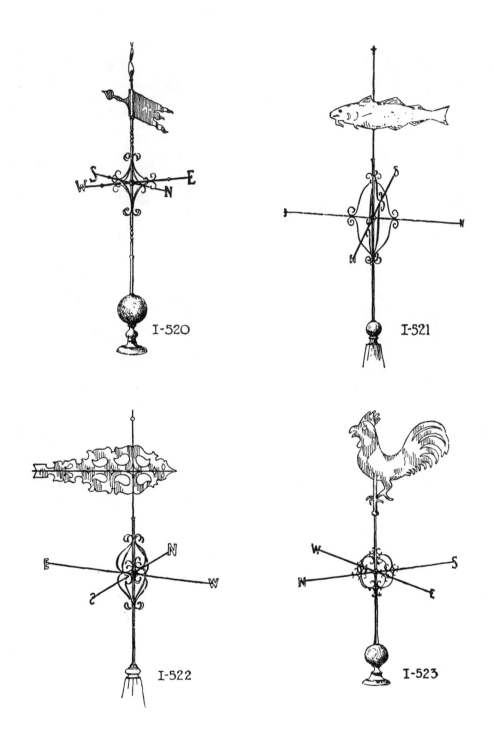

I-520

I-521

I-522

I-523

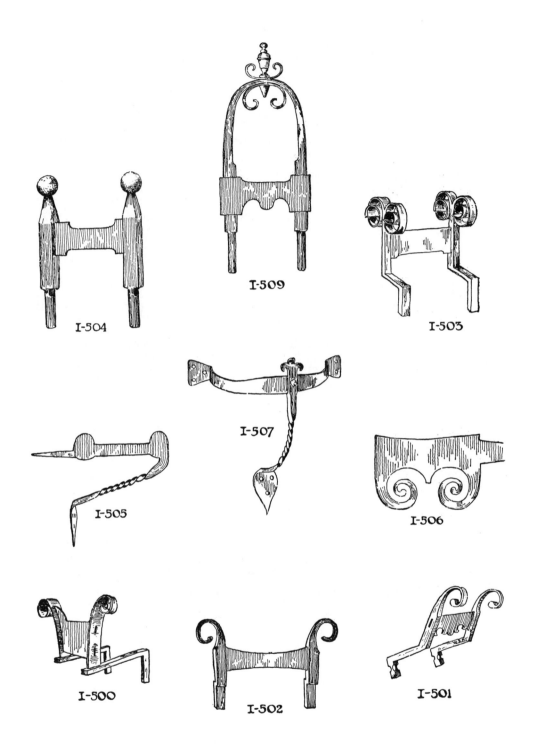

I-504

I-509

I-503

I-507

I-505

I-506

I-500

I-502

I-501

ON page 578 are shown the codfish weather vane, and the rooster vane, the latter on the First Church, Springfield. The other examples were found in America.

On page 579 are examples of door scrapers. The quaintest and best is 507. It was attached to the wide outside base board of the house. It was found in a Boston antique shop. 505 and 506 were similarly attached but are simpler models. 509 is a Philadelphia pattern. On a Saugus double step cut from one stone is on either side the scraper, 503. The other examples are more commonly seen. At a time when roads were nothing but mud, and no rubber shoes existed, scrapers were a necessity of civilization.

All the persons are very kind who have assisted by affording the writer opportunity to secure pictures. Their names are set forth at large through the volume.

Among the great number of pictures in this volume, are a very few which, collected through many years, cannot be traced. The indulgence of the owners of the articles pictured is begged by the author. Nothing could be farther from his intention that to fail of crediting an article to its owner. Certain friends who have assisted in the way of facts or pictures have declined to allow their names to be mentioned. They do good deeds secretly.

Finally the author begs a kindly judgment on his work, trusting it will be understood all has been guided by fidelity in dealing with the work of faithful artificers of the Pilgrim Century.

INDEX

A

Alden House, John, bed: 334; parlor: 450.
Andirons: 545-547.
Attic, Webb House: 485; Wentworth-Garden House: 535.
Author, the: *see* Nutting, Wallace.

B

Barrels: 536, 538.
Bates, Albert C., bowls and utensils: 533, 537, 538.
Beds: 322-334, 456, 486.
Behrend, B. A., boxes: 104, 105, 107, 110; candle-stands: 459, 460, 461, 464, 467; chairs, banister-back: 250—carved 254, Brewster transition: 188, Carver: 191, 194—reversed baby: 269, mushroom: 211, trundle: 229; chests: 19, 25, 31, on frame, small: 89, 96; desk: 114; parlor: 214; settle with rockers: 310; stand: 446, triangular: 442; tables, tavern: 417, 419, 420; trestle-board: 343.
Bellows: 538.
Betty lamps: 463, 539, 554.
Bible-box: *see* box.
Bigelow, Francis Hill, chairs, carved cane: 247, 248; looking glasses: 499, 502, 503, 504, 505, 506, 507, 509, 511, 512, 519; sconce glasses: 506; sconce reflectors: 491, 493.
Blair, Mrs. J. Insley, cupboard, court: 130, 136; table, heavy tavern: 407.
Blaney, Dwight, box: 100; chair, carved cane: 267, heavy, Pilgrim slat-back: 203; chest: 40, 41, 46; cupboard, press: 131; stools: 290; table, butterfly-trestle: 395.
Bolts: 540, 577.
Boston Museum of Fine Arts, cupboard: 167.
Boards and Trestles: 342.
Bowls: 531, 532, 533, 537.
Boxes: 90-111; band: 445; carved: 97-107, 109; decorated: 110; Friesian: 97, 106, 109; carrying: 445; cocked hat: 166; pipe: 526, 527, 528; tinder: 527; wall: 526, 527, 528, 539.
Brackets candles and lamps: *see* branches.

Branches: 556, 557, 559-562, 567, 569, 570.
Brinton, Francis D., chairs, five-back: 234, Pennsylvania six-back: 231, 233.
Broilers: 550.
Brooklyn Public Museum, cupboard, press: 126; spinet: 477.
Brown, G. Winthrop, candle-stand: 459; chair, banister-back: 265, carved cane: 236, high: 223, serpentine slat-back: 228; chests: 32, 36, 49; table, dressing (lowboy): 425, gate-leg: 374.
Brown, Mrs. Hulings Cowperthwaite, chest: 42.
Bryant, Mrs. G. C., cupboard, press: 142, 143; table, heavy tavern: 413.
Buek, G. H., 1.

C

Campbell, James N. H., chair, banister-back: 274; chest: 12, 29; cupboard, court: 133, 137.
Candle-stands, iron: 554, 563-565.
Candle-sticks: 554, 557, 558, 569.
Chairs: 175-284; baby high: 195, 196, 208, 209, 223, 263, 266, 269, 284; baby low: 198, 217, 269, 276, 277, 278, 279, 280; banister-back: 250, 251, 254, 258-265, 268, 269, 274, 275, 283; Brewster: 182-185; buffet: 272, 274; candle: 256; cane: 235-249, 252-255, 267; carved: 234; Carver: 189-201; Charles II: 235-255; children's, *see* baby; corner or buffet: 272, 273, 274, 277; Cromwellian: 218; Dutch: 277, 282, 283; English scroll-foot: 241, 242, 244; leather back: 219-221, 283; miscellaneous: 276; mushroom: 210-217; New England turned: 222, 225-228, 230, 256, 257, 268, 270-273, 275-281; Pennsylvania: 231-234; Pilgrim: 182-207, 217; late: 208, slat-back: 202, 203-207, 217; transition: 186, 188; rockers, later: 228; serpentine: 222; roundabout: 272-274; rush-bottom, banister-back: 259-266; 203, Spanish-foot: 240, 248, 251, 252, 253, 254, 258, 262, 263, 282, 283; spinning: 275; Standish, Myles: 185; tables: 336-341; wainscot: 175, 181; Windsor: 284; writing-arm: 281.